# Greek and Roman Mythology

## A to Z

THIRD EDITION

# MYTHOLOGY A TO Z

MYTHOLOGY A TO Z

# WITHDRAWN
# Greek and Roman Mythology

## A to Z

### THIRD EDITION

Kathleen N. Daly

Revised by Marian Rengel

**CHELSEA HOUSE**
PUBLISHERS
An imprint of Infobase Publishing

# Greek and Roman Mythology A to Z, Third Edition

Chelsea House
An imprint of Infobase Publishing
132 West 31st Street
New York NY 10001

ISBN-13: 978-1-60413-412-4

**Library of Congress Cataloging-in-Publication Data**
Daly, Kathleen N.
Greek and Roman mythology, A to Z / Kathleen N. Daly ; revised by Marian Rengel. — 3rd ed.
p. cm.
Includes bibliographical references and index.
ISBN 978-1-60413-412-4 (hc : alk. paper)
1. Mythology, Classical—Encyclopedias, Juvenile. I. Rengel, Marian. II. Title.

BL715.D26 2009
292.1'303—dc22        2009008243

Chelsea House books are available at special discounts when purchased in bulk quantities for businesses, associations, institutions, or sales promotions. Please call our Special Sales Department in New York at (212) 967-8800 or (800) 322-8755.

You can find Chelsea House on the World Wide Web at http://www.chelseahouse.com

Text design and composition by Lina Farinella
Cover design by Alicia Post
Maps by Patricia Meschino
Cover printed by Bang Printing, Brainerd, MN
Book printed and bound by Bang Printing, Brainerd, MN
Date printed: April, 2010
Printed in the United States of America

10  9  8  7  6  5  4  3  2

This book is printed on acid-free paper.

# CONTENTS

# INTRODUCTION

## WHAT IS MYTHOLOGY?

From earliest times, humans have had a need to explain the origins and wonders of the world: the mountains and the oceans, the changing seasons, the earthquakes and storms, volcanoes, floods, and the existence of animals, including humans. Early humans, in every culture on Earth, made up stories about these phenomena and invented gods and supernatural beings to provide comfort and instruction. Sometimes people such as the Greeks made up stories just for entertainment; for example, the story of PYGMALION and GALATEA explains nothing in nature or science, but it's a good story. It is the story in George Bernard Shaw's play *Pygmalion* (1913) and the musical and movie *My Fair Lady*.

As the ages passed, and tribes shifted from place to place, broke up, regrouped, increased in size, and migrated to different lands, they took their stories with them. As the stories were passed on, they changed with the language, climate, and local folklore of the people. Eventually people built shrines and temples to their gods and heroes. They prayed to them for help, made sacrifices to them and celebrated them with festivals. In some countries, such as ROME, rulers took on the status of gods. In GREECE, we find temples built in honor of ZEUS, ATHENE, APHRODITE, and other gods and goddesses. In the Roman empire, there are temples to JUPITER, JUNO, QUIRINUS, and other major and minor gods and goddesses. Their names live on in place-names, people's names, and history.

In the early mythologies of most cultures, women were the supreme gods. The EARTH MOTHER was the creator of new life. She was also the moon or sun goddess who ruled the skies, the seasons, and the harvests. As eons went by, people discovered that the male, as well as the female, was necessary for the procreation of the species. The Earth Mother and moon goddess were gradually replaced by male sky gods, and sun gods, often typified by BULLS or rams. The queen mother's decline is typified in Greek mythology by the attitude of Zeus toward his sister-wife, HERA. He was a mischievous, unfaithful, and disrespectful husband. His indiscretions and Hera's anger may reflect the conservative religious feeling (personified by Hera) against marriages or other liaisons (those of Zeus) between the new Hellenic chieftains and the local moon priestesses and NYMPHS.

Other stories were invented to explain new developments such as the introduction of grain cultivation, the making of bread and wine, and the breeding of domestic goats, pigs, and cattle.

## THE GREEKS: WHERE DID THEY COME FROM?

Greek mythology is extremely old. The Great Mother was worshiped in 2000 B.C., in the land that we now call Greece. Early invaders from ASIA MINOR brought with them an early form of Indo-European language and the worship of Aryan sky gods. They settled peacefully in THESSALY and central Greece and intermarried with the natives.

Next came the more destructive and aggressive waves of what HOMER called the Achaeans and Dorians, tribes from the north. These people were not peace-loving. In SPARTA, in the southern PELOPONNESUS, they enslaved the entire native population, using them to perform menial tasks. The Achaeans called these slaves Helots. The Achaeans spoke a dialect of ancient Greek and used a simple type of picture-writing scholars now call Linear B.

While savages and barbarians inhabited what we now call Greece, there was already a flourishing civilization on the island of CRETE, which lies to the south of Greece. Crete had long been trading with the even more ancient civilizations of Egypt and the East. This culture reached its height in about 1600 B.C., and was known as the Minoan culture. In 1400 B.C., the Minoan civilization collapsed, probably due to a natural phenomenon such as an earthquake, whereupon the Greeks took over Crete.

We find many instances of Cretan myths in Greek stories, such as those of the upbringing of the god Zeus in Crete, the story of EUROPA and the bull, and the MINOTAUR who was vanquished by THESEUS. However, the ancient divinities gradually took on the aspect of the invaders from Greece.

The Greek myths, as we know them, came from all over the ancient Balkan Peninsula: Thrace, BOEOTIA, ATTICA, the Peloponnesus, ARGOS, and MYCENAE, and many of the islands, including, of course, Crete, and also from Asia Minor and places farther afield, such as Babylon and Sumer. Homer, whose work may be that of several poets writing between 750 and 700 B.C., is considered the "supreme source" of the stories of Greece.

## GREEK MYTHOLOGY

Greeks were the first people to create gods and goddesses that looked like real human beings: beautiful men and women, old people with humor and dignity, and splendidly natural animals (as well as a few monsters). All the art and all the thought of Greece centered on human beings and human feelings.

The Greek gods and goddesses usually interacted with humans in towns and countries that are still familiar: Mount IDA, on the island of Crete, where the god Zeus was brought up, exists to this day; the hero HERACLES had his home in the city of THEBES; the exact spot where the goddess Aphrodite is said to have emerged from the sea can be pointed out near the island of Cythera.

Greek mythology tells of many heroes who defeated their enemies by superior wit. ODYSSEUS, for example, was said to have thought of the wooden Trojan horse, inside which were hidden invading Greek soldiers. Greek intelligence went much further than clever strategy. The Greeks had a clear-eyed curiosity about themselves and all creation. The playwright SOPHOCLES (496–406 B.C.) said, "Wonders are many and none is more wonderful than man."

### The Greek Creation Myth

All creation myths the world over have a certain similarity to one another, in that they explore the efforts of early humans to explain the origin of the Earth, the Sun, the Moon and the stars, and the creatures of the Earth, including men and women.

The best-known Greek creation myth is the one told by the renowned poet HESIOD (some time around 800 B.C.). It tells of the original chaos, a swirling, form-less mass, from which came GAIA, Earth Mother, and her son-consort, URANUS, the heavens. These two created all the animals and vegetation that covered the Earth.

They also created the TITANS, and the one-eyed CYCLOPES, and other monsters that Uranus banished underground.

Uranus was eventually ousted by his son, CRONUS. From Cronus and RHEA were born the 12 who would become the OLYMPIAN GODS, the great Greek pantheon of gods and goddesses.

## The Romans

Rome, which became one of the world's largest and most successful empires, famous for law-giving and material and cultural achievements, was a small, pastoral community when Greece was at its height.

The Romans' forbearers or ancestors, called LATIUMS, were simple folk, living in close-knit clans, but trading and intermarrying with other clans. For centuries they had been overrun by tribes from the north. First were the Ligurians, who originally came from North Africa and settled around the land still called Liguria, near Genoa. In the third millennium B.C. came the Terramara, people who lived in stilt houses and brought with them the art of making bronze artifacts and weapons, which ensured them military supremacy. In the 11th century B.C. came the Villanovans, named after a small town, Villanova, near Bologna, in northern Italy.

Also living on the Italian Peninsula were the Etruscans, who appear to have been native to the region but may have arrived early in the first millennium B.C. They could not only write, a skill rare in Italy, but they were also skilled in

The great Italian artist Sandro Botticelli (1445-1510) painted *Primavera* (Spring) in 1478. It captures the scene of the birth of Venus (center in red). The goddess is surrounded by (left to right) Mercury, The Three Graces, Flora, Chloris, and Zephyrus. The painting is in the Uffizi Gallery in Florence, Italy.

metalwork, sculpture, painting, and good living. Nobody knows exactly where the Etruscans came from. They may have come from Asia Minor, but their arrival was deep in prehistory. It seems certain that they had had contact with Greek culture.

Historians note with interest that the people of Rome were already sophisticated and discerning enough to adopt only those Etruscan morals and values that they thought would be useful to them. For instance, they eagerly embraced the idea of building temples to the deities; for an increasingly urban population, a temple was the logical place to worship, much better than the rocks and turf traditionally set up in a field. They also accepted the idea of divination, that is, the art of foretelling the future, often by means of animal sacrifice. The Romans of Latium ancestry were already a superstitious but cynical people; the idea that the future could be influenced by magic rituals, including sacrifices, and the casting of spells, fit in very well with their shrewdness and practicality.

The Romans, like all peoples, already had their gods: three chief gods—Jupiter, Mars, Quirinus—and many household Gods, such as Terminus and Cloacina. The Romans were practical people, not given to fantasizing about the family lives of their gods. The Romans paid homage to their gods, in return for which they expected protection, prosperity, fertility, good health, and more.

Jupiter started out his mythological life as a lump of stone, known as Jupiter Lapis. The worship of stones goes back to the Stone Age or earlier, when knives and ax heads were made from flint. Even in the Bronze Age, Jupiter continued to be worshiped as a terrifying flint figure.

Mars, who became associated with the Greek god of war, Ares, was at first worshiped as a god of fields and crops as well as a god of war. In early societies, the time for war came when the crops had been harvested and next year's growth did not yet need tending. The men were free to go to war between autumn and spring. In the temperate Northern Hemisphere, March, named after Mars, was the ideal month for war.

Quirinus, the third god of this early Roman triad, was also a war god, but eventually became known as the patron of citizenship. There were household gods, Lares and Penates, who presided over the hearth and pantry.

Greek gods were different from Roman gods. Greek gods were like human beings, only bigger and better and more beautiful. Roman gods were often thinly sketched characters such as Vulcan, who was feared and placated as the god of fire.

By borrowing mythologies from the Greeks and using the stories and beliefs for their own purposes, the Romans brought personalities and vividness to their religions. Jupiter took on the glory of the Greek Zeus, and was worshiped in Rome as Optimus Maximus (the best and greatest). Temples and statues were built to Jupiter and his consort, Juno, and Minerva, a goddess with no apparent relationship to Jupiter but important to the Romans. Juno, originally an ancient moon goddess, became assimilated with Hera. Minerva became assimilated with the Greek Athene. No Roman counterpart was found for Apollo, so he retained the same name in both Greek and Roman mythologies.

| Roman Names | Greek Names |
| --- | --- |
| **Gods:** | |
| Jupiter | Zeus |
| Neptune | Poseidon |
| Mars | Ares |
| Apollo | Apollo |
| Vulcan | Hephaestus |
| Mercury | Hermes |

**Goddesses:**

| | |
|---|---|
| Juno | Hera |
| Minerva | Athene |
| Diana | Artemis |
| Venus | Aphrodite |
| Vesta | Hestia |
| Ceres | Demeter |

## How to Use This Book

The entries in this book are in alphabetical order and may be looked up as in a dictionary. Alternate spellings are given in parentheses after the entry headword. Spellings given in FULL CAPITAL letters are variations of the names found in different translations. Those appearing in normal type with standard capitalization are English translations. Within the main text, cross-references to other entries, which contain additional information, are printed in SMALL CAPITAL letters. The index at the end of the book will also help you find your way around.

In case you are not familiar with Greek and Roman mythology, here is a list of the principal gods. If you look up the entries concerning these characters, you will find a general overview of Greek and Roman mythology.

THE OLYMPIANS GODS   The gods and goddesses who lived atop Mount Olympus, in Greece, were called the Olympians. As the influence of Greek myths grew in Rome and the empire it grew into, the people and their rulers adopted and adapted these Greek gods to meet their religious needs. In the following list the Greek name of each god is followed by the Roman name.

ZEUS/JUPITER   Zeus was the son of Titans. He was primarily a sky and weather god, with the thunderbolt as his emblem, but his presence was inescapable throughout Greek mythology.

HERA/JUNO   An ancient goddess, existing long before the time of the migrations and the new gods, including Zeus. She was the protector of women, children, and marriage. Her cult was so strong that the newcomers had to acknowledge it and absorb it into their own mythology by making Hera the consort of Zeus.

POSEIDON/NEPTUNE   The god of seas and of horses, and the cause of earthquakes ("The Earthshaker"). In ancient times, long before the appearance of Zeus, Poseidon was worshiped as a god of fertility and of herdsmen. His symbol, the three-tined trident, was also a symbol for the thunderbolt.

DEMETER/CERES   The goddess of fertility and the mother of PERSEPHONE, who was carried off to the UNDERWORLD by HADES. The winter months were dark and unfruitful, for that was when Persephone went underground. (See *Demeter and Persephone*, under DEMETER.)

HADES/PLUTO   The ruler of the dead and of the underworld. Since he did not live in OLYMPUS, his status as an Olympian is in dispute but as a brother of Zeus and Poseidon, he was a powerful force among the Olympians.

ATHENE/MINERVA   A goddess of war, but also a patroness of the arts and crafts; she was the goddess of wisdom and the patron goddess of the city of ATHENS.

APOLLO   The only god to have the same name in both Greek and Roman mythology. He has many functions: He was the god of poetry, music, archery, prophecy, and the art of healing. He was a sun god of great antiquity, just and wise and of great beauty.

ARTEMIS/DIANA   The sister of Apollo, goddess of the hunt and of beasts, of childbirth and of chastity. She is usually depicted with a bow and arrow.

HEPHAESTUS/VULCAN   The god of fire and of craftsmen, especially the smiths who worked in metal. He was known as "the divine artificer."

APHRODITE/VENUS   The goddess of love, Aphrodite was born of the sea foam that swirled around the flesh of Uranus that had been cast in the sea.

DIONYSUS/BACCHUS   A Greek fertility god of very ancient origin. He was famous for his frenzied festivities.

HERMES/MERCURY   The winged messenger of the gods, Hermes was also the god of merchants and thieves, roads, flocks, and luck.

© Infobase Publishing

# A

**ABSYRTUS** *Greek* Son of AEETES, who was king of Colchis; brother of the sorceress MEDEA.

In various tellings of the story of JASON and the GOLDEN FLEECE, Absyrtus' fate varies. In one version, Medea takes her brother hostage as she flees the kingdom of Colchis with Jason after he has stolen the fleece from Aeetes. Medea kills her brother and scatters his body parts over the road to delay pursuit by her father.

In another version, Absyrtus and his troops stop Jason and Medea at a river they must sail down as they flee. Jason breaks a truce with the prince and kills him, before making his escape.

**ACCA LARENTIA (1)** (ACCA LAURENTIA) *Roman* A minor divinity, perhaps originating in ETRURIA, honored in ROME during the annual festival of the Laurentalia, held on December 23. Known commonly as Larentia, this goddess appeared to have an association with the world of the dead and the early role of the LARES, guardian spirits of the dead. Scholars studying Roman writers agree that the god existed first and then, as Roman culture developed, stories grew up around Acca Larentia to explain her role in their culture.

The oldest stories say that Larentia was the wife of the shepherd FAUSTULUS, who found and brought to her the twins ROMULUS AND REMUS, so that she could nurse them and raise them as her own. She was also believed to have been a prostitute who changed her life and became revered as a saint, for the root of her name, *lupa*, means both she-wolf and whore. Through these similarities, it became convenient to connect this ancient goddess with the mythology surrounding these prominent twins, who, sons of MARS, were rescued by a she-wolf from the Tiber River and went on to found Rome.

**ACCA LARENTIA (2)** (ACCA LAURENTIA) *Roman* A prostitute with whom the god HERCULES spent the night in a Roman temple, after the priest of that temple played dice with the great hero and god and lost. Acca Larentia was the beautiful woman the priest found on the street and locked in the temple as a prize for Hercules.

After enjoying the night with her, Hercules told Acca Larentia to approach and be friendly with the first wealthy man she met upon leaving the temple. Some Roman writers say that Hercules influenced the man; others say that Acca Larentia used tricks of her trade to win his affections. As her role in the story of Rome continues, Acca Larentia married the rich man, and when he died, leaving her all of his wealth, she gave the fortune to Rome, the city she loved.

Ancient Roman writers and modern scholars are unsure of the relationship of the woman in this story with the Acca Larentia (1) who became the foster mother to ROMULUS AND REMUS. Some say it was the same woman; others say that familiarity with her name made it an easy one to give to the woman in this story from the Hercules legends.

**ACESTES** *Roman* Son of the Trojan woman Egesta and the Sicilian river god Crimisus; founder of Segesta, a city in Sicily.

Acestes welcomed to Sicily AENEAS, the hero from TROY, near the end of the hero's great journey following the TROJAN WAR. Aeneas' father, ANCHISES, died in Sicily. Acestes helped the hero bury his father, and a year later, helped Aeneas celebrate the games commemorating Anchises' death.

Acestes also provided a home in Sicily and founded cities there for the Trojan women who, after years of travel, refused to go any farther. According to some accounts, Acestes, who was born in Sicily, traveled to

Troy to fight in the great war with the Greeks, but returned to Sicily before the end of the war.

**ACHELOUS** *Greek*  A river god who turned himself into a serpent to overcome his rival, HERACLES, for the hand of DEIANIRA. Heracles finally subdued Achelous and won the maiden. Rivers and their gods were worshiped by the Greeks, who believed them to be the offspring of the gods OCEANUS and TETHYS.

ALCMAEON, one of the SEVEN AGAINST THEBES, cursed by his mother, finally found refuge on an island newly formed from silt carried down by the river Achelous.

**ACHERON** (River of Sadness) *Greek*  The "woeful river" of the UNDERWORLD (1) into which flowed the Phlegethon and the Coctyus. Acheron was the son of GAIA. He had quenched the thirst of the TITANS during their war with ZEUS, who then changed Acheron into a river. To cross the river Acheron, it was necessary to seek the help of CHARON, the ancient ferryman of the underworld.

Acheron is sometimes used as a synonym for HADES, the underworld.

**ACHILLES** *Greek*  The son of PELEUS and THETIS; married to DEIDAMIA; father of NEOPTOLEMUS. Achilles is the central figure of HOMER's ILIAD, the story of the TROJAN WAR, a 20-year battle between the Greeks and the Trojans after the abduction of HELEN by PARIS. Writers after Homer further developed the story of Achilles, and around this figure grew a series of great legends. A soothsayer prophesied that without the aid of Achilles the Greeks would never defeat the Trojans. Achilles went bravely into battle and indeed the Greeks won the war. Achilles was a hero in battle, and he has become a symbol of the fighting man doomed to die in war but glorying in the fulfillment of heroism and achievement. He is a vivid character, given to rages and revenge, such as his barbarous treatment of the body of the slain Trojan hero HECTOR.

**The Childhood of Achilles**  Thetis, the mother of Achilles, was a sea NYMPH who had been wooed by ZEUS and POSEIDON. She reluctantly married Peleus and left him soon after the birth of Achilles. Knowing that Achilles was destined to be a hero who would win glory but also die in battle, she bathed the infant in the river STYX, trying to make him invulnerable to wounds. But the heel by which she held the child remained dry, and it was from an arrow wound in that heel that Achilles eventually died. The arrow was shot by either APOLLO or Paris, in a battle near the end of the Trojan War.

As Achilles grew, Thetis put him in the care of CHIRON, the gentle and wise CENTAUR. Chiron fed the lad the entrails of lions and the marrow of bears to make him brave, and taught him the arts of riding and hunting as well as of music and healing.

When the Greek leaders began to prepare for war with TROY, Peleus, knowing that Achilles faced certain death in Troy, hid his son in the court of Lycomedes, king of Scyros, and disguised him as a girl. However, since the seer CALCHAS had prophesied that without Achilles the Trojans would never be defeated in the war, the Greeks were determined to seek out the young man. ODYSSEUS, another Greek hero, sent presents to the "girl," among them a superb spear and shield. When Achilles promptly and expertly took up these objects in a battle alarm, the Greeks recognized him for the man that he was and they led him off to the battlefield.

**Achilles at War**  Achilles had early training in the art of war (as well as of music and healing) from CHIRON. When he went to war against the Trojans, Achilles led his own army, unlike the rest of the Greeks, who acknowledged AGAMEMNON as their leader. It had been prophesied that without Achilles the Trojans would triumph over the Greeks. Therefore there was much dismay when Agamemnon and Achilles quarreled over the beautiful captive BRISEIS, who had been stolen away from Achilles by Agamemnon. In a fury, Achilles withdrew his army from the war, with disastrous results for the Greeks. This is the quarrel from which the events described in the *Iliad* commence.

When the Greeks began to lose ground in the battle against the Trojans, Achilles finally sent his troops back into war under the leadership of PATROCLUS, his dearest friend. Patroclus was killed by the Trojan hero HECTOR. Achilles then went back into the war and routed the Trojans. He slew Hector. Despite the anguished pleas of PRIAM (king of the Trojans and father of Hector), Achilles dragged Hector's body around the wall of Troy and the tomb of Patroclus. Achilles finally gave Hector's mutilated body to Priam in return for the warrior's weight in gold.

**ACTAEON** *Greek*  A hunter and the son of Autonoe and grandson of CADMUS. He aroused the anger of the goddess ARTEMIS when he saw her bathing naked in a river. Artemis changed Actaeon into a stag. His own dogs set upon him and tore him to pieces.

**ADMETUS** *Greek*  King of Phera in THESSALY; one of the ARGONAUTS. Admetus was a kind master to APOLLO, who had been his slave as a punishment for killing the CYCLOPS. When Apollo heard that Admetus was soon to die, Apollo went to the Fates and persuaded them to prolong Admetus's life. They agreed, on condition that someone else should be sent in his stead. Not even the parents of Admetus would give up their lives. His faithful wife, ALCESTIS, agreed to do so. She took a drink of poison and went down to HADES, but PERSEPHONE refused to let her stay. She sent her back to her husband and children. Another version of the story says that HERACLES went to the UNDERWORLD and wrestled with Hades for the life of Alcestis.

The story is the subject of a play, *Alcestis*, by EURIPIDES, and an opera, *Alceste*, by the German composer Christoph Willibald Gluck (1714–1787).

**ADONIS** *Greek* The beloved of APHRODITE and the personification of masculine beauty. His mother was the beautiful Myrrha; his father, King Theias, king of Syria, was the father of Myrrha. The strange parentage of Adonis came about because Aphrodite was jealous of Myrrha's beauty and caused the girl to unite with her own father. When Cinyrus found out that he had been tricked, he chased Myrrha with a sword, intending to kill her and her unborn child. Aphrodite, repenting of her deed, quickly turned the girl into a myrrh tree. The king's sword split the tree and out stepped the beautiful child Adonis.

Aphrodite hid the baby in a box and gave it to PERSEPHONE, queen of death, to look after. Persephone reared Adonis in the UNDERWORLD (1). He grew to be a handsome young man, whereupon Aphrodite claimed him back. Persephone refused to give him up. Appealed to by the two goddesses, ZEUS decreed that each should have him for half of the year. When he stayed in the underworld, it was winter. When he returned, the Earth blossomed into spring and summer.

In some versions of the story, when ARES hears that Aphrodite loves the youth Adonis, he changes himself into a wild boar and gores the boy to death. Anemones spring from the blood of Adonis and his spirit returns to the underworld. In response to the two tearful goddesses, Zeus determines that Adonis should stay with each of them in turn for half the year.

According to scholars, the death and resurrection of Adonis represents the decay and revival of the plant year. He was worshiped as a corn god, a god of grain crops, which were much more important to the ancient inhabitants of the Mediterranean lands than the berries and roots of the wilderness that nourished their primitive, pre-agrarian ancestors.

**ADRASTIA** (Inescapable One) *Greek* Daughter of Melisseus, king of CRETE; sister of IDA (1). With Ida and the goat-NYMPH AMALTHEA, Adrastia tended the infant god ZEUS on Mount IDA (2), in Crete. Later mythology identified Adrastia with NEMESIS, the goddess of vengeance.

**ADRASTUS** *Greek* King of ARGOS; the leader of the warriors known as the SEVEN AGAINST THEBES according to the tragedy written by the Greek poet AESCHYLUS. The attack on THEBES by rebels who supported Polynices in his attempt to force his brother, Eteocles, off the throne of Thebes was a disaster. Of the seven champions, only Adrastus lived, escaping on his winged horse, ARION.

Later, Adrastus made another attempt to gain Thebes, when the children of the Seven, called the EPIGONI, were old enough to become warriors. This time the battle was a success, but it was a sad victory for Adrastus because his only son, Aegialeus, was killed in the conflict.

**AEETES** *Greek* King of Colchis on the island of RHODES; his father was the sun god HELIOS and his mother the NYMPH Rhodos; brother of CIRCE, the witch goddess, and PASIPHAE; father with Eidyia, a daughter of the god OCEANUS, of MEDEA and ABSYRTUS.

Aeetes provided shelter to PHRIXUS when the youth arrived on Rhodes on the back of the ram with the GOLDEN FLEECE, and Aeetes became the guardian of that treasure. When JASON and his ARGONAUTS arrived in search of the fleece, Aeetes set challenges before the hero, who completed each one, but the king did not keep his word and would not give Jason the fleece. Jason, with the help of Medea, who was gifted in magic and prophecy, stole the fleece and fled on ship. Aeetes sent his navy after them.

According to one version of the story, Medea took ABSYRTUS hostage, then killed him and scattered his body over the road so that Aeetes would stop and pick up the pieces and allow Jason time to escape. According to the version in the *ARGONAUTICA*, Absyrtus led Colchian troops to a river the Argonauts would need to travel down to escape. Jason broke a truce, killed Absyrtus, then made his escape with Medea and the Argonauts. Aeetes never captured them nor retrieved the fleece.

Years later, Aeetes was deposed by another brother, but Medea returned to restore her father to the throne of Colchis.

**AEGEUS** *Greek* King of ATHENS and father of the hero THESEUS, with Aethra, daughter of King Pittheus of Troezen. Some say that the sea god, POSEIDON, was the father of Theseus, and that possibly Aegeus and Poseidon were one and the same.

When Aegeus left Troezen, Aegeus told Aethra that if a child should be born of their union, it was to be reared quietly in Troezen, with King Pittheus as guardian. Aegeus then hid his sword and sandals under a rock, telling Aethra that she was to lead the child, when it became old enough, to the hiding place so that he or she could recover the tokens of its identity.

When Aegeus thought that Theseus had been killed, he threw himself into the sea that today bears his name—the Aegean Sea.

**AEGINA** *Greek* An island in the Saronic Gulf, south of ATHENS; in Greek legend, named after Aegina, a lover of the god ZEUS. When plague struck the island, Zeus repeopled it by turning the ants of the island into humans, who were known as MYRMIDONS. The ancient Cretan deity BRITOMARTIS took refuge here from the attentions of King MINOS; the Aegeans called her DICTYNNA. Aegina was the birthplace of PELEUS, son of King Aecus.

**AEGIS** (Goat Skin) *Greek* The shield of ZEUS made by the smith-god HEPHAESTUS and covered with the skin of the goat-NYMPH AMALTHEA. The shield had the power to terrify and disperse the enemy. When Zeus shook it, the shield produced tremendous thunder and lightning storms. It also had the power to protect friends. The aegis was also worn by ATHENE, when it bore the head of the GORGON, MEDUSA, in its center. The aegis is a symbol of divine protection.

**AEGISTHUS** *Greek* Son of Pelopia and THYESTES. Aegisthus became the lover of CLYTEMNESTRA, the wife of King AGAMEMNON, after the king had gone off to the TROJAN WAR. Aegisthus and Clytemnestra killed Agamemnon when he returned from the war and were in turn murdered by ORESTES and ELECTRA, Agamemnon's children.

Aegisthus was one of the descendants of PELOPS and a victim of the curse laid upon the family by the murdered charioteer, MYRTILUS (see *Pelops and the Charioteer*, under Pelops).

When Pelopia realized that Aegisthus was the son not of her husband, ATREUS, but of her own father, Thyestes, she placed the infant on a mountainside to die. But the baby survived, suckled by a goat, and grew up to play his part in the tragic story of the house of Pelops. (See Atreus AND THYESTES.)

Eventually Aegisthus killed his supposed father, Atreus, and acknowledged Thyestes as his real father.

It was only at the death of Aegisthus and Clytemnestra that the FURIES were satisfied and put an end to the tragedies and atrocities that had stained the house of Atreus (the Atreids) and the descendants of Pelops.

There are several versions of the genealogy of this accursed family, involving further incest, murder, and intrigue.

**AEGLE (1)** (Brightness) *Greek* Daughter of ASCLEPIUS, the god of medicine, and Lempetia, a daughter of HELIOS, or of Epione. The origin of her name is unclear, though it may refer to the health of the human body. Her sisters had names that related to their father's role: PANACEA, which means *all healing*, and Iaso, whose name means *healthy*.

**AEGLE (2)** (Dazzling Light) *Greek* A DRYAD, or wood NYMPH; one of the sisters known as the HESPERIDES; either the daughters of EREBUS (Darkness) and NYX (Night) or the daughters of ATLAS and PLEIONE or Hesperis. Aegle's sisters, those named by people writing during the classic age of Greek mythology, were ERYTHEIA, ARETHUSA, and HESPERIA.

**AEGLE (3)** *Greek* The most beautiful of the NAIADS, fresh water NYMPHS who guarded springs, wells, brooks, and small bodies of water; daughters of ZEUS.

**AENEAS** *Greek and Roman* Son of ANCHISES, a prince of TROY, and the goddess VENUS; husband of CREUSA; father of ASCANIUS; a hero of HOMER's Greek epic the *ILIAD*, and, perhaps more importantly, of the Roman poet VIRGIL's the *AENEID*.

In the *Iliad* and other Greek writings, Aeneas is the leader of the Dardanians, descendants of DARDANUS, the founder of Troy. King PRIAM, for whom they were fighting, was Aeneas' uncle. Aeneas fought many battles against the Greeks who had declared war against Troy in an effort to rescue the beautiful woman HELEN. Venus and the god APOLLO frequently helped Aeneas in his battles, as did other gods.

As the Greeks were about to sack Troy, Venus warned Aeneas and insisted that he leave. Aeneas gathered up his family, carrying his lame father on his back. Aeneas also gathered up the family gods, including the PENATES, and his father carried them as his son carried him. Warriors and friends fled the city with Aeneas. Creusa, however, was killed in the crush of people. Aeneas returned for her but found only her ghost, who told him to journey forward, to fulfill his destiny of founding a new city in Italy. Aeneas fled Troy, taking with him shiploads of refugees, including many women and children.

The story of Aeneas arriving with his son Ascanius on the shores of Latium is recounted in this marble relief carved in the second century A.D. The marble sculpture is in the British Museum in London. *(Photograph by Marie-Lan Nguyen.)*

Their journey to Italy took years and included many adventures. Though they were beset with turmoil and hardship, the great gods Jupiter, Juno, Neptune, and Mercury watched over them, often intervening on their behalf.

Eventually, Aeneas and a small group of the strongest and bravest of his followers landed on the shores of Italy in the kingdom of Latium. (The rest of the group that had fled Troy had stayed on the island of Sicily.) There Aeneas was welcomed by King Latinus, who, fearing the might of the Trojan hero, betrothed his daughter Lavinia to Aeneas. This angered Turnus, the king of the nearby Rutuli people, to whom Lavinia had been betrothed. A war ensued which lasted years. Gods supported both sides and many heroes died in the combat. Eventually, Aeneas killed Turnus in one-on-one combat and the war came to an end.

Aeneas married Lavinia and founded the city of Lavinium, which he named after her. Years later, Aeneas died, and his mother, Venus, asked Jupiter to make him a god. The Roman people worshiped Aeneas as a founding figure and protector long before Virgil wrote the *Aeneid* in the first century B.C.

**AENEID** Roman The epic poem composed by Latin poet Virgil between 30 and 19 B.C. It is divided into 12 books and was considered unfinished by Virgil when he died. Nevertheless, the *Aeneid* is one of the cornerstones of world literature. It had enormous influence on Roman thought, for it centered on a genuinely Roman myth, glorifying Rome and foretelling its future prosperity. People of all classes knew it by heart and often quoted it.

Virgil was greatly admired in his own lifetime, for his contemporaries at once understood his greatness and the relevance of his epic to their own culture.Like the *ODYSSEY*, written by Greek poet Homer between the eighth and the ninth centuries B.C., the *Aeneid* is the tale of a hero who fought in the Trojan War.

Aeneas fought on the Trojan side. He fled the burning city carrying his father, Anchises, on his back. Part of his story is told in flashback to Queen Dido of Carthage, who falls in love with him. Ever the favorite of the gods, Aeneas learns from Jupiter (via his messenger, Mercury) that the hero must leave Dido, for his destiny is to establish an empire on the west coast of Italy.

When Aeneas deserts her, the lovelorn Dido kills herself with his sword. When Aeneas reaches the kingdom of Latium, at the mouth of the river Tiber, King Latinus gives him the hand of his daughter Lavinia in marriage. However, Lavinia has already been promised to Turnus, king of the RUTULI. War is declared between the rivals. Helped by EVANDER, leader of the Arcadians, and the goddess VENUS (who brings Aeneas a shield crafted by VULCAN) Aneas and his troops defeat TURNUS. Turnus and Aeneas agree to end the war in single combat. Despite the aid of the warrior maiden CAMILLA, Turnus is defeated and Aeneas is victorious.

**AEOLUS** *Greek* God of the winds, also king of the winds. In HOMER's *ODYSSEY*, Aeolus helped the hero ODYSSEUS by imprisoning the winds in a huge leather bag, leaving only the west wind free to blow the ships of Odysseus homeward to Ithaca. When the ships were near home, Odysseus fell asleep from exhaustion. The restless, curious crew of the ship opened the bag. The winds escaped and blew all the ships away from Ithaca and back toward the island of Lipara, where Aeolus lived. Aeolus was angry and refused to help Odysseus further.

**AEROPE** *Greek* Wife of ATREUS, a member of the PELOPS family, mother of AGAMEMNON and MENELAUS, and possibly of Anaxibia and Pleisthenes. Atreus threw Aerope into the sea for her adultery with his brother. (See *The Golden Fleece*, under ATREUS AND THYESTES.)

**AESCHYLUS** (525–456 B.C.) Greek poet and dramatist, held by many to be the founder of Greek tragedy.

His plays preserve some of the stories of Greek mythology. Aeschylus was the first dramatist to introduce a second actor onto the stage; before him, drama had only one actor appearing at a time. The innovative use of dialogue between the actors brought vividness to the stage. Aeschylus also developed the use of costumes and special effects. Only seven of his many plays survive, among them *The Seven Against Thebes*, *Prometheus Bound*, and *The Oresteia*, a trilogy that tells the epic drama of King AGAMEMNON and how his murder was arranged by his son ORESTES.

**AESON** *Greek* King of IOLCUS (in THESSALY); with Queen Alcimede, father of JASON; half-brother of PELIAS, who usurped the throne of Iolcus.

**AETOLIA** District of the southern Greek mainland. One of its chief towns was CALYDON, site of the CALYDONIAN BOAR HUNT. It was named after Aetolus, son of ENDYMION.

**AGAMEMNON** *Greek* King of ARGOS and MYCENAE, regions in the northern PELOPONNESUS; son of Atreus and AEROPE. He was the grandson of PELOPS

and the last member of a family doomed to one tragedy after another. He was the brother of MENELAUS and Anaxibia; and the husband of CLYTEMNESTRA, with whom he fathered Chrysothemis, ELECTRA, IPHIGENIA, and ORESTES. King Agamemnon was the leader of the Achaean (Greek) forces in the TROJAN WAR. He was eventually killed by Clytemnestra and AEGISTHUS.

Driven from Mycenae after the murder of their father, Atreus, Agamemnon and Menelaus fled to SPARTA. There Agamemnon wed Clytemnestra, and Menelaus wed HELEN. Agamemnon was chosen to lead the Greeks in the expedition to rescue his sister-in-law, Helen, after PARIS abducted her. The expedition was stalled when Agamemnon offended the goddess ARTEMIS. A soothsayer, CALCHAS, said that only the sacrifice of Iphigenia would appease Artemis and AEOLUS, the wind god. Agamemnon tricked his wife into sending their daughter to her death.

In another act of treachery, Agamemnon stole BRISEIS, the beloved of the hero ACHILLES, who then laid down his arms and withdrew from the Trojan War (though he later rejoined it).

When Agamemnon returned in triumph from the war, 10 years later, accompanied by the princess CASSANDRA as booty, both he and she were murdered by Clytemnestra and her lover, Aegisthus. Agamemnon was trapped in a net and drowned in a bathtub, an ignoble end for a hero.

Agamemnon was one of the principal characters in Homer's *ILIAD*. He was a brave and successful warrior but a selfish and treacherous man.

Historians believe that there was a real King Agamemnon in Argos or Mycenae, since Agamemnon appears often in Greek mythology and there were many cults of Agamemnon in various places in ancient Greece.

**AGDISTIS** *Greek* A Phrygian mother-goddess, sometimes known as CYBELE, goddess of fertility, and associated with RHEA, Greek Earth mother and mother of the Olympian gods.

**AGENOR** *Greek* King of Tyre (in PHOENICIA); son of the sea god POSEIDON and LIBYA; father of EUROPA, CADMUS, PHOENIX, and CILIX; husband of Telephassa. After the god ZEUS carried off Europa, Agenor sent his three sons in search of their sister. The sons did not find her, and settled down elsewhere to found new nations. Phoenix was the ancestor of the Phoenicians; Cilix of the Cilicians; and the celebrated Cadmus, who settled in Boeotia and built the Cadmea (a fortress), was the founder of the city of THEBES.

The dispersal of Agenor's sons seems to refer to the westward flight of the Canaanite tribe (early Phoenicians) in the second millennium B.C., under pressure from Aryan and Semite invaders.

**AGRICULTURAL GODS** *Roman* Agriculture was critical to the success of ancient ROME. Growing crops and herds to feed the people was essential not only to individual health but, almost more importantly, the success of a growing society.

The earliest cultures of central Italy recognized a multitude of gods and goddesses who watched over almost every aspect of growing plants and raising animals to feed the growing communities. As they did with their PERSONAL GODS, these ancestors of the Romans recognized forces beyond their control and gave these forces names. They then performed rituals to either ask for the deity's help for a good growing season, or to implore the deity to not harm their fields or animals.

Gods and goddesses oversaw the food supply as well. People asked them to keep the harvest safe from storms, volcanoes, and bad workmanship, to help turn grapes into wine and grain into bread, and to bring crops to market.

## Principle Roman Agricultural Gods

*This chart includes only the agricultural characteristics that pertain to the gods. Many of them, particularly those that became more important in Roman culture, had other functions in society than overseeing the production of food.*

| God/Goddess | Gender | Area of agricultural influence |
|---|---|---|
| BACCHUS | M | Grape vines, wine |
| BUBONA | F | Protected oxen and cattle |
| CERES | F | Grain crops, cereals (She had many assistants.) |
| CONSUS | M | Grains and full storage bins |
| DEA DIA | F | Growth |
| EPONA | F | Protected horses |
| EVENTUS BONUS | M | Success in agriculture |
| FAUNUS | M | Fertility |
| FAUSTITAS | F | Protected herds and livestock |
| FLORA | F | Fertility, especially associated with flowers |
| FORNAX | F | Bread and baking, to prevent burning |
| LACTANS | M | Promoted the growth of young grain crops |
| LIBER | M | Fertility and healthy growth of vines |
| LUPERCUS | M | Protected livestock |
| NODUTUS | M | Harvesting wheat |
| OPS | M | Wealth of the harvest |
| PALES | F | Guarded shepherds and their flocks |
| POMONA | F | Fruit orchards and gardens |
| PORUS | M | Abundance |
| PRIAPUS | M | Fertility of all gardens and flocks |
| PUTA | F | Guided the pruning of vines and bushes |
| ROBIGO | F | Protected crops, particularly corn, from diseases |
| ROBIGUS | M | Protected crops from diseases |
| RUNCINA | F | Weeding and harvesting the crop |
| SARITOR | M | Hoeing and weeding |
| SATURN | M | The sowing of seeds |
| SEMONIA | F | The sowing of seeds |
| SILVANUS | M | Fields, forests, and woods |
| SPINIENSIS | M | Protected farmers from thorns when they weeded |
| VERMINUS | M | Protected cattle from disease, especially worms |
| VERTUMNUS | M | The ripening of fruit with the changing of seasons |

The rituals began as private acts, small prayers or sacrifices conducted by the head of a family. Over time, some of the gods grew in importance and became major deities in Roman culture. By the eighth century B.C., the rituals of the growing season had become so much a part of early Roman culture, which by then included influences of the people from ETRURIA, LATIUM, and much of Central Italy, that the Roman calendar already contained the great seasonal festivals centered on agriculture. The most prominent were on April 19, the Cerealia, celebrating the goddess of grains, and on April 25, the Robigalia, asking the god of mildew to spare the crop. These days of honoring the gods were celebrated by special clergy and involved the entire Roman community in their pageantry and sacrifice.

See also HOUSEHOLD GODS; INDIGETES; PERSONAL GODS; STATE GODS

**AJAX (1)** *Greek* Son of TELAMON, king of Salamis. He was one of the heroes who sailed with the Greeks to the TROJAN WAR. He is represented in HOMER's *ILIAD* as second only to ACHILLES in bravery. Ajax is described as tall and strong, though perhaps slow-witted, prone to rages and madness. He lost the contest for the armor of Achilles and in a fit of despair took his own life.

**AJAX (2)** ("The Lesser") *Greek* Son of Oileus of TROY; Greek warrior in the TROJAN WAR. Unlike AJAX (1), he was a small man, but swift-footed and a skilled spearman. Ajax the Lesser drowned on his way home to Greece after the fall of Troy. Some say he was a victim of the sea god, POSEIDON. Some claim that he was the victim of the goddess ATHENE.

**ALBA LONGA** A city of ancient LATIUM, southeast of ROME. It is the site of the modern Castel Gondolfo. Tradition has it that ROMULUS AND REMUS were born in Alba Longa, thus making it the mother city of ROME.

**ALCESTIS** *Greek* Daughter of PELIAS. Married to ADMETUS, she was the symbol of wifely devotion. Alcetis willingly gave up her life for Admetus so that he could live a little longer. But PERSEPHONE, queen of the UNDERWORLD, refused to admit Alcestis and sent her back to Earth.

In another version of her death, HERACLES wrestles with HADES for the life of Alcestis, and wins the battle. Alcestis and Admetus are the subjects of a play, *Alcestis*, by EURIPIDES.

**ALCINOUS** *Greek* King of the Phaecians on the island of Scheria. In HOMER's *ODYSSEY*, Alcinous and his daughter, NAUSICAA, entertain the Greek hero ODYSSEUS, who has been shipwrecked on his way home from the TROJAN WAR.

**ALCIPPE** *Greek* Daughter of the war god ARES and the NYMPH Aglauros. Halirrhothius, a son of the sea god POSEIDON, ravished Alcippe. Ares killed Halirrhothius for this crime.

**ALCMAEON** *Greek* The son of AMPHIARAUS (one of the SEVEN AGAINST THEBES) and of ERIPHYLE; brother of Amphilochus. The sons of the seven fallen champions who had fought at THEBES were called the EPIGONI (descendants). They swore to avenge their fathers, and Alcmaeon rather reluctantly became their leader. He had been persuaded by his mother, Eriphyle, who in turn had been bribed with the coveted magic robe and amber necklace of HARMONIA.

When he learned that his mother had been similarly bribed to send his father off to war, Alcmaeon killed Eriphyle. Her dying curse was that no land would ever shelter Alcmaeon. Alcmaeon wandered from place to place, pursued by the FURIES, who gave him no rest. Finally, he found an island newly formed from silt brought down by the river ACHELOUS. Since the island had not existed when Eriphyle uttered her curse, Alcmaeon was able to find peace, at least for a while.

He married CALLIRHOË, the daughter of OENEUS, king of CALYDON. Callirhoë heard about the fabulous robe and necklace that had been given to Eriphyle, and as the wife of Alcmaeon, demanded that the treasures be given to her. She did not know that in his unhappy wanderings her husband had married Arsinoë, daughter of an Arcadian king, and given the treasures to her. Alcmaeon returned to ARCADIA and begged King Psophis to give him the treasure, as he wanted to place it in the shrine of APOLLO at DELPHI. The king could not refuse such a request; but when he heard the truth from one of Alcmaeon's servants, he had Alcmaeon killed.

Princess Arsinoë witnessed the death of her husband and, knowing nothing of his treachery, vowed vengeance on her father. The king sent the treasure to Delphi, in the hope that no further harm would come of it, but the treasure of Harmonia was accursed. Eventually King Phegeus and all his family died at the hands of the vengeful sons of Alcmaeon and Callirhoë.

**ALCMENE** *Greek* Daughter of Electryon, king of MYCENAE; granddaughter of the hero PERSEUS; wife and cousin of Amphitryon; mother of Heracles (by Zeus) and of Iphicles (by her husband).

While her husband was at war, the god Zeus disguised as Amphitryon, visited Alcmene. According to Hesiod, Alcmene was a most virtuous woman and would not have entertained Zeus had he appeared as himself. Zeus realized this, and wanting to sire a champion for both gods and humans, he wooed Alcmene as if he were her husband. It is said that the experience was so enjoyable that Zeus, with his magic, made one night last the length of three. The next morning, Amphitryon returned from war and mated with his wife, who then also conceived a mortal son, Iphicles. Alcmene bore the hero Heracles, son of Zeus on one day and his twin brother the next day.

When Alcmene died, many years later, Zeus had her taken to the Islands of the Blessed, where she married Rhadamanthus.

**ALOEIDS** (ALOADAE) *Greek* Giant sons of Iphimedia by Poseidon. Their names were Ephialtes and Otus; they were called the Aloeids after Aloeus, the husband of Iphimedia. The brothers grew at an enormous rate. By the time they were nine years old, they were 36 feet tall. These giants declared war on Olympus, the home of the gods. Ephialtes determined to capture Hera, wife of the great god Zeus. Otus swore he would capture Artemis, goddess of the hunt. First they seized Ares, god of war, and confined him in a bronze vessel, where he remained for 13 months until he was rescued by Hermes.

Then their siege of Olympus began: The giants piled Mount Pelion atop Mount Ossa (in Thessaly) to create a ladder to the heavens. They were not afraid of the gods, for it had been prophesied that neither gods nor men would kill them. Artemis tricked them by turning herself into a white doe and prancing before them. The brothers threw their spears at the doe, who skillfully darted away, and they accidentally killed each other with their spears. Thus the prophecy was fulfilled, for neither gods nor humans had killed them; they had killed each other. The souls of the Aloeids went down to Tartarus, where they were tied back to back on either side of a pillar, with cords that were living vipers.

The story of the Aloeids symbolizes the revolt of the giants against the gods. The imprisonment of Ares may symbolize a 13-month truce between two warring tribes of ancient Greece, when warlike tokens of both nations were sealed into a bronze jar to ensure peace.

In another version of the myth, in Homer's *Odyssey*, it is said that the brothers would have suc-cessfully stormed Olympus if the god Apollo had not slain them with his arrows.

The Aloeids were worshiped on the island of Naxos (where Artemis had appeared to them as a doe) and in the city of Ascra, in Boeotia, where they were regarded as founders of the city.

Myths of the Aloeids also appear in Homer's *Odyssey* and in Virgil's *Aeneid*.

**ALOEUS** *Greek* Son of Poseidon; husband of Iphimedia. Iphimedia had two sons, Otus and Ephialtes, by Poseidon. After she married Aloeus, the sons were known as the Aloeids (sons of Aloeus).

**AMALTHEA** (Tender) *Greek* The goat-Nymph that suckled the infant Zeus on Mount Ida (2) in Crete. Zeus was grateful to the goat-nymph. When he became lord of the universe, he set Amalthea's image among the stars as Capricorn (the goat). He also borrowed one of her horns, which were as large

The nymph Amalthea helped nurture the infant Zeus (known by the Romans as Jupiter) with the milk of a goat. Her story is portrayed in this statue by French artist Pierre Julien (1731-1804). The statue, known as *Amalthea and the Goat of Jupiter*, is in the Musée de Louvre in Paris.

and full as a cow's, and gave it to ADRASTIA and Ida (1), the ash nymphs who, with Amalthea, had tended the infant Zeus, as a CORNUCOPIA, horn of plenty. The horn would always be filled with food and drink for its owners. The AEGIS, the shield worn by Zeus, was covered with the skin of Amalthea.

**AMAZONS** *Greek* A legendary race of female warriors, supposed to live in ASIA MINOR or possibly Africa, or, as Greek navigators explored farther, "at the edge of the world." The Amazons were sometimes associated with ARTEMIS, goddess of the hunt, but no close connection exists except that the name of one Amazonian leader was Artemis. Some scholars say that the legend of the Amazon warriors may be connected with the invasion of beardless nomads from the Russian steppes.

The Amazons appear in several legends, including those of the hero HERACLES. The most famous queen of the Amazons was HIPPOLYTA, whose girdle Heracles stole, and who was vanquished by THESEUS, to whom she bore a son, HIPPOLYTUS. PENTHESILEA, an Amazon queen, fought valiantly for the Trojans in the TROJAN WAR. She was slain by ACHILLES.

The Greeks cited the conquest of the Amazons as a triumph of civilization over barbarism. Scholars have cited it as a triumph of male dominance over female independence.

Some say that the Amazon warriors cut off one breast in order to facilitate use of the bow. However, there are no known depictions of this phenomenon in ancient art.

**AMPHIARAUS** *Greek* Known as the seer of ARGOS, he was the brother-in-law of King ADRASTUS, leader of the SEVEN AGAINST THEBES. Amphiaraus foresaw that the war would be a disaster but was reluctantly persuaded to join the warriors by his wife, ERIPHYLE, the sister of Adrastus. Amphiaraus would have been killed by the Thebans but for the intervention of ZEUS. He vanished into a cleft in the Earth made by Zeus. The spot became famous as a shrine and oracle.

**AMPHION** *Greek* Son of ZEUS and ANTIOPE; twin brother of ZETHUS; husband of NIOBE. The twin brothers captured THEBES and decided to build a wall around it. Zethus found the stones and Amphion, who had been given a lyre by the messenger god HERMES, played so sweetly that the stones assembled themselves into a wall. Amphion married Niobe, with whom he had many children.

**AMPHITRITE** *Greek* A sea goddess; daughter of NEREUS or OCEANUS; wife of POSEIDON; mother of TRITON, Rhode, and Benthescyme. She was a female personification of the sea.

Amphitrite was not pleased when Poseidon tried to woo her. She fled into the Atlas Mountains, in North Africa. Poseidon sent delphinus to win her and eventually she consented to become Poseidon's wife. She bore him three children.

Amphitrite discovered that Poseidon was a faithless husband. One of his lovers was the beautiful NYMPH SCYLLA, whom Amphitrite changed into a terrible monster.

**AMPHITRYON** *Greek* Grandson of the Greek hero PERSEUS; husband of ALCMENE; father of IPHICLES and foster father of the hero HERACLES, who was the son of Alcmene and the supreme god ZEUS. His brother, Electryon, was the father of Alcmene, and king of MYCENAE. The brothers quarreled and Amphitryon accidentally killed Electryon. Amphitryon and Alcmene fled to THEBES and were given refuge by King Creon. In gratitude, Amphitryon helped to rid Thebes of a monster known as the Teumessian vixen, a fox that had terrorized the country by demanding the sacrifice of a child every month. With the help of Zeus and the marvelous hound LAELAPS, which could catch anything it hunted, Amphitryon rid the country of the dreaded fox.

**ANANKE** *Greek* An ancient goddess or personification of the absolute fate of all things, a force that even the great gods could not resist. According to some versions of her story, Ananke was formed independently from the forces of the cosmos, at the same time as CRONUS; together they formed all the parts of the cosmos. In other stories, Ananke was a daughter of Cronus.

Ananke was the mother of the MOIRAE or the Fates, and also the mother of ETHER, CHAOS, and EREBUS, the primeval forces of nature. She was part of the elaborate mythology that developed around ORPHEUS, a mythical hero from Thrace on the northern shores of the Aegean Sea, and the traditions of the origins of the cosmos that centered on this character.

The Roman goddess NECESSITAS eventually took on the origins and stories of Ananke.

**ANAXARETE** (Excellent Princess) *Greek* The central villain in a popular love story from Greek mythology. Anaxarete was a rich and beautiful but cruel maiden who lived in a city on the island of Cyprus.

The handsome young man Iphis loved Anaxarete, but she only laughed at his pledges of devotion. In final desperation, Iphis hanged himself in her doorway. Even that act brought no feelings of sadness to Anaxarete. The citizens of her city, though, were so touched by his unfulfilled love and his sad ending that they gave him a huge funeral procession. The crowd wound through the streets and passed the home of Anaxarete's family. Curious, and believing the crowd was honoring her, Anaxarete leaned out of the window. When she realized the people were honoring Iphis, she only laughed and scoffed at the dead young man.

APHRODITE, goddess of love, watched the procession, too. She knew of Iphis's unrequited love and shared the pity the crowd felt for him. When Aphrodite heard Anaxarete's callous laughter, the goddess grew furious and turned the maiden to stone in the very position of leaning out of the window. Discovering Anaxarete, the people of Cyprus placed the statue in a temple at Salamis, where it stood as a reminder of the girl's cruelty.

**ANCHISES** *Greek* A Trojan prince or king loved by the goddess APHRODITE, who bore him a son, AENEAS. When Anchises boasted that a goddess had loved him, the great god ZEUS struck him blind or lame (stories differ). His son, Aeneas, carried him away from the burning city of Troy on his shoulders. This story is told in VIRGIL's *AENEID* and is the subject of works of art by Italian artists Giovanni Bernini (1598–1680) and Raphael (1483–1520).

**ANDROGEUS** *Greek* Son of MINOS and PASIPHAË; brother of ARIADNE and PHAEDRA. Androgeus was a great athlete. He beat all his opponents at the OLYMPIC GAMES in Athens, whereupon the jealous King AEGEUS had him assassinated. Subsequently, King Minos of CRETE declared war on Athens.

**ANDROMACHE** *Greek* A touching, tragic figure in the TROJAN WAR. She was the daughter of King Thebe of Cilicia; wife of the Trojan hero HECTOR; mother of Astyanax. Andromache lost her father and brothers at the fall of Troy and was given as booty to NEOPTOLEMUS. Her son Astyanax was murdered by the victorious Greek hero ODYSSEUS. Andromache was cruelly treated by Hermione, the wife of NEOPTOLEMUS, but finally found peace with her fellow Trojan captive, HELENUS. Her story is told in *Andromache*, a play by EURIPIDES, and in HOMER's *ILIAD*.

**ANDROMEDA** (Ruler of Men) *Greek* The daughter of CEPHEUS and CASSIOPEIA OF ETHIOPIA, a country in northeast Africa; wife of the hero PERSEUS; mother of many sons, including PERSES, who is said to have founded the land of Persia.

The fates of Andromeda and Perseus became entwined. CASSIOPEIA had boasted of her daughter's beauty, claiming that it was greater than that of the sea NYMPHS, daughters of the god POSEIDON. Greatly angered, Poseidon sent a sea monster to ravage Ethiopia. AMMON, the ORACLE, declared that only the sacrifice of Andromeda to the monster could appease Poseidon and save the Ethiopians from flood and plague, so Andromeda was chained to a rock in the sea to await death. She was rescued by Perseus, who turned the monster into stone with the head of MEDUSA and claimed Andromeda in marriage. The wedding feast was interrupted by the arrival of PHINEUS, brother of CEPHEUS, to whom Andromeda had been promised in marriage. In the ensuing battle,

The hero Perseus rescues Andromeda from her seashore captivity in this painting by Flemish artist Peter Paul Rubens (1577-1640). The painting is now in the Museo del Prado in Madrid.

Perseus again used the Medusa's head to turn Phineas and his soldiers into statues of stone.

The dramatic rescue of Andromeda by Perseus inspired many artists, among them Peter Paul Rubens (1577–1640), the foremost Flemish painter of the 17th century; Titian (c. 1490–1576), a Venetian and one of the greatest painters of the Renaissance; and Jean-Auguste-Dominique Ingres (1780–1867), a French painter. An ancient fresco still surviving at Pompeii (near Naples, Italy) also shows the rescue.

The gods placed, Andromeda, Cassiopeia, and Cepheus among the stars as constellations. That constellation has been Andromeda for so long that some believe the Greeks invented the story to explain the stars.

**ANGERONA** *Roman*  An ancient goddess in Italy about whom little is clearly known. Scholars have sought since the late 1800s to understand this goddess and the statute of her that stood in ROME in classical times.

Most agree that in her earliest form Angerona was a goddess of winter, specifically of the winter solstice. The people of Rome celebrated her on December 21, the beginning of winter. It was on this day, people believed, that Angerona brought back the sun, for on this solstice, daylight hours began to increase and nighttime hours began to decrease.

In later years, Angerona became associated with secrets and quiet, though scholars today do not agree on this interpretation. Because the statue that stood in a temple near the Roman Forum showed her blindfolded and holding her finger to her mouth, some experts say Angerona encourages people to be silent and keep secrets. Other experts say that interpretation is simply a guess.

Some passages in the surviving histories of the time suggest Angerona was a goddess of fear and anguish, particularly as related to illness, though scholars today argue that her connection with disease is a modern misinterpretation of her name.

**ANNA PERENNA** *Roman*  An ancient fertility goddess, worshiped in a sacred woods north of ROME. Anna Perenna is the central deity in several stories from Roman mythology.

In the earliest stories, Anna Perenna took on the form of an old woman who made and sold cakes to starving Romans who had fled to the country to avoid political strife in the city. When they returned home, these people paid homage to Anna and celebrated in her honor.

In another story, she is the sister of DIDO, Queen of CARTHAGE, whom the Trojan hero AENEAS had loved but left on his journey from Troy to Italy. Some time after Aeneas had married LAVINIA and founded a city in her name, Anna Perenna arrived. Lavinia was jealous of the newcomer and threatened to kill her. Anna fled into the woods where she met Numicius, a Roman river god, who carried her off as his wife and transformed her into a NYMPH.

Her name means both the new year, Anna, and the whole year, Perenna, and Romans paid her honor in the great New Year's festival on March 15, the first day of the new year in the ancient Roman calendar.

**ANTICLEA** *Greek*  Daughter of AUTOLYCUS; wife of LAERTES; mother of ODYSSEUS. Autolycus was a son of the god HERMES. Anticlea died of grief when her son went off to the TROJAN WAR.

**ANTIOPE** *Greek*  Mother of AMPHION and ZETHUS, whose father was ZEUS; daughter of a prince of the city of THEBES or perhaps of the river god Asopus.

Zeus desired Antiope, and, disguised as a SATYR, raped her. She became pregnant. Fearing her father, Nycteus, Antiope fled Thebes, but, according to some stories, Epopeus, king of Sicyon, abducted her. In the meantime, Nycteus, in anguish over his missing daughter, killed himself after commanding his brother, Lycus to either punish or rescue Antiope. Lycus attacked Sicyon, rescued Antiope, and began the journey back to Thebes.

On the way, Antiope gave birth to her twin sons. Some sources say both were the children of Zeus, others say only Amphion was a god and that Zethus was the mortal son of Epopeus. Antiope left the children on the hillside to die, but shepherds found them and raised the boys.

Antiope then became the slave of Lycus' wife, Dirce, who treated her badly. Eventually, Zeus helped Antiope escape. She found her sons, now grown men, who avenged her treatment by conquering Thebes, and punished Dirce by tying her to the horns of a bull. The god DIONYSUS, angry at the death of Dirce, punished Antiope by driving her mad and causing her to wander, insane, across GREECE. Eventually, she was discovered by Phocus, grandson of SISYPHUS, who cured her then married her.

**ANTIGONE** *Greek*  In Greek mythology, the daughter of OEDIPUS and Jocasta; sister of Eteocles and Polynices. Antigone accompanied her blind father when he went into exile. Her two brothers

Antigone leads her father, Oedipus, from Thebes after his banishment from the city. The painting by French artist Charles François Jalabert (1819-1901) is in the Musée des Beaux Arts in Marseilles, France.

killed each other in the war of the SEVEN AGAINST THEBES. King Creon of THEBES forbade the burial of the rebel Polynices. Antigone disobeyed the king's order and performed her brother's burial service herself. In one version of the myth, Antigone finally hanged herself after Creon ordered her to be buried alive. In another version, Antigone was rescued by a son of Creon and sent to live among shepherds.

*Antigone* was one of SOPHOCLES' greatest plays. The tragic heroine appears also in Sophocles' *Oedipus at Colonus*, in AESCHYLUS' *Seven Against Thebes*, in EURIPIDES' *The Phoenician Women*, and in *Antigone* by Jean Cocteau (1889–1963), which has a 20th-century setting.

**APHRODITE** (Foam Born) *Greek* Goddess of love, beauty, and fertility. One of the 12 OLYMPIAN GODS; identified with the Roman VENUS and, much earlier, with the Near Eastern fertility goddesses Astarte and Ishtar. Aphrodite was an ancient deity, an EARTH MOTHER whose domain embraced all creation, vegetable and animal as well as human. She represented sacred love and marriage as well as sensuality and desire. Aphrodite was so beautiful that all men who saw her loved her.

The origins of Aphrodite are obscure. She is called "Foam Born" in an attempt to make her the offspring of GAIA (Earth) and URANUS (Heaven), who was cast into the sea after being mutilated by his son, CRONUS. She was supposed to have emerged from the sea foam that had formed around the remains of Uranus.

The myth of Aphrodite as a descendant of the TITANS probably refers to a goddess who preceded the peoples later called Greeks. When the migrating tribes settled in GREECE, they adopted Aphrodite into the Olympian family by making her the daughter of ZEUS and DIONE.

According to HOMER, in the *ILIAD*, Aphrodite was the daughter of Zeus and Dione. Also according to Homer, Aphrodite was married to the smith god, HEPHAESTUS. But Aphrodite was faithless and had many lovers.

This marble head of Aphrodite was found in the remains of an ancient gathering place in Athens. It may be a replica of a statue by the Greek sculptor Praxiteles, who worked in the fourth century B.C. The head is now in the National Archaeological Museum of Athens.

**The Loves of Aphrodite**  Aphrodite, goddess of love, was married to Hephaestus, but she had many other loves, among them ARES, god of war. She bore him Phobos (Fear), Deimos (Terror), HARMONIA (Peace or Concord) and, in some accounts, EROS (Love).

Although Hephaestus was a god, he proved himself capable of subtle revenge on Aphrodite and Ares by snaring them in a skillfully crafted golden net.

POSEIDON, god of the sea, fell in love with Aphrodite when he saw her entrapped in the golden net. With Poseidon, the goddess had two or three sons, Rhodus and Herophilus, and, some say, Eryx.

With HERMES, a son of Zeus, Aphrodite bore HERMAPHRODITUS and, some say, Eros. With DIONYSUS, god of the vine, another son of Zeus, she bore PRIAPUS. With the Trojan mortal ANCHISES, she bore AENEAS.

With another mortal, the beautiful ADONIS, Aphrodite spent the months of the year that symbolized fruitful spring and summer. Some accounts say that she bore him a son, Golgos, and a daughter, Beroe. From the legend of Aphrodite and Adonis comes the word *aphrodisiac*, meaning a potion or other agent that induces love.

Aphrodite was also beloved by PYGMALION, who created a statue of her so beautiful that he fell in love with it. And there were many other lovers, for Aphrodite inspired love in all who saw her.

**Aphrodite and Eros**  Aphrodite was often depicted with the infant god, Eros (Love), who some said was her son with Hermes. However, mythologists believe that Eros was an ancient god, an adult rather than a child. He was to become the plump, babyish CUPID (his Roman name), companion or son of Aphrodite, only in later times.

**Aphrodite and Paris**  The tale of Aphrodite and the young mortal hero PARIS is told in HOMER's *Iliad*. Paris was supposed to choose the fairest among three Olympian gods: HERA, ATHENE, and Aphrodite. Each goddess offered Paris a bribe. Aphrodite offered him the love of the most beautiful woman in the world, and Paris awarded Aphrodite a golden apple as reward. The beautiful woman turned out to be HELEN of Troy. The love affair of Paris and Helen was the leading cause of the TROJAN WAR.

**Aphrodite and Art**  Aphrodite was worshiped as a great beauty as well as a goddess of fertility. She is the subject of some of the world's art masterpieces, in which she is usually known by her Roman name, Venus. The most famous statue of her was by the Greek Praxiteles (c. 350 B.C.). The original has been lost but there is a Roman copy in Athens, and the Venus de Milo, at the Louvre, in Paris, France.

**APOLLO**  One of the greatest OLYMPIAN GODS and the only one to appear with the same name in both Greek and Roman mythology.

In Greek mythology, he was the son of ZEUS and LETO, brother of ARTEMIS, half brother of HERMES, and father of many, including ARISTAEUS and ASCLEPIUS. Apollo had many functions: he was the god of poetry, music, archery, prophecy, and healing. Associated with the care of herds and crops, Apollo was a sun god of great antiquity, yet he is represented as an ever-youthful god, just and wise and of great beauty. He has been the subject of many great paintings and statues throughout the ages; perhaps the most famous is the Apollo Belvedere, an ancient statue that now stands in the Belvedere Gallery at the Vatican.

Apollo was well loved among the gods. Only his half brother, Hermes, dared to play a trick on him when he stole Apollo's cattle.

As well as physical beauty, Apollo represented the moral excellence that we think of as civilization. His cult at DELPHI had enormous influence on matters of state and religion, as well as on everyday law and order. The influence of Apollo at Delphi helped to spread tolerance in all social ranks. Apollo was, above all, a god of justice, law, and order.

The many and varying functions of Apollo suggest that the god had many personalities derived from various origins. Some mythologists say that he was a sun god from Asia who merged with a pastoral god from the countries north of GREECE, known as Hyperborea, that is "the Far North."

**The Birth of Apollo**  According to the poet HESIOD, Apollo was the son of the great god Zeus and Leto, the gentle TITAN. HERA, the wife of Zeus, was jealous of her rival; familiar with the rages of Hera, no land would give Leto sanctuary in which to bear her child. At last Leto found refuge in the floating island of Ortygia, later called DELOS, which became firmly anchored only after the birth of her first child, Artemis. Artemis assisted Leto in the birth of her twin brother, Apollo.

Apollo was fed on nectar and ambrosia and quickly grew to manhood.

**Apollo and Python**  Apollo grew to manhood very soon after his birth. Supplied with arms by the smith god HEPHAESTUS, an expert metalworker, the young Apollo set off in search of the serpent PYTHON, who had tormented Apollo's mother, Leto, during her homeless wanderings. Apollo tracked down Python at Delphi and killed her, thus defiling a sacred place with blood. Zeus sent Apollo to be purified at the Vale of TEMPE. After his purification, Apollo returned to Delphi and took the shrine for himself. Python, or Pythia, was to be his ORACLE. The dramatic battle between Apollo and Python was later celebrated in the festival Septaria.

**The Loves of Apollo**  Apollo was one of the foremost gods of OLYMPUS and supremely handsome. Like all the gods and goddesses, Apollo had many loves, not all of them happy. The nymph DAPHNE fled from the god and turned herself into a laurel tree rather than submit to him. Apollo made the laurel tree his sacred tree and emblem.

With CORONIS, Apollo begat Asclepius, god of healing and medicine, but Coronis deserted Apollo for love of Ischyus. Apollo's sister, Artemis, killed Coronis with her arrows. Apollo snatched the infant

The god Apollo stands tall and strong in this Roman copy, created in the second century A.D., of a Greek statue which was made in the fourth century B.C. This statue is in the Vatican Museum. *(Photograph by Marie-Lan Nyugen.)*

Asclepius from the funeral pyre and gave him to Hermes, or, some say, to CHIRON, the CENTAUR.

Apollo fell in love with CASSANDRA, daughter of King PRIAM. He conferred on her the gift of prophecy, but Cassandra was untrue to Apollo who then breathed a kiss into her mouth that took away her powers of persuasion. From then on, no one believed the prophecies of Cassandra.

With the nymph CYRENE, Apollo begot Aristaeus, who was worshiped as a protector of flocks and crops and especially of the art of beekeeping.

Among Apollo's male loves was HYACINTHUS, a beautiful youth after whom the spring flower hyacinth is named.

**ARACHNE** (Spider) *Greek*  The daughter of Idmon of Colophon in LYDIA (ASIA MINOR). Arachne was a skillful weaver. Marveling at her work, people said that she must have been taught by ATHENE herself. Arachne denied this and rashly invited the goddess Athene to come and compete with her. Athene was annoyed but accepted the invitation. She became angry when she could find no fault in the maiden's clever weaving and amusing, if disrespectful, depictions of the antics of the gods and goddesses. Athene tore the work apart and destroyed the loom. Terrified, Arachne tried to hang herself. Athene turned Arachne into a spider, doomed to forever show off her artful weaving of cobwebs.

This story was told by OVID in *Metamorphoses*. Some scholars think that the explanation of this myth can be found in the commercial rivalry between the Athenians, represented by Athene, and the Lydians, represented by Arachne, for the export of textiles. The spider emblem was frequently found on the seals of sea lords and weavers.

**ARCADIA** *Greek*  In ancient GREECE, the central plateau of the PELOPONNESUS, surrounded by and dissected by mountains. It was inhabited mostly by shepherds and hunters who worshiped PAN and other nature gods.

In the myth of DEMETER, the corn goddess turns herself into a mare and hides in a herd owned by King Oncus of Arcadia. Nevertheless, the amorous sea god POSEIDON discovers her.

**ARCAS** (ARCTOS; Bear) *Greek*  Son of CALLISTO and ZEUS, married to the DRYAD Erato, father of many. Arcas was king of ARCADIA, an isolated, mountainous area in the PELOPONNESUS peninsula. He had been taught his skills by TRIPTOLEMUS, a favorite of the goddess DEMETER. Arcas taught the Arcadians agriculture and attendant arts, such as those of spinning wool.

Arcas was also a great hunter. In one story, he almost killed the she-bear Callisto, who was his mother in another guise. Zeus, to prevent Arcas from killing his own mother, turned Arcas into a bear and set him and his mother up in the stars as the Great Bear (Ursa Major) and ARCTURUS (Guardian of the Bear).

**ARCTURUS** (Guardian of the Bear) *Greek*  The brightest star in the constellation Boötes. It is named after ARCAS (Bear), who in Greek mythology is the Little Bear, son of CALLISTO (the Great Bear).

**ARES** *Greek*  The god of war; son of ZEUS and HERA. ERIS (Discord) was his sister and constant companion.

Ares was not a popular god. A vicious crowd followed him, among them Pain, Panic, Famine, and Oblivion. His sons, Phobos (Fear) and Deimos (Terror), prepared his chariot. Thus were the horrors of war symbolized.

Although usually identified with the Roman god of war, MARS, Ares bore little resemblance to the noble Mars.

The grisly followers of Ares, Zeus's hatred of him, and the humiliation and defeats that plagued him all symbolized the horror that the Athenians felt toward Ares, the personification of senseless war and brutality. For them, war was to be waged only for a good and noble reason. For Ares, war did not have to have any reason at all for he liked battle and violence for their own sakes.

**Ares, the Unloved God**  Ares, god of war, was bloody and brutal. Even his father, Zeus (in HOMER's ILIAD), declared that he hated his son for his perpetual violence and aggression.

Ares was not always successful in battle and was often thought of as cowardly and inept. Helped by the wisdom of the goddess ATHENE, DIOMEDES (1), one of the heroes at the siege of TROY, defeated Ares. ATHENE, although a goddess of war and half-sister of Ares, despised Ares's behavior. She wounded him so that he was forced to leave the field, bellowing with rage and pain. On another occasion, Ares was severely wounded by HERACLES, with whom he fought in defense of his son, CYCNUS.

The brother of Ares was HEPHAESTUS, the smith god. Hephaestus defeated Ares not in violent battle, but by using his subtle cleverness.

Otus and Ephialtes, known as the ALOEIDS, also despised Ares. They managed to imprison him in a bronze jar, where he remained trapped for 13 months until the god HERMES found him and released him. This myth is thought to symbolize a historical 13-month truce between two warring tribes of ancient GREECE when warlike tokens of these nations were sealed in a bronze jar and kept inside a temple.

**Ares and Aphrodite**  Ares was not a popular god, but APHRODITE, fickle goddess of love, perversely favored the warlike god over her gentle husband, Hephaestus. HELIOS (the Sun), who saw everything, discovered that Ares and Aphrodite were lovers, and informed Hephaestus of this. Hephaestus, famous for his skills and artistry in metal-working, created a golden net so fine that it was invisible. He placed it on the couch where he knew Aphrodite and Ares would lie; then he announced that he was going for a few days to Lemnos, one of his favorite retreats. As soon as he had gone, Aphrodite summoned Ares, and the two lay upon the couch. Then Hephaestus, with a crowd of the OLYMPIAN GODS and goddesses, burst in upon them. Ares and Aphrodite tried to leap up but became hopelessly entangled in the invisible golden net. The gods and goddesses delighted in this scene, laughing and pointing and making crude remarks. Thus was Ares made to look ridiculous to all. It was a subtle revenge for Hephaestus. This story is told in Homer's ODYSSEY.

**ARETE** (Virtue) *Greek* The goddess, or perhaps only the personification, of virtue or excellence of character. She was said to have lived high on a mountain, close to the gods themselves.

Arete was depicted as a tall woman standing straight and wearing a white robe. Some ancient Greek writers suggest that battle and wars were fought by men trying to prove their worth in the eyes of this minor goddess.

Her counterpart was Kakia (Cacia), the personification of vice and weak morals. In the few depictions of her in Greek literature, Kakia is plump, vain, and self-centered, and strives to entice people away from the influence of Arete.

**ARETHUSA (1)** *Greek* A NAIAD or NYMPH of fountains and rivers. In one legend, told by OVID in *Metamorphoses*, the nymph is pursued by the river god Alpheus. Arethusa calls to the goddess ARTEMIS for help; Artemis turns Arethusa into a fountain at Syracuse on the island now called Sicily, where the Fontana Arethusa still exists.

**ARETHUSA (2)** *Greek* One of the sisters known as the HESPERIDES; either the daughters of EREBUS (Darkness) and NYX (Night) or the daughters of ATLAS and PLEIONE or Hesperis. Her sisters, those named by people writing during the classic age of Greek mythology, were AEGLE (2), ERYTHEIA, and HESPERIA.

**ARGO** *Greek* The ship in which JASON and the ARGONAUTS sailed in quest of the GOLDEN FLEECE. ARGUS (2), son of PHRIXUS, built the vessel, with the help of the goddess ATHENE. Within the ship was a beam cut from the divine tree at DODONA (an oak or a beech), a shrine to the god ZEUS and the Dodona ORACLE. It was said that the beam could help foretell the future.

**ARGONAUTICA** *Greek* A major epic poem by Apollonius Rhodius (Apollonius of Rhodes) a Greek scholar at the Library of Alexandria in Egypt. *Argonautica* tells in four books the story of JASON's quest

for the GOLDEN FLEECE, the treachery of MEDEA, who possessed the fleece, and the journey of the ARGONAUTS to return home. It is the best known version of the story of Jason and the Argonauts.

Apollonius composed the poem in the 200s B.C. and based his story on the works of other Greek poets as well as the stories he knew. Apollonius relied on the understanding of his audience of the stories of Greek myths and legends.

**ARGONAUTS** (Sailors of the *Argo*) *Greek* The crew gathered by the hero JASON to sail on his ship, the *Argo*. There were 50 oars and 49 men and one woman, ATALANTA. It is said that never before or since was so gallant a company gathered together. Their quest was to capture the GOLDEN FLEECE, and this they did, after many adventures.

**Names of the Argonauts** Many different names have been included in the muster roll of the *Argo*, the ship sailed by Jason in his quest for the Golden Fleece. The following 50 names are those "given by the most trustworthy authorities," according to scholar Robert Graves (1895–1985).

Acastus, son of King PELIAS
Actor, son of Deion, the Phocian
ADMETUS, prince of Pherae
AMPHIARAUS, the Argive seer
Ancaeus of Samos
Ancaeus of Tegea, son of POSEIDON
ARGUS (2), the builder of the *ARGO*
Ascalaphus, son of ARES
Asterius, a Pelopian
Atalanta of CALYDON, the great huntress
Augeias of Elis
Butes of ATHENS
Caeneus the LAPITH
Calais, winged son of BOREAS
Canthus the Euboean
CASTOR, one of the DIOSCURI
CEPHEUS, son of the Arcadian Aleus
CORONIS the Lapith
Echion, son of HERMES
Erginus of Miletus
Euphemus of Taenarum
Euryalus, son of Mecisteus, one of the EPIGONI
Eurydamus the Dolopian
HERACLES of TIRYNS, the strongest man who ever lived
Hylas, companion to Heracles
Idas, son of Aphareus of Messene
Idmon, the Argive, son of APOLLO

Iphicles, son of Thestius
Iphitus, brother of King Eurystheus of Mycenae
Jason, the captain
laertes, son of Acrisius the Argive
Lynceus, brother of Idas
Melampus, son of Poseidon
Meleager of Calydon
Mopsus, the Lapith
Naupilus the Argive, son of Poseidon, a noted navigator
Oileus, father of the hero Ajax (2)
Orpheus, the poet
Palaemon, son of Hephaestus
Peleus, the myrmidon
Peneleos of Boeotia
Periclymenus, son of Poseidon
Phalerus, the Athenian archer
Phanus, the Cretan son of Dionysus
Poeas, son of Thaumacus the Magnesian
Polydeuces, one of the Dioscuri
Polyphemus, son of Elatus, the Arcadian
Staphylus, brother of Phanus
Tiphys, the helmsman of the *Argo*
Zetes, brother of Calais

**ARGOS** *(Argolis)* A district in Greece, part of the northern Peloponnesus, today known as the Argive Plain. For many centuries Argos dominated the Peloponnesus, rivaling Athens, Sparta, and Corinth. It was known as Hera's city from the magnificent temple built in her honor. In mythology, Argos was known as the place where the 50 daughters of Danaus killed their bridegrooms, except for one, who became the ancestor of Perseus. Another descendant of these women was the hero Heracles. Agamemnon was the famous king of Argos and Mycenae who fought in the Trojan War.

**ARGUS (1)** *(Argos)* *Greek* A giant with 100 eyes. He was set by the goddess Hera to watch over the maiden Io, who had been transformed into a beautiful white heifer by the god Zeus. Zeus sent Hermes to rescue Io. Hermes played upon his lute and sang songs until all the eyes of Argus closed in sleep. Then Hermes slew Argus and set Io free. Hera placed the eyes of Argus on the tail of the peacock, where they remain to this day. The peacock was sacred to Hera.

**ARGUS (2)** *(Argos)* *Greek* The builder of the ship *Argo* and one of the Argonauts.

**ARGUS (3)** *(Argos)* *Greek* The faithful old dog of Odysseus, who alone recognized his master after 20 years of absence.

**ARIADNE** *Greek* Daughter of Minos and Pasiphaë of Crete; sister of Androgeus, Phaedra, and others.

Ariadne fell in love with the hero Theseus when he came to Crete to kill the Minotaur, a monstrous creature, half human, half bull, that lived in the tortuous labyrinth. The labyrinth had been invented and built by Daedalus so that no one, once inside, could find the way out. Ariadne gave Theseus a ball of string to trail behind him so that he could follow it and escape. After Theseus had done battle and slain the dreaded beast, he emerged triumphantly from the Labyrinth and carried Ariadne off.

Some stories say that Theseus deserted Ariadne on the island of Naxos. Other stories say that it was the god Dionysus who commanded Theseus to leave because he wanted the beautiful Ariadne for himself. Scholars think that the second version of the tale is an attempt to make the great hero Theseus less of a scoundrel for deserting Ariadne. Still other versions of the story say that Ariadne was slain by the goddess Artemis; or that she was pregnant and died in childbirth. All of the different stories seem to indicate that part of the original story of Ariadne was lost.

In any case, it is said that Zeus gave her a crown and set her among the stars.

**ARION** *Greek* The swiftest of all horses, possibly winged. He was born from the union between Demeter (who changed herself into a mare) and the sea god Poseidon, who changed himself into a stallion. Arion belonged first to the hero Heracles, and then to Adrastus, king of Argos. In the war called the seven against Thebes, Adrastus was the only one to survive, thanks to the wonders of Arion.

**ARISTAEUS** *Greek* An ancient rural deity, native to Thessaly. Son of Apollo and the Nymph Cyrene. Aristaeus was brought up by the nymphs of the god Hermes (half brother of Apollo), who taught him beekeeping, cheese-making, and the cultivation of olives. Later, the Muses taught him healing, hunting, and the care of herds and flocks.

Aristaeus tried to force his attentions on the Dryad Eurydice. The gods punished him by destroying his bees. Aristaeus sought the advice of Proteus, who advised him to sacrifice cattle to the gods. Aristaeus followed the counsel of Proteus and was rewarded when swarms of bees emerged from the rotting corpses of the slain cattle.

Aristaeus was honored as a god in ancient GREECE because of the great knowledge of his crafts that he passed on to humans.

**ARTEMIS** *Greek* Goddess of the hunt and of childbirth and chastity; also associated with the moon; daughter of ZEUS and LETO; sister of APOLLO; one of the OLYMPIAN GODS. Her origins are very old, probably derived from the EARTH MOTHER mythologies. She is identified with DIANA in Roman mythology.

Artemis was armed with a bow and a quiver of arrows made by the smith god, HEPHAESTUS. Like Apollo, she had many sides to her nature—she could be wild and destructive with her arrows; she could cause deadly disease in animals. Artemis was a deity of sudden death. On the other hand, Artemis could be benevolent: with ilithya, she was helpful to women in childbirth. Like Apollo, Artemis loved music, song, and dancing.

Artemis was worshiped throughout GREECE, especially in ARCADIA, and also in CRETE, ASIA MINOR, and MAGNA GRAECIA.

**Artemis, the Vengeful One** Artemis was not only pure and virginal herself; she punished any of her attendant NYMPHS who fell in love and she punished any man who approached her or her nymphs with amorous intent.

After Zeus fell in love with CALLISTO, who bore him a son, ARCAS, Artemis grew angry at her departure from chastity. Artemis changed Callisto into a she-bear.

ACTEON, a hunter, saw Artemis bathing and gazed at her with admiration. Outraged, Artemis changed Acteon into a stag, then set his own pack of hounds upon him; they tore him to pieces.

The ALOEIDS, two giants who were determined to overthrow the OLYMPIAN GODS, swore to capture both HERA and Artemis. In one legend, Artemis turned herself into a white doe and pranced between the brothers. The Aloeids aimed their darts at the doe and inadvertently killed each other, and thus were punished for lusting after the goddesses.

NIOBE, the mother of 12 children, was foolish enough to boast that she was superior to Leto, the mother of Apollo and Artemis, who had borne only two children. Enraged, Apollo and Artemis killed all Niobe's children.

When Artemis at last fell in love, it was with ORION, another great hunter. One day Orion went swimming and swam so far from shore that his head looked like a rock in the sea. Jealous of his sister's love for Orion, or perhaps wanting to preserve his sister's chastity, Apollo challenged Artemis to hit the rock with her arrow. The arrow of Artemis pierced Orion's head, killing him. Another legend says that Artemis sent a scorpion to sting Orion, as a punishment for having gazed upon her amorously.

See also "The Birth of Apollo" under APOLLO

**ARTEMIS (2)** *Greek* A prominent leader of the AMAZONS, a mythical race of female warriors, worshiped at EPHESUS, in Ionia, part of ASIA MINOR (today's western Turkey). The temple built to Artemis (c. 550 B.C.) was considered one of the Seven Wonders of the Ancient World.

**ASCANIUS** *Roman* The son of AENEAS and his wife, CREUSA (2). When TROY fell (see TROJAN WAR), Ascanius fled with his parents and his grandfather, ANCHISES. He is said to have founded ALBA LONGA, a city of ancient LATIUM near Lake Albano, southeast of ROME. Since he is also called Iulus or Julus, the family of Julius Caesar, the mighty Roman emperor, claimed descent from him. The story of Ascanius is told by the Latin poet VIRGIL in the *AENEID*.

**ASCLEPIUS** *Greek* God of medicine and healing; son of APOLLO and CORONIS; father of HYGEIA and others. The Roman spelling of his name is Aesculapius.

According to legend, Asclepius learned the art of healing from CHIRON, the wise and gentle CENTAUR. He mastered his craft so well that eventually, it was said, Asclepius could raise the dead. The great god ZEUS, afraid that mere humans might become immortal, struck Asclepius with a thunderbolt, but then made him a minor god in charge of medicine and healing.

The center of his cult was EPIDAURUS (northeast PELOPONNESUS), but there were many others, including Cos and Pergamum, where treatments were given to the sick. Snakes, symbols of renewal because of the frequent shedding of their skin, to reveal glossy new skin underneath, were his emblem, usually depicted as twined about a wand called a CADUCEUS.

**ASIA MINOR** The peninsula at the extreme tip of western Asia, usually synonymous with Asian Turkey or Anatolia. It is washed by the Black Sea in the north, by the Mediterranean in the south, and by the Aegean Sea in the west. It was the intersecting point between East and West in ancient times: to the east lay Mesopotamia and China, to the west, Europe, especially nearby GREECE. It was the site of the ancient kingdoms of LYDIA and PHRYGIA. At the entrance to the DARDANELLES, the sea passage that led from the Mediterranean to the Black Sea, stood the city of TROY.

**ASTERIA** (ASTRIOS; Of the stars) *Greek* A second-generation TITAN goddess; daughter of COEUS and his sister PHOEBE; mother with the Titan PERSES of the goddess HECATE. Asteria was the goddess of prophecy, or night dreams, and of communication with the spirits of the dead (necromancy).

After the OLYMPIAN GODS defeated the Titans, Asteria was not sent to TARTARUS, as were most of the Titans. Instead, ZEUS, the greatest of the Olympians, pursued her, but she resisted his advances. To hide, she changed herself into a quail, then threw herself into the sea. Some say she became the island that was later known as DELOS, the island where her sister, LETO, came to give birth to her twins, APOLLO and ARTEMIS (1).

**ASTERION** (ASTERIUS; Starry) *Greek* King of CRETE who married EUROPA and adopted her three sons: MINOS, RHADAMANTHUS, and SARPEDON.

**ASTRAEA** (ASTRIA; Starry night) *Greek* The virgin goddess of justice and fairness; daughter of ZEUS and THEMIS, who was also a goddess of justice.

When her father brought the gods to Earth to dwell among mankind, Astraea often walked through towns and cities, smiling at people, helping them to treat each other well. After Zeus, frustrated with how poorly people treated the gods and themselves, took the gods back up to the heavens, Astraea lingered behind, always hopeful.

Eventually, though, as people became more evil and meaner to each other and stopped listening to her, Astraea, too, rose up to the heavens where she sat at her mother's right hand, still watching mankind, still trying to help them be just and fair. Some sources say Zeus transformed Astraea into the constellation VIRGO, with the famous scales she always carried placed next to her in the sky as the constellation Libra.

Some modern experts equate Astraea with DIKE, the personification of justice, while others see these as two separate beings in Greek literature and history. Also, a few writers from the classical period say that Astraea was the daughter of the TITANS ASTRAEUS and Eos.

**ASTRAEUS** (Starry) *Greek* A second-generation TITAN god and father of the WINDS and the stars. His wife was Eos, goddess of the dawn. Astraeus was the son of the Titans CRIUS and EURYBIA.

**ATALANTA** *Greek* A renowned huntress, daughter of Iasus, king of ARCADIA, and CLYMENE. Disappointed at the birth of a daughter, Iasus put the infant on Mount PARNASSUS and left her to die. (This was a common fate for female infants in ancient GREECE.) ARTEMIS, goddess of the hunt, sent a she-bear to suckle the baby. The child was then reared by a band of hunters who found her on the mountainside.

Her hunting skills were so great that Atalanta dared to join the all-male group of hunters who were going after the Calydonian Boar at the request of MELEAGER, prince of CALYDON. Atalanta scored the first thrust at the ferocious boar. Meleager killed the boar and presented its coveted hide and tusks to Atalanta, thus causing anger and strife among the men. (See CALYDONIAN BOAR HUNT.)

Now that she was famous, King Iasus recognized Atalanta as his daughter. He insisted that she must marry. Atalanta, having been warned by an ORACLE that she would find no happiness in marriage, set a condition on her marriage. Her suitor must be able to beat her in a foot-race, or else die. Many tried to win her but failed and died. Finally MELANION, a prince from Arcadia, sought the help of APHRODITE, goddess of love. She gave him three golden apples that he dropped, one at a time, throughout the race. Atalanta could not resist picking them up and lost the race. Atalanta bore Melanion a son, Parthenonpaeus.

In some versions of this legend it is said that Atalanta and Melanion were turned into lions by Aphrodite and forced to pull the chariot of CYBELE, a goddess of Earth and nature.

It is said that Atalanta was one of the ARGONAUTS, a fabled crew of sailors who sought the GOLDEN FLEECE.

**ATHAMAS** *Greek* One of the sons of AEOLUS; brother of SISYPHUS and Salmoneus; king of Orchomenus in BOEOTIA. With NEPHELE he had two sons, PHRIXUS and Leucon, and a daughter, HELLE.

Athamas tired of the phantomlike Nephele and took INO, daughter of CADMUS, to be his second wife. It was this marriage and the subsequent flight of Phrixus and Helle that brought about (a generation later) JASON's quest for the GOLDEN FLEECE, for the

The goddess Athena hovers behind Prometheus as the Titan passes fire to humans, an act for which he was later punished. The scene was painted in 1802 by Jean-Simon Berthélemy (1743-1811) in a ceiling mural in the Louvre in Paris. *(Photograph by Marie-Lan Nyugen. Used under a Creative Commons license.)*

two youngsters had fled from Boeotia on the back of a winged ram that bore a Golden Fleece.

Athamas and Ino looked after the infant DIO-NYSUS, son of ZEUS and SEMELE. For this they earned the gratitude of Zeus but also the wrath of his wife, HERA, who visited madness upon Athamas and Ino.

Athamas and Ino had two sons, Learchus and Melicertes. In a fit of madness, Athamas killed Learchus and ate his still-warm flesh. Stricken with grief, Athamas left his kingdom and wandered from country to country. After many years, he founded a city called Alos, in EPIRUS, an ancient country of GREECE, on the Ionian Sea.

The conflict between the two wives of Athamas, Nephele (made by ZEUS in the likeness of HERA) and Ino, may represent the conflict between early Ionian farmers (who worshiped the corn goddess) and later Aeolian invaders, who reared sheep and worshiped the thunder god Aeolus, represented by the cloudlike Nephele.

**ATHENE** (ATHENA) *Greek* Daughter of ZEUS and METIS. One of the most important OLYMPIAN GODS. Identified with MINERVA by the Romans.

Athene was a deity of many different functions and attributes. On the one hand, she was a goddess of war, the female counterpart of ARES. However, she was also associated with peace and compassion. She was a patron of the arts and crafts, especially spinning and weaving (see ARACHNE); a patron of cities, notably ATHENS, which was named after her; and a goddess of wisdom.

The cult of Athene went back to the Cretan civilization, which predated that of classical GREECE by about 1,500 years. In CRETE and MYCENAE, she was an Earth goddess. However, the Athenians firmly claimed her as their own, and dedicated the Parthenon, the temple on the Acropolis in Athens, to her. Athens acknowledged Athene as the ancestor of their first king, ERICHTHONIUS (1).

Athene appears in innumerable myths, but none better displays her unique intellectual qualities than her role in the *ODYSSEY* as the constant friend and adviser of the clever and imaginative ODYSSEUS. She also offered help to heroes, such as JASON and DIOMEDES (1). Other myths associated with Athene include those of BELLEROPHON; PERSEUS and the MEDUSA; ARGUS and the ship *ARGO*; CADMUS and the dragon's teeth; and heroes HERACLES, DIOMEDES (2), and Tydeus.

**The Birth of Athene**   There are many different stories about the birth and parentage of Athene. In the most familiar story, she sprang fully armed from the head of Zeus when HEPHAESTUS split it open with an ax. Zeus had previously swallowed his consort, METIS, on learning that she would soon bear a child who would rule the gods. Metis was renowned for her wisdom. The myth may be a way of saying that when Zeus came to power he absorbed wisdom (Metis), and from this wisdom came the knowledge from which the arts (Athene) developed. This myth in some tellings develops the story of Zeus having violent headaches that made him howl with pain and rage. HERMES found him on the banks of the Triton River and summoned Hephaestus to help relieve his pain.

In Crete, they said that the goddess Athene had been hidden in a cloud and that by striking the cloud with his head, Zeus had caused Athene to emerge. This event was supposed to have happened beside a stream called the Triton.

According to the Pelasgians (prehistoric peoples inhabiting Mediterranean lands), Athene was born beside the lake or river Triton, and nurtured by three NYMPHS. As a girl, Athene accidentally killed her playmate, Pallas. In a token of her grief, Athene set the nymph's name before her own, and is often known as Pallas Athene. This legend probably dates to pre-Hellenic times.

**Athene and Poseidon**   In this myth, Athene challenges the sea god POSEIDON over who should reign over Athens. Zeus judged Athene the winner because she bestowed upon Athens the olive tree, while Poseidon produced only a salty stream. The rivalry for the possession of Athens may have been a folk memory of the collision between new people (migrants) with their new gods, and the ancient people (symbolized by Athene, Earth goddess). The triumph of the ancient EARTH MOTHER figure over the male god Poseidon shows that the myth goes back to archaic times, long before the HELLENES (Greeks) and other migrants arrived on the peninsula (the PELOPONNESUS), bringing with them a belief in dominant male gods.

**ATHENS** *Greek*   Capital of modern GREECE situated in ATTICA. It was named after the goddess ATHENE. Athens was inhabited even before the Bronze Age (2000–1000 B.C.). It is the site of many architectural and archaeological wonders, such as the Acropolis, an ancient fortress, and the Parthenon, one of many temples surviving from antiquity. Athens was (and is) the cultural center of the Greek world.

**ATLAS** *Greek*   A TITAN, the son of IAPETUS and CLYMENE. He was the leader of the Titans in their battle against the OLYMPIAN GODS. (See *The War with the Titans*, under ZEUS.) The Titans were defeated and all but Atlas were confined to TARTARUS, a section of the UNDERWORLD. Atlas's punishment was to carry the sky upon his shoulders throughout eternity.

During one of his 12 famous labors, the great hero HERACLES took the burden from the shoulders of Atlas so that the Titan could fetch for him the golden apples of the HESPERIDES. When Atlas returned, Heracles tricked him into taking back the weight of the heavens. In another myth, the hero PERSEUS turned the Titan into stone by showing him the head of MEDUSA. Because of his gigantic size, the petrified Atlas became a mountain range.

**ATREUS AND THYESTES** *Greek*   The sons of PELOPS and HIPPODAMEIA. The Pelops family, of which they were a part, was doomed to tragedy and bloodshed through the generations until the fall of MYCENAE and the death of their descendants, AGAMEMNON and MENELAUS. The stories concerning the tragedies of the house of Pelops are sometimes called the Atreids, after Atreus. One of the stories tells how Atreus became king of Mycenae.

**The Golden Fleece**  The people of Mycenae had been advised by an ORACLE to choose a ruler from the house of Pelops. They considered Atreus and Thyestes, the sons of Pelops and Hippodameia. The brothers had been rivals since childhood.

Atreus laid claim to the throne, being the older brother and also the owner of the lamb with the GOLDEN FLEECE that had been given to the brothers by the god HERMES. Atreus sacrificed the lamb to the gods but kept the valuable fleece for himself.

Thyestes then persuaded AEROPE, the wife of Atreus, to steal the GOLDEN FLEECE for him. Because he possessed the valuable fleece, the elders of Mycenae chose Thyestes as their ruler, but ZEUS revealed to them that Thyestes had obtained the fleece by treachery. Thyestes fled in terror of punishment, leaving his home and children behind. The throne of Mycenae was awarded to Atreus.

Not content with his victory, Atreus plotted revenge on his brother. He invited his brother back from exile, pretending forgiveness, and served him a banquet that consisted of Thyestes' own children. When he found out what he had eaten, Thyestes went mad with grief. He threw a curse upon the house of Atreus, thus compounding the one already laid upon it by the charioteer MYRTILUS, who had been tricked by Pelops. The children of Atreus, Agamemnon and Menelaus, would suffer greatly from these curses.

Thyestes then consulted an oracle and was advised to beget a child upon his own daughter, Pelopia, the only one not cooked in the stew served up by Atreus. Thyestes, in disguise, seduced his daughter, who managed to wrest his sword from him. Years later, when Thyestes was a captive of Atreus, a boy of seven appeared before him bearing a sword. Thyestes recognized the sword as his own, and the boy, AEGISTHUS, as his son with Pelopia. Aegisthus, upon learning the truth of his ancestry, was persuaded to acknowledge Thyestes as his true father and to turn the sword upon Atreus.

Thyestes then reigned as king of Mycenae, with Aegisthus as his heir. But this being the accursed house of Pelops, Agamemnon (the eldest son of Atreus) drove Thyestes out of Mycenae and deposed Aegisthus. Only at the death of Aegisthus and CLYTEMNESTRA were the FURIES and Fates satisfied. They removed the curses, stopping the atrocities of murder and incest that had plagued the house of Pelops and of Atreus.

**ATTICA** *Greek*  A triangular area at the eastern end of central GREECE. Its capital is ATHENS.

**ATTIS** *Greek*  A Phrygian vegetation god, the beloved of the great goddess CYBELE. Attis was born of a virgin mother, Nana, by springing from a ripe almond or pomegranate that she had placed on her bosom. As a young man, he was beloved by Cybele, but Attis reneged on his vows to the goddess and fell in love with the daughter of a river god. In some accounts, Cybele struck Attis in jealous anger, and in the ensuing frenzy Attis wounded himself and bled to death, whereupon Cybele (or ZEUS) turned him into a pine tree. Around the tree grew masses of violets, nourished by his blood. According to another tradition, Zeus set a wild boar upon Attis, and Attis was gored to death.

In any case, Attis went to the UNDERWORLD. All through the dark months of winter, Attis was mourned. Then, in the spring he returned to the Earth and was worshiped, only to be sacrificed again at the end of the season.

In ancient times, the birth, death, and resurrection of Attis were celebrated with wild music and bloody rituals in the shrines sacred to Cybele. The cult flourished in Rome, where Attis was regarded as a supreme deity.

The myth of Attis, like that of ADONIS, is plainly the development of an ancient fertility festival that celebrated the corn god, born anew each year, then killed and planted underground, only to reappear the following spring.

**AURORA** (Dawn) *Roman*  The Latin word for "dawn" and the name the Romans gave to Eos, who was the Greek goddess of that time of day. Aurora's history in Italy may include early Etruscan influences, but this goddess appears to have had no following in ROME before the arrival of the Greek religions.

Aurora returned the gift of sight to the giant god ORION after he traveled to the dawn on the advice of an ORACLE.

The bands of light that can be seen in the night sky of far northern and far southern latitudes when electrically charged particles hit the Earth's atmosphere take their name from this goddess. The aurora borealis are the northern lights and the aurora australis are the southern lights.

**AUTOLYCUS** *Greek*  Son of the god HERMES and CHIONE, described by OVID as a "wily brat"; father, with Amphithea, of ANTICLEA, who was the mother of ODYSSEUS.

Autolycus was known as a master thief and an expert liar. He would steal goats and sheep and offer them to Hermes as sacrifices, a tribute which the god then rewarded. Hermes gave his son the ability to transform objects to help disguise them. Autolycus would change the color of cattle, or put horns on animals that had none or remove horns from horned animals. He could also, some say, make himself and the things he stole invisible.

In one story, he stole cattle from his neighbor, Sɪsʏᴘʜᴜs, by changing their spots. At first Sisyphus could not understand how his herd could be shrinking, but since he never saw the cattle wandering off, he decided to carve a mark in the hooves of the cattle he still had. The next time Autolycus came to steal cattle, he changed their color but not their hooves and Sisyphus caught the thief. In revenge, Sisyphus slept with Anticlea shortly before she married Laertes, and therefore some say he is the father of Odysseus.

Autolycus is said to have taught the hero Hᴇʀᴀᴄʟᴇs to wrestle and to have joined Jᴀsᴏɴ and become one of the Aʀɢᴏɴᴀᴜᴛs. Some sources, however, say this Autolycus came from Tʜᴇssᴀʟʏ and was not the son of Hermes.

**BACCHANALIA** *Roman* The Latin name for the orgiastic rites of BACCHUS (see DIONYSUS). The excesses of drunken and violent behavior of the people who followed this cult led to a senatorial decree banning them in Italy in 186 B.C. In spite of severe penalties, people continued to celebrate these rites for centuries. Numerous paintings depict the bacchanalia; among the most famous are those by Flemish painter Peter Paul Rubens (1577–1640) and French painter Nicolas Poussin (1594–1665).

**BACCHANTS** (BACCHANTES) *Roman* The women (also called MAENADS) who followed the god DIONYSUS. In their ritual orgies, the Bacchants were said to sacrifice wild animals and humans, tearing them apart and eating their flesh. The *Bacchae*, a tragedy by EURIPIDES, deals with the cult of the Bacchae.

**BACCHE** *Greek* One of the five NYMPHS who looked after the infant DIONYSUS on Mount Nysa. The other nymphs were Macris, Nysa, Erato, and Bromie.

Nymphs celebrate a Bacchanalia, or wild party in honor of the god Bacchus, in front of a bust of the god Pan in this 1635 work by French painter Nicolas Poussin (1594-1665). It is located in the National Gallery in London.

The Italian painter Michelangelo Merisi da Caravaggio (1571-1610) painted his vision of Bacchus, the Roman god of wine and excess, in the late 1500s. The painting hangs in the Uffizi Gallery in Florence, Italy.

Collectively they were called the BACCHANTS; later their name was used to describe followers of Dionysus.

In gratitude for the nymphs' service in rearing Dionysus, ZEUS placed their images among the stars, naming them the Hyades, a cluster of stars in the constellation Taurus.

**BACCHUS** *Roman* The name for the Greek god DIONYSUS. He was also known as LIBER. Dionysian religion spread across Italy in the second century B.C., causing alarm to the Romans. The rites were suppressed in 186 B.C., but the cult of Bacchus continued for many years.

Bacchus was portrayed by many artists, including the Italian painter Caravaggio (1571–1610), who portrayed him in *The Young Bacchus* as a sensual youth, the god of wine and revelry.

Roman BACCHANALIA were festivals in honor of Bacchus, characterized by wild and drunken revelry.

**BELLEROPHON** *Greek* Son of the Corinthian king GLAUCUS (2); grandson of SISYPHUS. In one story, Bellerophon, a very handsome young man loved by many women, is sent on a seemingly impossible mission to kill the CHIMERA, a fire-breathing monster with the head of a lion, the body of a goat, and a serpent's tail. The seer Polyeidus advises the young hero to capture the winged horse, PEGASUS. Bellerophon succeeds, with the help of the goddess ATHENE, who gives him a golden bridle. Pegasus and Bellerophon kill the monster.

Bellerophon and his fabulous horse have many adventures, but the young man makes a mistake when he decides to ride Pegasus up to OLYMPUS, the home of the gods. Stung by a gadfly sent by ZEUS, Pegasus throws his rider and Bellerophon falls to Earth. He spends the rest of his life as a cripple and an outcast.

**BELLONA** (War) *Roman* The goddess of war, prominent in ancient ROME from the 300s B.C., but likely originally a goddess of the SABINES, a neighboring people who eventually became part of the Roman culture.

In the earliest references to Bellona, she appears to be a personification of powerful force and determination, the force needed to lead an army into a successful battle and war. During the early years of the Roman Republic, Bellona was recognized as a powerful deity, known to be fearsome and unrelenting against her enemies. Some Roman historians and poets described her as having snakes for hair, and carrying a bloody whip in one hand and a lance in the other.

Bellona was considered a companion, lover, or wife of the war god MARS. Eventually, as Greek mythology gained influence in Rome and Italy, her traits and powers merged with those of ENYO, the Greek goddess of war, a companion of ARES, the Greek god of war.

In 296 B.C., a military leader of the Roman Republic, Appius Claudius Caecus, vowed to build a temple honoring Bellona and thanking her for her support in defeating the Etruscans, a people who lived to the north of Rome. He built the temple outside of the city proper, so the goddess could help Rome fend off invaders. Outside stood a pillar. In memory of Bellona, and to summon her help, Roman leaders threw a lance over the pillar as a formal declaration of war against an enemy.

**BIA** (Force) *Greek* The personification of bodily force; a demigod or lesser goddess; daughter of the TITAN PALLAS and the water NYMPH STYX; sister of NIKE (Victory), CRATUS (Strength), and ZELUS (Zeal).

When their mother sided with ZEUS in his great battle against his father, CRONUS, and the Titans, Styx brought Bia, Nike, Cratus, and Zelus into service with her, though their father was a Titan. After that war, the sisters and brothers, often portrayed as winged beings, lived with Zeus and stood beside his throne, fulfilling his commands.

With her brother Cratus, Bia received the assignment to carry out the punishment of PROMETHEUS, the god who brought fire to humans. They chained him to a rock high on a mountain and each day a vulture plucked at his liver and each night the organ grew back.

Bia's Roman equivalent was the goddess, Vis, a name that appears to be a mere translation.

**BOEOTIA** An ancient region of central GREECE north of ATTICA and west of Megara and the Gulf of CORINTH. The early inhabitants were from THESSALY. The city of THEBES dominated the region. DELPHI, the most celebrated ORACLE of antiquity, had her abode in Boeotia, on Mount PARNASSUS. Mount HELICON, sacred to the god APOLLO, was home to the nine MUSES. It was from Boeotia that the children of King ATHAMAS fled, leading to the quest for the GOLDEN FLEECE. See *Jason and the Argonauts* under JASON.

**BONA DEA** (The good goddess) *Roman* A prominent goddess of women, ultimately seen as a version of Mother Earth.

The goddess was known for her influence over good health, fertility, and fecundity, which is the ability to have many offspring. People called upon Bona Dea to influence these aspects of life in agriculture and in the family. Bona Dea also brought strength to slaves and was a goddess of freed slaves.

Some historians and poets equated her with the goddess FAUNA, which would have made Bona Dea the sister or daughter of the god of fertility, FAUNUS. In this role, she was also known as Fenta Fatua.

Bona Dea was honored in a ceremony in early December, where the female head of a household would gather the other women of the family and they would close themselves in a room, away from the men, where they would conduct the ritual.

A temple to the goddess stood on the Aventine Hill. Here, VESTAL VIRGINS worshipped Bona Dea and in May, a special priestess offered sacrifices to her for the protection and service she would provide to the state of ROME. Men were not allowed to participate in these services.

**BOREAS** *Greek*  The North WIND, son of the dawn goddess, Eos, and the TITAN ASTREUS. He was the father of the fleet footed Calais and Zetes, who sailed with JASON and the ARGONAUTS.

**BRISEIS** (HIPPODAEMIA) *Greek*  The daughter of a Trojan priest, Briseus. A captive and lover of the Greek hero ACHILLES, she was stolen from him by AGAMEMNON, the leader of the Greek army, by an act of trickery. Furious, Achilles withdrew his troops from the battle (see TROJAN WAR), causing the Greeks to lose ground to the Trojans. These acts marked the beginning of HOMER's *ILIAD*, his great epic about the Trojan War.

**BRITOMARTIS** (Sweet Virgin) *Greek*  An an-cient Cretan deity, later said to be a daughter of the god ZEUS. A huntress, Britomartis pursued wild beasts in the forests of CRETE. King MINOS of Crete fell in love with her and pursued her for nine months though she always fled to avoid his advances. Finally Britomartis flung herself off a cliff into the sea, but fishermen caught her in a net and rescued her. She escaped to the island of AEGINA, where she was given the name DICTYNNA (Lady of the Nets). The goddess ARTEMIS (also a virgin huntress) rewarded her chastity by making her immortal. Legends say that Britomartis appears at night to navigators to guide them. In Greek mythology, Dictynna-Britomartis is called the Cretan Artemis.

**BULL**  A common animal featured in Greek and Roman mythology.

Bulls were sacred to ZEUS, the supreme OLYMPIAN GOD. He turned himself into a snow-white bull to enchant EUROPA, the daughter of the king of PHOENICIA. Zeus had fallen in love with the maiden and he carried her away in his disguise.

The vicious monster of CRETE, known as the MINOTAUR, was said to have the body of a man but the head of a bull. He consumed the young Athenians brought to him as sacrifices until the hero THESEUS killed the monster.

In Roman mythology, MARS, a god of war, was known as the "bull god" and often portrayed as having the ears and horns of a bull.

Ancient artists from GREECE and ETRURIA, a region in north-central Italy, often painted bulls on pottery. The bull was a powerful symbol for the farming societies that preceded the development of the cities of ATHENS and ROME. People commonly sacrificed bulls to the gods and goddesses. They also used bulls as a way to torture other people.

The Sumerian word for bull was *taurus*. The Greeks used this as a surname, or last name, for some of their gods. POSEIDON, for example, was given the last name of Taureus because he gave green pastures to bulls. The constellation Taurus is the second sign of the zodiac.

# C

**CACUS (1)** *Greek* A halfhuman lesser god, a maneating ogre, the son of HEPHAESTUS.

**CACUS (2)** *Roman* First an early god of the people of ETRURIA, perhaps a HOUSEHOLD GOD of the hearth, or a PENATE. In his earliest representations, Cacus was a beautiful young man, a shepherd, and singer with the gift of seeing into the future. His image survives on an early Etruscan mirror made of bronze.

Over time and in various stories, Cacus was also the villain in the Roman story of HERCULES' adventures with the cattle of GERYON. Two important Roman poets portray Cacus differently as they tell the story of Cacus's theft of the cattle as Hercules rested near a river. According to LIVY, Cacus, a local shepherd, was a strong, fierce man. According to VIRGIL, Cacus was a dangerous, evil monster who ate humans and littered his cave with their skulls and bones. In both versions, Hercules kills Cacus while rescuing the cattle. The traditional site of this conflict became ROME's famous cattle market, the forum Boarium.

In another story, Cacus was the slave of King EVANDER. Cacus stole the sheep of a Greek colonist.

**CADMUS** (From the East) *Greek* The founder of the city of THEBES in BOEOTIA. He was the son of King AGENOR and Telephassa; brother of EUROPA, CILIX, and PHOENIX; married HARMONIA; father of INO, Agave, Antonoë, and SEMELE (daughters), and Polydorus (a son). After ZEUS, disguised as a white bull, carried off Europa, Agenor sent his three sons to search for her, warning them not to return home without their sister. Not being able to find Europa, each of the brothers settled down elsewhere. Cadmus, on the advice of the Delphic ORACLE, eventually founded Thebes and married Harmonia.

**Cadmus and the Delphic Oracle** When Cadmus searched for his sister after she had been stolen away by a white bull, he and a few companions crossed the sea to DELPHI to consult the Oracle who resided there. The pythoness-oracle told Cadmus that he would found a city, and that he should give up the search for his sister and follow the tracks of a cow that would show him where to build the city. After a battle with a dragon and years of slavery under the war god ARES, Cadmus established Thebes.

**Cadmus and the Dragon** Cadmus, with a few companions, followed a cow that had moon-shaped markings on its head. The cow went deep into Boeotia before she rested. Cadmus knew that her resting place was to be the site of the citadel, or fortress, of the city that the oracle had told him he would found. He decided to sacrifice the cow to ATHENE, goddess of wisdom. He sent his companions to get some purifying water from a nearby spring. A dragon, the guardian of the spring, killed them all before Cadmus could reach them. Cadmus crushed the dragon's head with a rock. He sacrificed the cow and Athene rewarded him a visit. She told him to pull out the dragon's teeth and plant them in the ground. Cadmus did this, and in a very short time a host of fully armed men sprang up eager to fight, for the dragon was sacred to ARES, the god who loved to fight. The men were called the Spartoi (Sown Men).

Cadmus threw a stone into the midst of the Spartoi and at once the men started to attack each other, bellowing, until all but five were dead.

Ares was angry with Cadmus for killing his serpent-dragon and a divine court sentenced Cadmus to become the slave of Ares for "a Great Year," which may mean as much as eight years.

**Cadmus Builds the Citadel** Cadmus served many years of slavery under Ares, who was angry because Cadmus had killed one of his dragons. When the term of bondage ended, Cadmus and the Spartoi (the warriors born from the dragon's teeth) built the great citadel, or acropolis, called Cadmea in honor of Cadmus. Around the fortress rose Thebes. The Spartoi were to be the ancestors of the Theban nobility.

**Cadmus Marries Harmonia** After Cadmus founded Thebes, he married Harmonia, the daughter of Ares and APHRODITE. This was the first wedding of mortal beings ever attended by all 12 of the OLYMPIAN GODS. Cadmus had 12 golden thrones set up for them in his house. All the gods brought gifts: Aphrodite gave Harmonia a golden necklace made by HEPHAESTUS that would make her irresistibly beautiful; Athene gave her a golden robe that would make her wise; HERMES gave her a lyre; and all the gods blessed Harmonia.

Cadmus and Harmonia had four daughters; Ino, Agave, Antonoë, and Semele, and a son, Polydorus.

In their old age, the royal house of Thebes was destroyed and Cadmus and Harmonia made their way to Illyria, an ancient region of the Balkan Peninsula, generally taken to mean the Adriatic Coast north of Albania and west of the Dinaric Alps. There they eventually turned into serpents.

**Cadmus and the Alphabet** Cadmus, founder of Thebes, is said to have introduced the alphabet, and therefore writing, into GREECE from his native PHOENICIA. It is known that early Greek alphabets were derived from the Phoenician alphabet.

**CADUCEUS** *Greek* The wingtopped staff with two snakes winding around it, carried by HERMES and, in Roman mythology, MERCURY. Two snakes intertwined is an ancient symbol, associated since Babylonian times (third millennium B.C.) with fertility, wisdom, and healing. Greek heralds and ambassadors carried this staff as a symbol of peace and neutrality.

In later times, the staff became the emblem of ASCLEPIUS, god of healing. Today the caduceus is the insignia of the medical profession in many countries, including the United States and Great Britain.

**CALCHAS** *Greek* The sinister seer who prophesied doom throughout HOMER'S *ILIAD*. He was a priest of APOLLO and was called the son of Thestor. Calchas accompanied the Achaeans (Greeks) on their expedition to Troy during the TROJAN WAR. It was Calchas who advised AGAMEMNON to sacrifice his daughter IPHIGENIA to gain fair winds for the expedition to Troy, and it was Calchas who asserted that there would be no victory for the Greeks without the help of ACHILLES.

**CALLIOPE** (Beautiful Voice) *Greek* One of the MUSES, generally considered as the first and most important. Calliope was the patron of epic (heroic) stories and poems. She was the daughter of MNEMOSYNE and ZEUS and, some say, the mother of ORPHEUS. She is portrayed in art with a tablet and stylus and sometimes with a trumpet.

**CALLIRHOË** *Greek* Daughter of OENEUS, king of CALYDON. Callirhoë married ALCMAEON, not knowing that he was already married to Arsinoë, a princess of ARCADIA. However, Callirhoë learned about the fabulous treasure of HARMONIA, a necklace and a robe, that Alcmaeon had inherited from his greedy mother, ERIPHYLE. As Alcmaeon's wife, Callirhoë demanded that the treasure be given to her.

**CALLISTO** *Greek* The handmaiden of the goddess ARTEMIS and the lover of the god ZEUS, with whom she bore a child, ARCAS, the ancestor of the Arcadians. Artemis, angry at Callisto's loss of virginity, changed her into a she-bear. One day, as the grown-up Arcas was hunting in the woods, he saw the she-bear and was about to kill her. Zeus, to prevent the young man from killing his own mother, changed them both into stars. Callisto became Ursa Major, the Great Bear. Arcas became ARCTURUS, Guardian of the Bear.

**CALYDON** A town of AETOLIA, in western GREECE. In Greek myth, it was founded by AETOLUS and was the site of the CALYDONIAN BOAR HUNT.

**CALYDONIAN BOAR HUNT** *Greek* The boar was a ferocious creature sent by the goddess ARTEMIS to ravage CALYDON, an ancient city in AETOLIA, in western GREECE. OENEUS, the king of CALYDON, had offended the goddess by failing to offer her proper sacrifices. She sent the boar as punishment. MELEAGER, the son of Oeneus, sought to kill the boar. He sent messengers far and wide asking princes and sportsmen to come to his aid. Among those that came were the hero of ATHENS, THESEUS; his friend Peirithous; JASON; and ATALANTA. Atalanta, the only woman in the hunt, was the first to wound the boar, which was finally killed by Meleager. He presented the boar's hide to Atalanta, thus causing anger and quarrels among the men.

The Calydonian Boar Hunt is a heroic saga that first appears in HOMER'S *ILIAD*.

**CALYPSO** *Greek* In Homer's *Odyssey*, the Nymph-queen of the island of Ogygia in the Ionian Sea. Calypso detained the shipwrecked Odysseus for seven years but finally, at the command of the god Zeus, helped him on his way home to Ithaca.

**CAMENAE** *Roman* Spirits or Nymphs who tended the freshwater springs that supplied water to Rome, and specifically to the Vestal Virgins.

Part of their story is that King Numa, who succeeded Romulus as king of Rome, dedicated a grove of trees to the Camenae after they inspired him to develop wise laws for the young kingdom. A spring arose in this grove and it is here that the Camenae are said to have made their home.

Once Greek mythology began to strongly influence Roman religion, the Camenae merged into the stories of the muses, daughters of Zeus who brought inspiration to humans.

**CAMILLA** *Roman* A heroine of an ancient Roman legend. Camilla's father, Metabus, the king of the Volscians, saved his daughter's life as they were being pursued from their city by his enemies. Stories conflict as to Camilla's age—an infant or a little girl?—but as the father and child fled, they came to the river Amesenus in Latium. To save Camilla, Metabus fastened her to either a large stake or an arrow. He said a prayer for his daughter's safety to Diana, goddess of the woods and hunting, and threw or shot Camilla across the river. Metabus swam across the river and found that Diana had granted his prayer: his daughter was safe. Together they hid in the woods, where they lived for years.

Later, Camilla became a warrior, very fast, very strong, and devoted to Diana. She fought against Aeneas, the Trojan hero, in his battle with Turnus, a prince of the Rutuli people. Camilla died in battle.

Virgil tells the story of Camilla in the *Aeneid*, where he described her as so swift that when she ran over a field of corn, not a blade bent, and when she ran over the sea, her feet did not get wet. Some experts, however, believe Virgil based his story on an ancient legend, popular in central Italy before writing became common.

**CAPRICORN** (The Goat) A constellation between Sagittarius and Aquarius; the 10th sign of the zodiac. Capricorn is named after the goat-Nymph Amalthea who, in Greek mythology, tended the god Zeus when he was an infant. In gratitude, Zeus set Amalthea among the stars.

**CARDEA** *Roman* Goddess of door hinges, a protective deity who helps watch over the family.

Cardea was first a virgin huntress or perhaps a Nymph who tricked suitors by sending them to a cave and telling them that she would soon follow, while she turned and went the opposite way. Janus, a principle god in the Roman pantheon, could see forward and backward and marked the beginnings and ends of things. When he fell in love with Cardea, she pulled her trick on him, but he saw her flight and pursued her, catching her and making her his lover.

In return, Janus bestowed on Cardea the power to watch over and influence door hinges and doorways. He also gave her power over the whitethorn, or hawthorn bush, which had a reputation for protecting children against witches and vampires. In this way, Cardea became a prominent household goddess.

**CARMENTA** (CARMENTIS) *Roman* Originally, a goddess of childbirth, particularly of the position of the child, who could be born head first, *prorsa*, or feet first, *postversa*. Romans celebrated a festival to Carmenta on January 11 and 15, during the first month of the year, a symbol, perhaps of the beginning of life.

As Roman religion changed under the influence of Greek mythology, Carmenta's stories shifted. From a goddess, she became a Nymph of fresh waters, one of the Camenae of Roman mythology. In this role, Carmenta was known as the mother (perhaps the wife) of the hero Evander, which would have made her a Greek nymph. She and her son fled Arcadia, a region of Greece, and sailed for Italy. Through her powers of prophecy, Carmenta advised her son to settle on the Palatine Hill, one of Rome's seven hills. She was also known for giving the gift of writing to the people of Central Italy.

While the events of Carmenta's story were believed to have taken place long before Aeneas arrived in Italy after the Trojan War, some scholars suggest that Roman writers developed this story to explain the connection between Greek and Roman religions.

**CARTHAGE** An ancient city on the north shore of Africa, near modern Tunis. In mythology, as told in Virgil's *Aeneid*, Dido established Carthage and became its queen.

**CASSANDRA** *Greek* Daughter of King PRIAM of TROY and of Queen HECUBA; sister of HELENUS, PARIS, and HECTOR. The god APOLLO gave Cassandra the gift of prophecy, but when she rejected his advances, he ordained that no one would ever believe her prophecies (which were always accurate). Before the fall of Troy, Cassandra warned the Trojans that the gift-horse of the Greeks was a trick, but no one believed her, and the Trojans suffered defeat (see TROJAN WAR). At the fall of Troy, Cassandra was given as booty to the victorious AGAMEMNON, king of ARGOS and MYCENAE. Cassandra warned the king that his wife, CLYTEMNESTRA, would kill him, but Agamemnon would not believe her. He took Cassandra back to Mycenae. Clytemnestra murdered Agamemnon and Cassandra.

The word *Cassandra* has come to mean someone who is a prophet of doom.

**CASSIOPEIA** *Greek* Wife of King CEPHEUS of ETHIOPIA; mother of ANDROMEDA and of Atymnius, by ZEUS. Cassiopeia boasted that she and her daughter were more beautiful than the sea NYMPHS, or NERE-IDS, daughters of the god POSEIDON. This aroused the wrath of Poseidon, who sent a monster to punish Ethiopia. An ORACLE declared that only the sacrifice of Cassiopeia's daughter, Andromeda, would appease the monster and save the country. Cassiopeia, along with Cepheus and Andromeda, became constellations visible in the Northern Hemisphere.

**CASTOR AND POLLUX** ("The Heavenly Twins") *Greek and Roman* The twin gods known to the Greeks and Romans as the DIOSCURI (Sons of ZEUS).

The story of these brothers began in GREECE, where Pollux was known as Polydeuces, and where they are the subjects of many popular stories. The Romans, as they became familiar with the twins, developed a strong liking for these two characters. Castor, as a warrior and horseman, and Pollux, as a boxer, represented traits important to the Romans, who eventually created a powerful empire throughout much of Europe and the Mediterranean region.

One Roman story tells of people seeing the twins riding on magnificent white horses and fighting on the side of ROME in the battle at Lake Regillus (496 B.C.), although this was after Zeus had made them immortal and placed them in the heavens as the constellation Gemini. They disappeared from the battlefield as mysteriously as they had arrived.

In a story dating from 300 years later, they are said to have appeared on their horses and announced to a citizen on a road in Rome the victory of a Roman commander fighting across the sea in Macedonia, north of Greece, on the day of the battle. Again, the twins disappeared from the roadside, though their message proved, days later, to have been true.

Romans celebrated the twins on July 15 and built splendid temples in their honor.

**CELEUS** *Greek* Legendary king of ELEUSIS; father of DEMOPHON and TRIPTOLEMUS; husband of Metaneira. He and his wife were hosts to the goddess DEMETER when she wandered the Earth in search of her daughter PERSEPHONE. Celeus is described as the first priest and his daughters as the first priestesses of Demeter at Eleusis.

**CENTAURS** *Greek* These were creatures half human and half horse, sons of CENTAURUS. IXION, a LAPITH of THESSALY, loved the goddess HERA, wife of ZEUS, who became jealous. Zeus fashioned a likeness of Hera out of a cloud and called her NEPHELE. Ixion, convinced that the beautiful cloud-woman was Hera, mated with her. Nephele produced a son, Centaurus. This son mated with the mares of Thessaly, producing creatures that were half man and half horse—the centaurs.

Usually depicted as unruly, the centaurs are notorious in legend for their disorderly behavior among the Lapiths, the mythical people of Thessaly. The result was a battle. The centaurs were expelled from their native Thessaly and took refuge on Mount Pindus, on the frontiers of EPIRUS. Centaurs are often associated with the SATYRS and Sileni, followers of the wine god, DIONYSUS. However, CHIRON, the most famous of the centaurs, was wise and gentle.

The myth of the centaurs probably stems from the time of the migrations and the coming of the horse to GREECE in about 2000 B.C. The horse was enormously important to migratory people and was a cult animal in many parts of the world. In remote regions where wild horses lived, there must have been primitive peoples who were so skilled at catching, taming, and riding the horses that the sight of them awed all who saw them. Many may have believed that they were looking at a single, magical creature, with the head and trunk of a human and the hindquarters of a horse.

A female centaur decorates this first century A.D. metal cup which is in the National Library of France in Paris. *(Photograph by Marie-Lan Nguyen. Used under a Creative Commons license.)*

**CENTAURUS** *Greek* Son of IXION and NEPHELE; father of the CENTAURS, which were created after Centaurus mated with the mares of THESSALY. Centaurus is a constellation of the Southern Hemisphere.

**CEPHALUS** *Greek* Son of HERMES; husband of Procris, who was a daughter of ERECHTHEUS; love interest of the dawn goddess Eos. Eos tricked Cephalus into leaving his beloved wife. The unhappy Procris sought the protection of ARTEMIS, goddess of the hunt. By the devious methods of Artemis, Cephalus was presented with two magnificent gifts, a spear that never missed its mark and a hound named LAELAPS that never lost the scent of its quarry. Cephalus inadvertently cast the spear at Procris and killed her. He then killed himself by leaping from a cliff into the sea.

**CEPHEUS** *Greek* King of ETHIOPIA, husband of CASSIOPEIA; father of ANDROMEDA, who was to marry the hero PERSEUS. After their deaths, Cepheus, Cassiopeia, and Andromeda were all set among the stars as constellations.

**CERBERUS** *Greek* The hound of HADES, guardian of the UNDERWORLD (1). Cerberus was the offspring of TYPHON and ECHIDNA. In some accounts, Cerberus had three heads; in others, as many as 50. He was a fearsome creature, but music and offerings of food calmed him.

For HERACLES, bringing Cerberus from Hades to the upper world was his 12th and most difficult labor. When he was captured, the monstrous dog dripped venom from his fangs and thus infected certain HERBS, including aconite, called wolfsbane. Evil magicians then used these herbs to prepare poisonous brews.

The idea of a fearsome guardian dog probably had its origin in the custom of the Egyptians, who guarded the graves of the dead with large, dangerous dogs. Cerberus is associated with HECATE, an ancient goddess of death.

**CERCOPES** *Greek*   Twins, sons of the TITANS OCEANUS and THEIA. They were mischievous, clever thieves, sometimes depicted as monkeys. The Cercopes teased the great hero HERACLES, who took them captive and tied them onto a pole that he carried across his shoulders. Heracles was so disarmed by the jokes and good humor of the twins that he set them free.

**CERES** *Roman*   An ancient goddess of living things, of grains and other plants. The cult of Ceres appears to predate 600 B.C. when she was likely seen as a foundation goddess, a variation of the EARTH MOTHER. Ceres provided protection for the life cycle of plants, a very important function in an agricultural society. Legends give Ceres credit for being the first to harvest grains.

Romans celebrated Ceres during the festival of Cerialia on April 19, which was part of the oldest Roman religious calendar.

Despite her ancient popularity, Ceres was one of the first deities of Italy to be influenced and finally absorbed by Greek mythology (see HELLENIZATION).

According to one prominent story, the citizens of the young city of ROME were under attack by their neighbors from ETRURIA. The leaders consulted an ORACLE, who advised them to bring to Rome worship of the Greek goddess DEMETER and the god DIONYSUS. The worship of those two deities would save Rome from the attackers.

In about 496 B.C., the Romans built a temple on the Aventine Hill and dedicated it to Demeter and Dionysus, whom they came to call BACCHUS. From that time on, the identity of Ceres, her responsibilities, and her cults merged into those of Demeter. Most of the myths of Ceres, the stories and family relationships, were those of Demeter using the Roman names for the Greek gods. In this form, Ceres was the mother of PROSERPINA.

The word *cereal*, which in its broadest sense means grass or edible grains, comes from the name of this Roman goddess.

In astronomy, Ceres is the largest known Earth-orbiting asteroid, 1,000 kilometers in diameter, which was discovered in 1800.

**CETO** (Whale) *Greek*   An ancient Greek sea goddess. Ceto was a daughter of GAIA and PONTUS, the earliest personification of the sea. Some scholars suggest that the Greeks considered Ceto a sea monster or a whale.

She is most famous for her monstrous children. With PHORCYS, one of her many brothers, Ceto conceived and gave birth to the GORGONS, three female monsters, of whom STHENO and EURYALE were immortal and MEDUSA became mortal; the three sisters known as the GRAEA, who represented old age; and LADON, the dragon who guarded the apples of the HESPERIDES.

As one of the many original children of Gaia, Ceto was also sister and aunt to many ancient mythical creatures, including THAUMUS, father of the HARPIES, and NEREUS, father of the NEREIDS, or NYMPHS of the sea.

**CHAOS** *Greek*   The empty, unfathomable space at the beginning of time. GAIA, the original EARTH MOTHER, sprang from Chaos, as did NYX (Night) and EREBUS (Darkness). Eventually *chaos* came to mean a great confusion of matter out of which a supreme being created all life.

**CHARON** *Greek*   The ferryman of the UNDERWORLD (1). Son of EREBUS (Darkness) and NYX (Night). The hideous old man ferried the shades, or spirits, of the dead across the rivers Acheron and STYX. If not presented with an *obolus*, a small coin, or bribe, the old man would drive away the dead soul, who was then condemned to wander the bleak shores of Acheron and Styx. Hence comes the custom of the Greeks (and others) of placing a coin on the mouth or eyelids of the dead.

**CHIMERA** (She-Goat) *Greek*   A fire-breathing monster with a lion's head, a goat's body, and a serpent's tail; the offspring of the monsters ECHIDNA and TYPHON. BELLEROPHON destroyed the Chimera by riding his winged horse, PEGASUS, and shooting the monster with arrows or lumps of lead. The origin of this creature may be a volcano in LYCIA, ASIA MINOR, whose eruptions created as much havoc as did the mischief of Chimera.

The word *chimera* is used in English for an illusory fantasy or a wild, incongruous scheme.

**CHIONE** *Greek*   Daughter of Daedalion who was the son of Phosphorus (Lucifer), mother of AUTOLYCUS by HERMES and of Phillamon by APOLLO.

**CHIRON** *Greek* A CENTAUR of great wisdom and kindness, friend of both humans and gods. Possibly the son of CRONUS and Phylira, Chiron lived on Mount PELION in THESSALY. He received his education from the divine twins, APOLLO and ARTEMIS. In turn, the gods entrusted him with the education of ASCLEPIUS, god of healing, and the heroes JASON and ACHILLES.

HERACLES inadvertently wounded Chiron during a brawl with the centaurs, who were mostly wild and unruly. Heracles rushed to the side of Chiron but there was nothing either he or Chiron could do, for the arrow of Heracles had been dipped in the poisoned blood of HYDRA, the many-headed water serpent. Since Chiron was immortal, he was doomed to suffer eternal pain. ZEUS solved the dilemma by allowing Chiron to confer his immortality on PROMETHEUS in return for the peace of dying. Zeus then placed Chiron in the heavens as part of the SAGITTARIUS or Centaurus constellations.

Chiron, half human and half horse, represented ancient wisdom. He was the symbol of the wild horse, full of strength, tamed to be of enormous help to humans.

**CHRYSEIS** *Greek* The daughter of Chryses, a priest of APOLLO. During the TROJAN WAR, the Greek war hero ACHILLES took her prisoner. Considered as war booty, Chryseis was then seized by AGAMEMNON, leader of the Greeks. Her father, Chryses, came to the Greek camp to rescue his daughter, but Agamemnon defended against the attack. Thereupon Apollo sent a plague among the Greeks. Many died and Agamemnon at last released Chryseis to her father to appease Apollo's anger.

**CILIX** *Greek* Son of AGENOR and Telephassa, brother of CADMUS, EUROPA, and PHOENIX. When ZEUS stole Europa, King Agenor sent his three sons to search for her. The brothers could not find her, and not daring to return to their father, settled down elsewhere. Cilix is said to have founded the nation of the Cilicians, an ancient region of southeast ASIA MINOR. Modern Cilicia is an area of southern Turkey lying between the Mediterranean Sea and the Taurus Mountains.

**CIRCE** *Greek* Daughter of the sun god HELIOS, sister of PHAETON and AEETES. The witch-goddess of HOMER's *ODYSSEY*, Circe cast powerful spells. She turned all ODYSSEUS's men into swine. Odysseus escaped the curse with the help of an HERB called *moly* and spent a year with the enchantress. Eventually he persuaded Circe to restore his men to their former shapes and they all escaped from the witch. Circe also appears in the story of JASON.

In post-Homeric stories, Circe bore Odysseus a son, TELEGONUS.

**CLAUDIA QUINTAS** *Roman* A heroine of considerable fame. As the poet OVID told her story, Claudia had a bad reputation among the citizens of ROME for wearing too much makeup and fancy hairdos. People spread rumors that she was not a virgin. She was a follower of CYBELE, a Greek goddess of fertility. When the citizens of Rome decided to bring the cult of Cybele to Italy, they sent a ship to GREECE to bring back a statue of the goddess. When the ship returned, it became caught in the mud of the riverbank. Claudia stepped out of the waiting crowd, prayed loudly to Cybele to bring her strength, but only if Claudia was innocent of the accusations people made and worthy of the goddess's love. Then Claudia gave a great tug at the rope fastened to the ship and freed the ship from the mud. She became the leader of a new Roman cult.

**CLOACINA** *Roman* A specialized goddess who presided over and protected the sewers of ROME. As Rome became the home to more people, they needed to move more and more significant amounts of waste out of the city. They invoked Cloacina and her power to help them build and maintain the great sewer system to clean the city. The greatest of these sewers was the Cloaca Maxima. People built and dedicated a temple to her in the Roman Forum, an area that grew in prominence in part due to the sewer system there and Cloacina's protection of that resource.

Eventually, Cloacina's traits merged with those of the goddess VENUS, whom the Romans fashioned after the Greek goddess APHRODITE.

**CLOELIA** *Roman* A heroine of early ROME. Her story is told by many historians and poets, though some of the details vary.

Cloelia was a Roman citizen taken hostage with a group of others by Lars Porsenna, the legendary leader of the people of ETRURIA who laid siege to Rome in 509 B.C. One day, Cloelia gathered a group of young women together and went to bathe in the river. She convinced the guards to turn their backs while the women unclothed. Then the women hurried into the water and swam across the river while the guards hurled spears at them. The women safely reached the shore held by Roman forces and Cloelia received great honors for her courage. Lars Porsenna protested the escape as a violation of the truce and the Romans returned all of the women. However, Porsenna changed his mind and admitted that Cloelia was very brave and granted freedom to her and a group of hostages (whom she would choose). Cloelia chose the boys who had not yet reached puberty, arguing that her reputation and their safety at the hands of their captors made them the only group she could take with her. The Romans honored Cloelia's loyalty to the city and its people by dedicating in her honor a statue of a horse.

These events supposedly happened early in Rome's history, but the story of Cloelia survived for centuries as a symbol of loyalty and courage as the city-state expanded into an empire. Some scholars and historians said the Romans invented the story to explain the dedication of the equestrian statue after people had forgotten why it was dedicated to someone named Cloelia.

**CLYMENE** *Greek* An OCEANID, or ocean NYMPH; one of the eldest daughters of the TITANS OCEANUS and TETHYS, and, as such, considered a second-generation Titan; married IAPETUS and with him was the mother of still more Titans: ATLAS, PROMETHEUS, EPIMETHEUS, and MENOETIUS.

Clymene was also considered by some sources to be the mother of PHAETON and his weeping sisters, the Heliads, whose father was HELIOS, the OLYMPIAN GOD who drove the sun across the sky.

Clymene was known as the goddess of both fame and infamy. In some sources, she is named Asia, and considered a goddess of the region ASIA MINOR, also known as Anatolia.

**CLYTEMNESTRA** *Greek* Daughter of Tyndareus, king of SPARTA, and of LEDA, sister of HELEN and CASTOR AND POLLUX. Clytemnestra was the mother of Chrysothemis, IPHIGENIA, ELECTRA, and ORESTES.

Clytemnestra married AGAMEMNON, king of ARGOS and MYCENAE, of the accursed house of PELOPS. When Agamemnon went to the TROJAN WAR as commander of the Greek forces, Clytemnestra became the lover of AEGISTHUS, another descendant of Pelops. Clytemnestra hated Agamemnon, for he had sacrificed their daughter Iphigenia to ARTEMIS, and to the wind god, AEOLUS, in order to get fair winds for the Greek fleet to sail to TROY and many years of war.

When the victorious Agamemnon returned from Troy, he brought with him Princess CASSANDRA as one of the spoils of war. He and Cassandra were murdered by Clytemnestra and Aegisthus, who were themselves murdered by Electra and Orestes.

Although Clytemnestra has little mythology of her own, she is a major tragic figure in the plays of AESCHYLUS, SOPHOCLES, and EURIPIDES.

**COEUS** *Greek* A first-generation TITAN; son of URANUS and GAIA; father, with his sister PHOEBE, of ASTERIA and LETO, who would become the mother of APOLLO and ARTEMIS (1).

While best known in his role as a parent, Coeus was considered the god of intelligence and thinking. He was also the pillar of heaven around which the constellations evolved and, as such, the keeper of heavenly oracles.

With his siblings, Coeus was banished by ZEUS, the greatest of the conquering OLYMPIAN GODS, to TARTARUS, the depths of the UNDERWORLD.

**COMUS** *Roman* A god of joy and mirth, of feasting and revelry. Comus was often represented as a young man with wings, who was rather sleepy, perhaps drunk, after a large meal. Romans associated him with DIONYSUS, the Greek god of fertility, wine, and pleasure. Comus loved wine, dance, and song.

**CONCORDIA** *Roman* The goddess who personified concord, or harmony, particularly between citizens and the state or government. The oldest temple to her was built in 367 B.C. at the foot of the Capitoline Hill, and represented an agreement between the commoners and the members of the ruling families. The Roman Senate often met in Concordia's temple. She is pictured on coins, which were usually minted after a rebellion or civil war, as a matron, sitting, wearing a long cloak, and holding a saucer, cornucopia, or olive branch. Concordia was known as Harmonia in Greek mythology, and she had a temple in Olympia, site of the OLYMPIC GAMES. (See also PAX and EIRENE.)

**CONSUS** (The Storer) *Roman* An ancient but little-known Roman god of storage who protected the harvest once it was placed in silos, which were underground chambers in ancient ROME; an important god during the early agricultural days of Central Italy.

The cult that worshiped Consus faded from importance as Rome became a major city and empire. Consus was also known as the consort of OPS, an ancient goddess of plenty.

Rome celebrated Consus during horse races and during an annual harvest festival known as the Consualia when horses, mules, and other draft animals were decorated with flowers and allowed to rest.

Worshipers built an altar to Consus underground, beneath the middle of the Circus Maximus, a huge

A corner of the Temple of Apollo in Corinth, Greece, probably built in the sixth century B.C., still stands on a hilltop. It is now a prominent tourist attraction.

stadium with seating for 150,000 people. Here Rome held very popular horse races. Another temple to Consus stood between the Palatine and the Aventine hills.

**CORINTH** *Greek* A city in the northeast PELO-PONNESUS, strategically situated on the isthmus connecting Peloponnesus with central GREECE. Corinth was one of the largest and most powerful cities of ancient Greece, a rival of ATHENS and traditionally allied with SPARTA. Corinth traded with east and west and established numerous colonies.

**CORNUCOPIA** (Horn of Plenty) *Greek* The horn of the goat-NYMPH, AMALTHEA, who had tended the infant ZEUS. The horn was as large and full as that of a cow's, and would remain forever filled with food and drink for its owners. Zeus gave the horn to the ash nymphs, ADRASTIA and IDA (1), who, along with Amalthea, had tended him when he was an infant. The cornucopia remains a symbol of plenty, generosity, hospitality, and general well being.

**CORONIS** *Greek* Daughter of Phlegyas, king of the LAPITHS of THESSALY; mother of ASCLEPIUS, with the god APOLLO.

Apollo fell in love with Coronis when he saw her bathing in a lake. Coronis seemed to accept the love of Apollo. He left a white crow to watch over her, but Coronis then fell in love with Ischus. The crow sped off to tell the news to Apollo, who struck the crow in his anger and turned its white feathers to black.

ARTEMIS, the sister of Apollo, shot her arrows at the faithless Coronis and killed her, but Apollo managed to snatch the infant ASCLEPIUS from the funeral pyre. The child was brought up by the god HERMES, or, some say, by CHIRON, the gentle CENTAUR, to become a god of healing and medicine.

**CORYBANTES** *Greek* The worshipers of CYBELE who celebrated their goddess with wild dances and loud music. They were identified with the GALLI and later with the Cretan CURETES.

**COW** The cow, like the BULL, was a common farm animal found in Greek mythology. It was an animal important to the worship of some gods and used in ceremonies or initiation rites.

Zeus, the supreme Greek god, fell in love with Io, the daughter of a river god and a priestess to Hera, wife of Zeus. Furious at her husband's infidelity, Hera threatened Io, so Zeus turned the maiden into a white cow or heifer, who then wandered and grazed over the Earth.

Cadmus, son of King Agenor and founder of the city of Thebes, took the advice of the Oracle he consulted and followed a specific cow until she stopped. On that spot, Cadmus built a fortress that would become the center of Thebes.

In some cult ceremonies, girls being initiated into service as priestesses to Hera had their hair cut short and their skin painted white and were sent to wander in the hills. This was to re-create the story of the three young girls, known as the Proetides or Proitids, whom Hera had turned into cows after they had made fun of a statue of her.

Followers of Zeus, Pan, Demeter, and Athene, often sacrificed cows to these deities.

**CRATUS** (Cratos; Kratos; Strength) *Greek* The personification of strength; a demigod or lesser god; son of the Titan Pallas and the water Nymph Styx; brother of Nike (Victory), Bia (Force), and Zelus (Zeal).

Cratus and his siblings, winged creatures who moved very quickly, served as guards and attendants to Zeus. Their mother had sided with the great god in his battle with Cronus and the Titans, and had brought her children, Cratus, Nike, Bia, and Zelus, to serve with her.

To Cratus and Bia fell the task of carrying out the punishment of the god Prometheus, who had given fire to humans. They chained him to a rock high in the mountains, where each day a vulture plucked at his liver and each night the organ grew back.

The Roman counterpart to Cratus was Potestas.

**CRETE** *Greek* An island southeast of Greece in the eastern Mediterranean. Crete had one of the world's earliest civilizations, and one of the most brilliant: the Minoan civilization, named after the legendary king Minos. It is believed to be the birthplace of classical Greek language and literature. In mythology, Minos was the son of the god Zeus and Europa. He married Pasiphaë, who fell in love with a bull. Pasiphae gave birth to the Minotaur, half human and half bull. In order to hide the Minotaur, Minos had Daedalus build the famous labyrinth. Young men and maidens were said to be sacrificed to the bull. In the great palace of Knossos, beautiful murals depict these young people vaulting over the back of the Minotaur. Minoan culture was at its prime between 2200 and 1450 B.C.

**CREUSA (1)** (Glauca) *Greek* Daughter of King Creon of Corinth. Creusa married the hero, Jason. In jealous revenge, Medea, Jason's first wife, used her magic powers to kill Creusa. Medea sent Creusa a wedding dress soaked in poison. When Creusa put on the dress, it burned into her flesh and killed her. Creon, Creusa's father, also perished from the poison.

**CREUSA (2)** *Roman* Wife of Aeneas, a hero of the Trojan War who went on to become a founding figure in Roman mythology, and mother of his son, Ascanius. When Aeneas was fleeing Troy as it burned, Creusa was lost in the crush of people. When he discovered this, Aeneas went back to find her, but only her shade, or ghost, appeared to him. Creusa's spirit told Aeneas that he would embark on a great journey before establishing a great city, which would be Lavinium, near Rome. Creusa begged her husband to raise their son well.

**CRIUS** (Krios) *Greek* A first-generation Titan; son of Uranus (Heaven) and Gaia (Earth); with Eurybia, a daughter of Pontus and Gaia, the father of Astraeus, Pallas, and Perses.

Little is known of Crius other than his role as a father. However, hints in the writings of ancient Greeks suggest that he was a god of leadership and domestic animals and is associated with the ram, or male sheep. Some suggest that Crius became the constellation Aries, the ram.

**CRONUS** (Kronus) *Greek* A Titan, the son of Uranus (Heaven) and Gaia (Earth). With his sister-wife, Rhea, Cronus fathered daughters: Demeter, Hestia, and Hera, and sons: Hades, Poseidon, and Zeus, who became Olympian gods. Cronus dethroned his father, Uranus, and was in turn dethroned by his son, Zeus.

Cronus was probably a corn god in ancient times and is often depicted holding a sickle or scythe—the same weapon that he used to render Uranus impotent. The Roman Saturn is identified with Cronus.

**Cronus Overthrows Uranus** Uranus and Gaia had many children, including the Titans, the Cyclopes, and the Hecatoncheires (Hundred-Handed Ones).

Uranus grew jealous of his children and had them confined under the Earth. Gaia was very unhappy about losing all her children. Finally, she gave a sickle to her bravest son, Cronus, and encouraged him to use it on his father. This Cronus did, mutilating his father horribly so that Uranus became impotent. From his blood were born the furies and the giants; from parts of his flesh, which Cronus had cut off and thrown into the sea, arose the goddess APHRODITE. The defeated Uranus left his realm to Cronus, but warned that one of his sons would in turn overthrow him.

**The Children of Cronus**  Cronus married his sister, Rhea, with whom he fathered daughters Demeter, Hestia, and Hera and sons Hades, Poseidon, and Zeus. Remembering the prophecy of his defeated father, Uranus, Cronus swallowed his children as soon as they were born so that none could overthrow him. In despair, Rhea sought the advice of Gaia, who advised her to give Cronus a stone to swallow the next time a child was born to her. When Zeus was born, Rhea hid him away and presented Cronus with a large stone wrapped in baby clothes. Cronus promptly swallowed the stone, thinking it was his child.

When Zeus grew to be a young man, he tricked Cronus into coughing up all the siblings—and the stone—that he had swallowed. Then the siblings gathered together with Zeus, the Cyclopes, and the Hecatoncheires to fight a long war with Cronus and finally defeat him. The era of the Titans ended and Zeus and his brothers and sisters founded the Olympian dynasty.

There are various versions of the story of Cronus. The oldest and most often cited is found in the writings of HESIOD.

**CUPID** (Desire) *Roman*  God of love, son of VENUS and possibly of VULCAN, the fire god. Cupid is usually represented as a winged boy or fat baby, often blindfolded to denote his irresponsible nature, and carrying a bow and arrows, used to shoot his victims. Cupid is a Roman adaptation of the Greek god EROS. He was of no great importance except to writers such as VIRGIL (in the *AENEID*) and to many artists.

**CURETES** (Young Men) *Greek*  The young Cretan warriors, possibly sons of RHEA, who guarded the infant ZEUS when he was hidden on Mount IDA (2) in central CRETE. The young men danced wildly and clashed their weapons together to drown out the sound of the infant's crying. Some sources suggest that there was a cult in Crete devoted to the god Zeus as a youth (*kouros*) and that its devotees were the

Curetes. There is further mention of the Curetes in several Greek myths, including that of ZAGREUS.

The Curetes were sometimes identified with the CORYBANTES who performed with dancing, shouting, and clashing of armor at the rites of the goddess CYBELE.

See also GALLI.

**CYBELE** *Greek*  A Phrygian (Asiatic) goddess of fertility who found favor in GREECE (in the fourth or fifth century B.C.) and ROME (in the third century B.C.). She was sometimes associated with RHEA, the ancient TITAN, as she, too, personified the Earth in its primitive state. Cybele was sometimes known as AGDISTIS, who had some of the attributes of both a male and a female. Her attendant god was ATTIS; her priests were the GALLI. The cult of Cybele had a strong appeal for women. With Gordius, king of PHRYGIA (ASIA MINOR), Cybele bore a son, MIDAS.

**Cybele and Attis**  Attis was a lesser god with whom the great goddess Cybele fell in love. He is represented as a young, handsome shepherd. Cybele chose Attis as her priest and imposed upon him a vow of chastity. Attis broke his vow and in a fit of rage, Cybele changed him into a pine tree, or an almond tree. The death of Attis and his rebirth as a tree were celebrated every year in ancient Greece, and later, in Rome. This myth of Attis obviously has its origins in ancient fertility rites, based on the belief that Cybele or Agdistis, as a personification of the Earth, kills and then resurrects vegetation.

**Cybele and Midas**  The goddess Cybele mated with Gordius, king of Phrygia, with whom she bore a son, Midas. Midas inherited his father's throne. By the god DIONYSUS, Midas was granted the wish that everything he touched should turn to gold.

**CYCLOPES (1)** (Singular: CYCLOPS; Round-eyed) *Greek*  Three sons of URANUS and GAIA, large and strong, each with one eye in the middle of his forehead; siblings of the HECATONCHEIRES, hundred-handed giants, and the younger TITANS. Their names were Brontes (Thunder) Steropes (Lightning), and Arges (Thunderbolt); they were best known most for making lightning and thunder.

Their father, Uranus, hated them, and banished them to TARTARUS, the deepest pit below the underworld, but Gaia convinced Uranus to free their sons. However, after CRONUS, a Titan and the youngest of their siblings, revolted against and defeated Uranus, he once again banished back to Tartarus these three fearsome brothers, sometimes referred to as the Uranian Cyclopes.

When his time came to overthrow Cronus, ZEUS, having learned in a prophecy that he could not win his battle against his father and the Titans unless he had the aid of the Cyclopes, freed Brontes, Steropes, and Arges. In return, they helped Zeus defeat Cronus. The three then forged great treasures for the OLYMPIAN GODS: thunder and lightning, which they gave to Zeus; a helmet of invisibility, which they gave to HADES; and a great trident, which they gave to POSEIDON. From that time forward, these one-eyed brothers were greatly admired and respected by the Olympians.

Brontes, Steropes, and Arges died at the hands of APOLLO, who killed them for making the thunderbolt which Zeus had used to kill Appolo's son ASCLEPIUS.

Later Greek mythology tells of a group of one-eyed beings who lived under Mount Aetna and helped the smith god HEPHAESTUS forge thunder, lightning, and armor for the gods. Some sources consider these to be the three sons of Uranus and Gaia. Other sources suggest that they are a separate group of Cyclopes.

## CYCLOPES (2) (Singular: CYCLOPS) *Greek*

The poet HOMER describes the Cyclopes in the *ODYSSEY* as a tribe of gigantic, one-eyed shepherds who lived on an island in the Mediterranean Sea. Some sources suggest the tribe is made up of the off-spring of the sea god POSEIDON and a water NYMPH.

These Cyclopes are cannibals, wild and ruthless, and pose a great threat to humans stranded on their shores. The most famous among them was POLYPHEMUS, who captured ODYSSEUS and his men and held them in a cave, then began eating some of them each day. (See "Odysseus and the Cyclops" under *Odyssey*).

## CYCLOPES (3) (Singular: CYCLOPS) *Greek* A

race of very strong men, who were known to be master builders, perhaps having come from Thrace, a region on the northern shores of the Aegean Sea.

These Cyclopes served King PROETUS of the city Tiryns. For him, they built the great walls of the city. They built similar walls around the city of MYCENAE and the famous Lion Gate there. The stones they used were so massive that the term "cyclopean" has come to mean gigantic. They were also called "belly-hands" for they worked for their livings.

## CYCNUS *Greek* Son of ARES by Pelopia or by

Pyrene. Cycnus was cruel and aggressive like his father, the god of war. Cycnus attacked and killed travelers in the region of Tempe, in THESSALY. He used their bones to build a temple for his father. One day he challenged HERACLES. In the fearsome battle that followed, Heracles killed Cycnus and severely wounded Ares, who had tried to help Cycnus.

## CYRENE *Greek* Thessalian NYMPH, carried off

by the god APOLLO to the country that came to be called Cyrenaica. There she bore Apollo a son, ARISTAEUS.

# D

**DAEDALUS** (Cunningly Wrought) *Greek* A legendary Athenian, descendant of the god HEPHAESTUS, who was known as "the divine artificer." Daedalus was a great craftsman, architect, sculptor, and inventor. His nephew, TALUS, was also a gifted craftsman and became the apprentice of Daedalus. When the boy invented the saw, Daedalus became jealous, murdered his nephew, and fled from ATHENS to the island of CRETE.

Daedalus entered the service of King MINOS of Crete, for whom he constructed the amazing LABYRINTH, or maze, in which the MINOTAUR lived, The Minotaur, or monster, was half human, half BULL, and was the offspring of Minos's wife PASIPHAË and a bull.

Once the Labyrinth was completed, Minos kept Daedalus prisoner so that he could not reveal the secret of the maze to anyone. Daedalus made wings from the feathers of birds and wax and escaped from Crete with his son, ICARUS. Icarus ignored his father's advice and flew too near the Sun, which melted the wax and rendered the wings useless. Icarus fell into the sea and drowned.

Daedalus landed in Sicily and entered the court of King Cocalus, where he constructed beautiful and imaginative toys for the king's daughters.

Minos went in search of Daedalus. He carried with him a triton shell and a piece of linen thread, saying that he would reward the person who could thread the linen through the shell. Minos knew that only the talented Daedalus could find a way to do this impossible task. Sure enough, when he reached Sicily, King Cocalus boasted of the wonderful inventor at his court and asked Daedalus to perform the task. Daedalus did this by boring a minute hole in the triton shell, smearing it with honey, and sending an ant, harnessed to the thread, through the hole and all the way through the shell's spirals to its opening.

Minos demanded the surrender of Daedalus, but with the help of Cocalus's daughters, Daedalus contrived for Minos a horrid death in a hot bathtub.

The story of Daedalus ends there. Scholars do not know whether there was a real Daedalus, so skillful that legends grew around his memory, or whether he was purely fictitious.

**DANAE** *Greek* Daughter of Acrisius, king of ARGOS; mother of PERSEUS, who would one day kill his grandfather in fulfillment of a prophecy made by an ORACLE. The oracle had told Acrisius that he would be killed by a son of Danae. Acrisius imprisoned Danae in a tower or chamber of bronze, safe from the advances of men, but the great god ZEUS was undeterred in his amorous pursuit of Danae. He appeared to her in her prison as a shower of gold, which impregnated her. She bore a son, Perseus.

Scholars think that the story of Zeus and Danae is a pastoral allegory, in which water is the "gold" of the Greek shepherd or farmer. Hence Zeus was thought to send thunder and showers onto the Earth (Danae) to make her fertile.

**DANAUS** *Greek* A king of Egypt who had 50 daughters who were demanded by their cousins in marriage. Danaus fled with his brood to ARGOS, where he became king. The cousins came in pursuit. Danaus gave a dagger to all of his daughters so that they could murder their bridegrooms. Only one of the yong men, Lynceus, survived. He became the king of Argos after he had killed Danaus, and he became the ancestor of PERSEUS. As for the daughters, according to legend, they were punished in TARTARUS by being compelled to try and fill a sieve with water for all eternity. The daughters are sometimes known as the danaids.

**DAPHNE** (LAUREL) *Greek* A DRYAD or tree NYMPH, daughter of the river god LADON, or of Peneus, and GAIA. Pursued by the god APOLLO, Daphne begged her mother for help. Gaia opened up the Earth and Daphne disappeared. In her place, a laurel tree sprang up. Apollo embraced the tree and adopted it as his sacred tree and emblem. The poet OVID tells Daphne's story.

In some legends, Leucippus, a mortal man, loved Daphne. He disguised himself as a girl to pursue the nymph, but she discovered him to be a man when he went bathing with the maidens. The angry nymphs tore Leucippus to pieces.

**DAPHNIS** *Greek* The son of HERMES and a Sicilian NYMPH; inventor of simple, countrylike poetry. In one account, Daphnis was untrue to the nymph, Nomia, who loved him, so she blinded him in revenge. After that, Daphnis sang the sad but beautiful songs that are associated with pastoral music. His father, Hermes, at last took pity on his son and led him up to OLYMPUS. Another account has it that Daphnis was incapable of love, a fact that made APHRODITE, goddess of love, so angry that she afflicted him with everlasting sadness and longing.

Some say that PAN taught Daphnis to play the pipes, and that Daphnis was a love interest of APOLLO and hunted with ARTEMIS, though other accounts have it that it was Daphnis's father, Hermes, who enjoyed these privileges.

**DARDANELLES** *Greek* The strait between Europe and Asian Turkey, connecting the Aegean Sea with the Sea of Marmara. It is 40 miles long and one to five miles wide. In ancient times, it was called the HELLESPONT, which means "bridge to the HELLENES," or GREECE.

**DARDANUS** *Greek* The founder of the city of TROY, according to HOMER. Dardanus was the son of ZEUS. His son was ERICHTHONIUS (2), the richest king on Earth, who owned thousands of horses. The son of Erichthonius was Tros, who had three sons: Ilus, GANYMEDE, and Assaracus. King PRIAM of Troy was a descendant of Ilus.

**DEIANIRA** *Greek* Daughter of OENEUS, king of CALYDON, sister of MELEAGER. She became the second wife of the hero HERACLES and unwittingly caused his death. Deianira killed herself in despair at what she had done to Heracles.

**DEIDAMIA** *Greek* The wife of the Greek hero ACHILLES, though some experts suggest the two were never married.

Deidamia was the daughter of King Lycomedes, of the island of Skyros. When Achilles' mother, THETIS, a sea NYMPH, asked Lycomedes to hide her son to protect him from having to fight in the TROJAN WAR,

the king dressed Achilles as a girl and hid him among his daughters. Deidamia and Achilles fell in love, and while he was still in hiding, she bore him a son, Pyrrhus, who came to be known as NEOPTOLEMUS.

The couple sailed away together but were blown back to the island kingdom.

**DEIFICATION** In mythology, the process of bestowing upon a mortal the status of a god; also, the process a mortal goes through to transform into a god. Deification could be granted by a god, such as ZEUS or JUPITER, to a worthy mortal or to a hero who was half mortal and half god, such as HERACLES. It could also be granted by members of a culture, such as the Romans, who in their mythology believed that ROMULUS, the founder of ROME, became a god after he died. In Roman history, emperors were also deified after their deaths. People would then build temples to these new gods and worship them in formal ceremonies.

**DEIPHOBUS** *Greek* Son of PRIAM and HECUBA. He married HELEN (or took her by force) after the death of PARIS, his brother. Deiphobus died at the hands of MENELAUS at the fall of TROY (see TROJAN WAR), or, some say, Helen killed him.

**DELOS** *Greek* The smallest of the Greek islands known as the Cyclades, in the Aegean Sea. One legend says that Delos was a drifting island until ZEUS anchored it so that LETO could comfortably give birth to their children, ARTEMIS and APOLLO.

**DELPHI** *Greek* The most venerated shrine in ancient GREECE and probably the oldest. It lies on the remote slopes of Mount PARNASSUS, high above the Gulf of CORINTH, which separates mainland Greece from the PELOPONNESUS. The oldest objects found at Delphi date from 1600 B.C., but archaeologists believe this cleft in the hills was sacred long before that time. The ruins of the temple of APOLLO, the presiding god, still stand on the hills. Nearby is the stadium where the PYTHIAN GAMES were held in honor of the ancient PYTHON whom Apollo vanquished.

**The Origins of Delphi** According to one myth, ZEUS set two eagles free, one from each end of the Earth. Where they met, he established Delphi as the center of the world. A stone (OMPHALOS in Greek) marked the place from which the ORACLE—a wise being, capable of speaking words of the gods and foretelling the future—would speak.

Long before that, the site of the shrine was sacred to GAIA. At that time, Delphi was called Pytho. A female serpent-dragon, Python, guarded the shrine. The young god Apollo slew Python and commanded her spirit to be his oracle at Delphi.

Delphi was in fact Apollo's chosen land. Having killed the serpent Python, he built an altar in the sacred grove. According to one legend, Apollo was looking for priests to minister to his shrine when he saw a ship manned by Cretans, an ancient race (see CRETE). Apollo turned himself into a dolphin and sped after the ship. He captured the ship and persuaded the sailors to guard his temple, which they then called Delphi in honor of the dolphin (Greek *delphin*).

The decline of Delphi and its oracle is paralleled by the decline of Greece and of the justice and moral excellence represented by Apollo. Some efforts were made to restore Delphi's influence but finally, in A.D. 385, the Emperor Theodosius, a Christian, closed the site in the name of Christianity.

**DEMETER** *Greek*   Daughter of CRONUS and RHEA, one of the 12 great deities of OLYMPUS. With her brother ZEUS, she became the mother of PERSEPHONE. Demeter was goddess of Earth, agriculture, and crops, especially corn, who, in ancient rites, presided over the harvest. Her Roman name is CERES.

**Demeter and Persephone**   Demeter is most famous for her suffering over the loss of her daughter Persephone. Unbeknownst to Demeter, Zeus had promised Persephone to HADES, god of the UNDERWORLD. One day, when the maiden was gathering flowers in the fields of Nysa, the Earth opened and Hades seized Persephone and dragged her underground.

Demeter suffered great grief at the loss of her daughter. She wandered the Earth, searching for her child, until at last HELIOS (the Sun, who sees everything) told her what had happened. In anger and grief at the treachery of Zeus, Demeter left Olympus and went to live among mortals, disguised as an old woman. Demeter's sojourn at ELEUSIS was the chief episode in the course of her wanderings on Earth.

Meanwhile, the Earth suffered from Demeter's grief and bore no fruit. Finally Zeus sent HERMES into the kingdom of Hades to bring Persephone back to her mother. Before leaving the underworld, Persephone had been persuaded to eat four seeds of a pomegranate. In ancient mythology, to eat the fruit of one's captor meant that one would have to return to that captor or country, so Persephone was doomed to return to the underworld for four months of the year. She was allowed to spend the remaining two-thirds of the year with her EARTH MOTHER, Demeter.

There was great rejoicing on Earth at Persephone's return, for now Demeter allowed the Earth to bear crops once again.

This myth has its basis in the four seasons of the Northern Hemisphere. The time when Persephone goes underground is winter; the time when she returns is spring, which leads to the fruit of summer and the seeds of autumn, which in turn lead inevitably to the new growth of the next spring.

**Demeter's Suitors**   Demeter, the corn goddess, was loved by Zeus and bore him a daughter, Persephone. The sea god, POSEIDON, pursued her even after she had turned herself into a mare and hidden in a flock owned by King Oncus of ARCADIA. Demeter bore Poseidon a daughter, Despoena.

Demeter, in turn, loved Iasion, and bore him a son, PLUTUS. Zeus, jealous of Iasion, struck him with a thunderbolt. Some say that Iasion lived for a long time with Demeter and introduced her cult into Sicily.

**Demeter at Eleusis**   Demeter wandered the Earth in search of her daughter, not knowing that Hades had carried her off into the underworld. One day Demeter arrived in Eleusis, at the palace of King CELEUS. Demeter disguised herself as an old woman, wearing a hood. The king's wife, Metaneira, welcomed Demeter and asked her to look after her newborn son, DEMOPHON.

Demeter nourished the infant on ambrosia (food of the gods) and each night placed him in the fire in order to destroy all that was mortal in him, so that he would grow up like a god. One night, Metaneira spied upon her nurse and saw her place the child in the fire. Metaneira screamed with terror. Demeter was angry at the intrusion. Demeter threw back her hood and revealed herself as the goddess. She demanded that a temple be built for her in Eleusis. In some accounts Metaneira's screams broke the magic spells and the child was destroyed in the flames.

Before she left the palace of Eleusis, Demeter showed her gratitude to Celeus and Metaneira by giving TRIPTOLEMUS, Celeus's elder son, the first grain of corn. She taught him how to sow it and harvest it. In some accounts Triptolemus is identified with Demophon.

**Demeter and the Eleusinian Mysteries**   According to legend, Persephone was the embodiment of the corn seed that hides underground until its rebirth in the spring, when it returns to Demeter, Earth Mother.

The disappearance and the return of Persephone were the occasions of great festivals in ancient GREECE, among them the Eleusinian rites, whose secrets were so closely guarded that little is known about them today. Some experts believe the rites, or mysteries, fostered the idea of a more perfect life after death, and thus helped to lay the groundwork for the coming of Christianity, which upholds the idea of everlasting life.

## DEMONS OF THE KILNS (DAIMONES KERAMI-KOI; Ceramics Demons; Potter's Demons) *Greek* Potters were very important in Greek culture, for the functional ware they produced as well as for the artistic pottery they crafted that celebrated the gods and the stories of their interactions with human cultures.

So important was success to these artisans that they recognized a separate group of pesky semi-gods, or demons, that they prayed to before firing a new batch of pottery. When things went wrong, potters blamed these demons for the damage to the pottery and then appeased them with more prayers to ensure that the next firing went well.

Each demon was named for the damage he created in the kiln. They were:

Asbetus (Asbetos) – Char – who burned pottery;
Sabactes (Sabaktes) – Crash – who broke pottery;
Smaragus (Smaragon) – Smash – who dropped pottery;
Suntrobus (Suntrobos) – Shatter – who exploded clay;
Omodamus (Omodamos) – Crudebake – who caused pottery to harden poorly.

As a wild force from the heavens, this troop of demons would also come to destroy the kiln of an unfair, unworthy potter.

The *daimones keramikoi* are best known from the poetry of HOMER, who wrote a prayer for potters, calling upon ATHENA, who, among other things, was the goddess of pottery. He asked her to help potters if they were fair and honest, but he threatened the potters with destruction by these demons if the potters cheated customers or acted unfairly.

## DEMOPHON *Greek* The son of Metaneira and King CELEUS of ELEUSIS. DEMETER, the sorrowing mother of PERSEPHONE, found refuge at the court of the king and his wife, who asked her to look after their infant son, Demophon. This Demeter did, performing some goddesslike magic along the way.

## DEUCALION *Greek* A son of PROMETHEUS, the TITAN champion of humankind. Prometheus warned Deucalion that ZEUS was so angry with the evils of humanity that he was plotting its annihilation. Deucalion, the Greek equivalent of the Old Testament's Noah, built an ark. After nine days of rain, the ark landed safely on Mount PARNASSUS. Deucalion and his wife, PYRRHA, gave sacrifice to Zeus. The spirit of the Titan THEMIS told them to repeople the Earth. This they did by casting stones (the bones of GAIA) behind them. Those cast by Pyrrha became women; those cast by Deucalion became men. HELLEN, the eldest son, was the patriarch of the race of HELLENES, later called the Greeks.

Scholars say that the deluge in this myth is undoubtedly the same as the flood quoted in the Old Testament and the Gilgamesh epic of Babylon, and reflects a dim memory common to the peoples of the Mediterranean.

## DIANA (Bright) *Roman* An ancient Roman, perhaps Etruscan, goddess of the Moon. In the Roman PANTHEON, Diana was the daughter of JUPITER and the twin sister of APOLLO.

Diana's name means "bright" and comes from the Latin word for "god." With such a name, she was also considered the goddess of light, woodlands, women, and childbirth. Diana also protected wild animals. Women worshiped her in groves and woods, in temples on the Aventine Hill in ROME, and in EPHESUS, an ancient city in ASIA MINOR. Slaves and members of the lower classes of Roman society were particularly attracted to the worship of Diana.

With her special attachment to wild areas, Diana was portrayed carrying a bow and arrows and in the company of hunting dogs.

As early as 600 B.C., Diana, though keeping her Roman name, took on the stories and characteristics of the Greek goddess ARTEMIS.

## DICTYNNA (Lady of the Nets) *Greek* An ancient Cretan goddess, perhaps the goddess of Mount Dicte, which was later known as the birthplace of the Greek god ZEUS. She was the EARTH MOTHER of CRETE, later associated with BRITOMARTIS, the huntress and patron of navigators.

## DICTYS *Greek* The fisherman, some say the brother of POLYDECTES, who rescued the hero PERSEUS and his mother, DANAE, from the sea. Dictys took the mother and child to the court of King Polydectes of the island of SERIPHOS, in the Aegean Sea. Later he rescued Danae once again, this time from the unwelcome attentions of Polydectes. Perseus turned Polydectes into stone with the head of MEDUSA as his weapon, and Dictys became the new king of Seriphos.

## DIDO *Greek* The founder and queen of CARTHAGE, also known as Elisa. She was the daughter of the Tyrian

One of the many sculptures in the gardens of the royal palace in Caserta, Italy, near Naples, shows the Roman goddess Diana (center) frolicking with her attending nymphs. *(Photograph by Japiot. Used under a Creative Commons license.)*

king Belus, and sister of Pygmalion. According to the Roman poet Virgil, Anna Perenna was also Dido's sister. Dido was married to her wealthy uncle Acerbas. After Pygmalion murdered Acerbas, Dido fled to Carthage. Here she was allowed to purchase as much land as could be enclosed with the hide of a Bull. Dido cleverly had the hide cut up into narrow strips so that the area they enclosed was great. Her citadel was called Byrsa, and the city of Carthage arose around it more.

The best-known story about Dido is Virgil's account of her love for the hero Aeneas, told in the *Aeneid*. In it, she hears tales of the adventures of the hero and falls in love with him. Aeneas deserts her to pursue his destiny and Dido kills herself. The story of Dido, dating back at least to the second century b.c., is much older than the *Aeneid*, which was written in the first century b.c.

**Dike** (Dice; Justice) *Greek*  The personification of justice, particularly under the law. Dike was a daughter of Zeus and Themis. As one of the three Horae, guardians of the seasons, Dike was the sister of Eirene (Peace) and Eunomia (Order). She was the mother of Hesychia (Quiet, Tranquility).

Dike was the avowed enemy of falsehood and protected the fair treatment of people by the laws of society. She often served as an emissary and counselor for the great god Zeus. He would send her among mankind to watch them closely and report back to him on their crimes, their poor behavior, and their injustice to one another. After hearing of their indiscretions, Zeus would punish them. Dike watched judges very carefully and sought the help of Zeus in punishing them for acts of unfairness. She carried a sword with which to pierce the hearts of the unjust. Her counterpart was Adicia (Injustice), whom Dike is often portrayed as beating with a club.

As a member of the Horae, Dike helped watch over the four seasons, aiding farmers, helping them meet the agricultural needs of society, bringing prosperity to mankind. The sisters' names all relate to social order and the development of lawfulness, a concept that was closely related to farming in classical mythology, showing the importance of agriculture to society.

Some modern scholars identify Dike as the same as the goddess Astraea, for both ruled over justice. However, others see Dike as distinct from Astraea, with distinct stories for each in Greek mythology.

**DIOMEDES (1)** *Greek* Son of Tydeus and successor of ADRASTUS as king of ARGOS. Diomedes sailed against TROY in the TROJAN WAR, and was, next to ACHILLES, the bravest of the Greeks. The war goddess ATHENE favored him.

**DIOMEDES (2)** *Greek* A son of ARES; king of the Bistones in Thrace. Diomedes raised maneating mares, which HERACLES carried off and tamed after he killed Diomedes and fed him to the mares.

**DIONE** *Greek* An obscure, ancient divinity of prehistoric GREECE, said to be a daughter of OCEANUS and TETHYS, closely associated with the cult of the god ZEUS. Scholars point out that her name is a feminine form of the name Zeus. Homer said that she was the mother, with Zeus, of the goddess APHRODITE, though most sources say that Aphrodite, goddess of love and fertility, was born from URANUS and GAIA. Dione was venerated at DODONA as the consort of Zeus.

**DIONYSUS** *Greek* A fertility god, god of vegetation, especially the vine, god of wine and later of the pleasures of civilization. Son of ZEUS; his mother is variously thought to be SEMELE, DEMETER, PERSEPHONE, or IO, DIONE, or LETHE. The most common myth identifies his mother as Semele. The Romans called him BACCHUS.

In early times, Dionysus was associated with orgiastic rites and generally wild behavior. As the cultivation of grape vines spread throughout GREECE, so did the worship of Dionysus and the ensuing orgies, called Dionysian or Bacchic festivals. Later, however, Dionysus was also celebrated as a cultivator of the soil, a lawgiver, a peacemaker, and a patron of tragic art.

Among his followers were the CENTAURS, MAENADS, SATYRS, and sileni, all of whom were depicted in ancient art as enthusiastically—sometimes frighteningly—demented, carrying staffs and wearing animal skins and crowns of ivy and grape leaves.

The young Dionysus was not honored as a god and he was forced to flee from Greece. He traveled through Europe, ASIA MINOR, and North Africa. Many adventures marked his passage as he spread his knowledge of the cultivation of the vine and the making of wine. Dionysus learned to use the divine power he had inherited from his father, Zeus. He inspired devotion, especially among women, and finally returned to Greece in triumph as a true god. APOLLO, the beautiful god of the arts, admitted Dionysus to his shrine at DELPHI. Thus Dionysus joined the OLYMPIAN GODS.

The acceptance of Dionysus into Greece after many struggles may refer to the conflict between old and new religions in the ancient world. Dionysus represents the ancient cult of the spirit of nature and fertility. It found expression in human sacrifice, nature worship, and orgiastic rites. Apollo represents the Dorians and other migrants who invaded peninsular Greece. These newcomers brought with them their own gods and cults but learned to accept the ancient deities and rites.

Dionysus was often depicted as a seminude, youthful god, his head crowned with vine leaves and grapes, and carrying a goblet of wine in one hand and a staff topped with a pinecone in the other. In earlier art, he was shown as a mature, bearded man crowned with ivy.

**The Birth of Dionysus** Though the identity of Dionysus's mother is in doubt, the most common myth identifies her as Semele. Zeus had come down to Earth disguised as a mortal. He wooed and won Semele. HERA, the wife of Zeus, was jealous. When Semele was six months pregnant, Hera, disguised as an old nurse, persuaded Semele to ask Zeus to reveal himself in his true form. This she did. At first Zeus refused Semele's request, but he finally presented himself in all his glory as a mighty god, flashing lightning and hurling thunderbolts. No mortal could withstand such power, and Semele perished in flames. Zeus snatched the unborn child from the fire and sewed it into his thigh so that it could mature for another three months. In due course, Zeus gave birth to a boy, Dionysus, who is sometimes called DITHYRAMBUS (Child of the Double Door), referring to his two births, once from his mother's body and again from his father's body.

Some scholars believe that this myth represents Zeus asserting his power over mortals by killing Semele and taking her child under his protection.

**The Childhood of Dionysus** Zeus entrusted the care of his newborn child to Semele's sister, INO, or perhaps to the NYMPHS or Mount Nysa. Although her rival, Semele, was dead, Hera was still jealous; she transferred her hatred to Dionysus. Hera caused the child's foster parents to become insane, but Dionysus survived their madness, and Zeus gave him to HERMES to take to the nymphs of Nysa, which may have been a mountain near HELICON, the highest point in BOEOTIA, or a purely imaginary spot. The nymphs were BACCHANTS. They took good care of the child and Dionysus grew to manhood in Nysa.

Hera's hatred of Dionysus and his mother may reflect conservative opposition to the ritual use of wine and the extravagant orgies of the Bacchants and MAENADS. Dionysus was eventually admitted to OLYMPUS.

**DIOSCURI** (Sons of Zeus) *Greek*  A title used in Greek and Roman mythology for the twin brothers CASTOR and Polydeuces, whose Roman name was Pollux. They were the sons of the mortal woman, LEDA, who was married to Tyndareus, king of Lacedaemonia (SPARTA).

There are several legends about the parentage of these two favorite characters. One says that ZEUS seduced Leda and conceived Polydeuces on the same night that she and her husband conceived Castor. Polydeuces was thus a god and immortal and Castor was a mortal. In some of the legends, Castor and Polydeuces are the brothers of HELEN of TROY and CLYTEMNESTRA. In others, neither Leda or Zeus is their parent.

In Greek myths, the twins rescued Helen from the hero THESEUS and took part in the expeditions of JASON and the ARGONAUTS. POSEIDON, god of the sea, is said to have given Castor and Polydeuces special powers, after which mariners and sailors honored the twins as their guardians.

One story, told by the Greek poet PINDAR, says that Castor was mortally wounded in battle. Polydeuces begged his father, Zeus, to allow him to share his brother's suffering. Zeus granted them a single life, to be shared and lived on alternate days. To keep them together forever, Zeus put them in the sky as the constellation Gemini in the northern celestial hemisphere. CASTOR and POLLUX are the two very bright stars that form the heads of the constellation.

The Dioscuri do not enter into the stories of the TROJAN WAR, though the abduction of their sister Helen started the conflict, for Zeus had made them divine and placed them in the heavens before the war began.

**DIS** (DIS PATER, DISPATER) *Roman*  The richest of the ancient Roman gods; a god or king of the UNDERWORLD (2), the realm of the dead. Dis's wealth came from his possession of the precious metals and gemstones hidden beneath the Earth's surface, part of the kingdom of the underworld.

Dis was the husband of PROSERPINA, goddess or queen of the underworld. They were honored together in hymns, songs, and ceremonies that featured singing by 27 virgins. The people of ROME held athletic games once a century to honor Dis and to bring protection against pestilence, plague, and death.

One popular story tells of a father who went out in search of the gods to help his children, who had fallen seriously ill from a plague. In his journeys, the father found a hot spring flowing near the Tiber River. When he searched for the source of the water, he found a cave in which stood an altar to Dis and Proserpina.

**DITHYRAMBUS** (Child of the Double Door) *Greek*  A name for the god DIONYSUS, referring to the legend that he was born twice.

In literature, a dithyramb is a Greek song or chant of wild character and irregular form, originally sung in honor of Dionysus, god of wine. Verse described as dithyrambic is most irregular in form.

**DODONA** *Greek*  The oldest and most famous sanctuary of the god ZEUS, situated in EPIRUS, in northwestern GREECE. Since the times of the Pelasgians, the most ancient peoples of the land that is now called Greece, people had come here to consult the ORACLE who was said to live in a sacred oak tree (some said it was a beech tree) and to represent Zeus. People also worshiped the ancient goddess DIONE at Dodona. Her presence at Dodona suggests that the oracle of Dodona was of greater antiquity than Zeus himself.

**DORIS** (Bounty) *Greek*  An OCEANID, or ocean NYMPH; one of the eldest daughters of the TITANS OCEANUS and TETHYS; herself considered a second-generation Titan. Doris, as a sea nymph, married the Titan sea god NEREUS and with him was the mother of the group of sea nymphs known as the NEREIDS.

Doris was sometimes associated with the bountiful fishing grounds commonly found at the mouths of rivers.

**DRYADS** (NYMPHS; Tree) *Greek*  The lives of some were entwined with specific trees; they lived and died with that tree. Others were connected with groves of trees or specific types of trees.

The main categories of Dryads are:

- The Meliai, NYMPHS of the ash tree. They were born from the drops of blood from URANUS which GAIA caused to spill on the Earth after CRONUS killed his father.
- The Hamadryads, nymphs of poplar and oak trees. According to some stories, the Hamadryads were born with and died with specific trees.
- Meliades, nymphs of apple trees. The HESPERIDES, who guarded HERA's golden apples, were Meliades.
- Daphnaie, nymphs of the laurel tree, who were named after DAPHNE, whom her father, a river god, transformed into a laurel tree to rescue her from the pursuits of the god APOLLO.

Eirene was also considered the goddess of health. She is often pictured on coins holding a CORNUCOPIA, shafts of wheat, or an olive branch. A burning pile of weapons and armor represents Eirene on some artifacts. In ROME, she was worshiped as PAX.

## ELECTRA (1) *Greek* Daughter of AGAMEMNON

and CLYTEMNESTRA; sister of IPHIGENIA and ORESTES. Agamemnon was the leader of the Achaean (Greek) forces in the TROJAN WAR. While her husband was gone to war, Clytemnestra took a lover, AEGISTHUS. When Agamemnon finally returned, he brought with him the lovely CASSANDRA. Aided by Aegisthus, Clytemnestra murdered both Agamemnon and Cassandra. To avenge their father's death, Electra and Orestes murdered Clytemnestra and Aegisthus. Electra eventually married Pylades.

Many great playwrights tell the story of this tragic mythical family, including AESCHYLUS, SOPHOCLES, and EURIPIDES, and in modern times Eugene O'Neill (1883–1953) in *Mourning Becomes Electra.*

## ELECTRA (2) *Greek* One of the PLEIADES;

daughter of ATLAS and PLEIONE; mother, by ZEUS, of DARDANUS, the founder of TROY. Some say that Electra was the lost Pleiad, who faded away with grief after the TROJAN WAR and the destruction of Troy.

## ELECTRA (3) (AMBER) *Greek* A sea NYMPH, or

OCEANID, daughter of OCEANUS and TETHYS; one of the eldest of this group of nymphs, which numbered in the thousands; considered one of the second-generation TITANS. She married THAUMUS, a son of GAIA and PONTUS, and with him was the mother of IRIS (Rainbow) and the HARPIES (Winds).

Electra was considered a bright shining nymph who shone with an amber glow and was thought to live among the clouds, which would be appropriate since she was mother of rainbows and the spirits of sharp strong winds.

## ELEUSIS Ancient city in ATTICA, in ancient GREECE,

famous for being the site of the Eleusian Mysteries (see *Demeter and the Eleusinian Mysteries,* under DEMETER).

## ELYSIUM *Greek* A conception of afterlife, the

pre-Hellenic paradise that the Greeks identified with their mythical Islands of the Blessed, located at the ends of the Earth—"the far west." People, or their shades, who were transported there led a blessedly happy life rather than remaining in the oblivion of the truly dead of the UNDERWORLD. RHADAMANTHUS

and CRONUS were joint rulers of this paradise. In HOMER, Elysium was a place for elite heroes; in HESIOD, it was a place for the blessed dead; and from the time of PINDAR, it was believed that admission to Elysium was the reward of a good life. Elysian, which means "in Elysium," still refers to paradise in the phrase "Elysian fields."

## ENDYMION *Greek* According to various sources,

the son of ZEUS and Calyce or the shepherd son of Aethlius; prince or king of Elis, a region of the PELOPONNESUS; he was a beautiful young man, loved by Selene (Moon).

In one myth, Endymion begged Zeus to give him immortality so that he could be with Selene forever. Zeus granted his request with the condition that he remain eternally asleep. Another myth has it that Selene herself imposed eternal sleep on Endymion so that she might enjoy his beauty forever. In another story, it is said that Selene had 50 daughters by Endymion. Selene visited Endymion on many nights of the month, personifying the gentle radiance of the Moon that caresses the sleep of mortals.

## ENYO (1) *Greek* A goddess of war, specifically

known for sacking cities and towns of the enemy; daughter of ZEUS and HERA; depicted as the sister, daughter, or mother of the war god ARES, often included as a companion of Ares when he went into battle.

Enyo was most known for her terrifying war cry and was portrayed carrying a lance and torch with which she incited troops to do battle. She was known to be the force sent to destroy cities. In Roman mythology, she took on the traits of BELLONA, an ancient goddess of warfare.

## ENYO (2) *Greek* One of the three GRAEA, who

were daughters of CETO and PHORCYS; sister of Pemphrado and Dino and of the GORGONS. Between them, the three Graea shared one eye and one tooth, which they passed to each other as they needed it.

## EOS (Dawn) *Greek* The goddess of dawn. She

was the daughter of HELIOS (Sun), or, some accounts say, the sister of Helios and SELENE (Moon), begotten by the TITANS, HYPERION and Theia. The Romans called her AURORA. Eos was married to TITHONUS, but she had many other lovers. Eos is depicted as a beautiful young woman, sometimes riding the dawn skies on the winged horse, PEGASUS, sometimes in a chariot drawn by two horses.

With the Titan Astraeus as their father, Eos was mother to the winds Zephyrus and Boreas and various astral bodies.

Memnon was one of her sons with Tithonus. Cephalus was one of her partners in a tragic love affair.

**EPAPHUS** *Greek* The son of the god Zeus and Io. Epaphus was born in Egypt. Hera, wife of Zeus, was jealous of Io and tormented her endlessly until Io, in the shape of a young white cow, eventually escaped to Egypt, where Zeus restored her to her human shape. There, Io bore her son. Hera, still jealous, ordered the Curetes to kidnap Epaphus. This they did, but Zeus destroyed the Curetes and rescued the child. Epaphus later became king of Egypt, where he built the great city of Memphis, capital of the Old Kingdom of ancient Egypt.

**EPHESUS** *Greek* An ancient Greek city of Asia Minor (today, Turkey, south of Izmir). Once a wealthy seaport, Ephesus was the site of a temple to the goddess Artemis (Roman Diana); the temple was considered one of the Seven Wonders of the Ancient World.

**EPIDAURUS** *Greek* A city in southern Greece (northeastern Peloponnesus) celebrated in ancient times as the sanctuary of Asclepius, god of medicine and healing. Epidaurus is also famous for its magnificent theater, dating from the fourth century B.C.

**EPIGONI** (Descendants, the younger generation) *Greek* The sons of the Seven Against Thebes, an expedition launched by Adrastus and Polynices to capture the throne of Thebes. The effort failed and Adrastus was the only survivor. When the sons of the Seven, the Epigoni, were old enough to bear arms, Adrastus rallied them to make a second attack. This one succeeded. Thebes was destroyed. It was a bitter victory for Adrastus, for his son Aegialeus was killed.

**EPIMETHEUS** (Afterthought) *Greek* Brother of Prometheus, a Titan. Epimetheus accepted Pandora as his wife, in spite of the warnings of his wiser brother. Pandora had been created by the gods to punish humankind for accepting the forbidden gift of fire from Prometheus.

**EPIRUS** *Greek* An ancient country of Greece on the Ionian Sea, west of Macedonia and Thessaly. Epirus was the home of the Oracle at Dodona and refuge of the Centaurs when they were expelled from their native Thessaly.

**EPONA** *Roman* A goddess who protected horses, donkeys, and mules, and paid special attention to foals and mares during the birthing process.

Epona was most popular among the soldiers of the Roman armies, who placed images celebrating her, often small statues, in their stables. Epona was said to be the daughter of a mare and a human.

The name, Epona, which is the source of *pony*, comes from the Celtic language of the British Isles. Some scholars suggest that Epona was a goddess of those northern people and later became a favorite in Rome after the Empire expanded into England in the first century. Epona is credited as the only Celtic god to be welcomed into the Roman pantheon.

Other scholars, however, argue that a Roman goddess of horses was a very old deity in Central Italy and only her name changed after contact with the British Isles.

**EREBUS** (Darkness) *Greek* The personification of darkness. Erebus sprang from Chaos at the beginning of time. He was the father of Charon, Nemesis, and others. His name was given to the gloomy underground cavern through which the dead had to walk on their way to the Underworld.

**ERECHTHEUS** *Greek* The son of Dardanus, the founder of Troy. Erechtheus was said to be the richest king on Earth. He owned thousands of magnificent horses, the offspring of Boreas, the North Wind. He was the father of Tros and the grandfather of Ilus, Ganymede, and Assaracus. King Priam of Troy was a descendant of Ilus.

**ERICHTHONIUS** *Greek* Legendary king of Athens. According to Homer, Erichthonius was the son of the lame god, Hephaestus, and Gaia. He grew out of semen spilled by Hephaestus when he tried to force his attentions on the goddess Athene. Earth nourished the seed and the child, Erichthonius, was born.

In a later story, Athene placed the child in a basket and gave him to the daughters of Cecrops, legendary first king of Athens, to look after. She forbade them to open the basket but the women could not resist. When they saw what was inside, they ran off screaming, for the child was half serpent. It is common in Greek mythology for men born of the soil to be represented as half serpent, for serpents were regarded as the essential Earth creatures in ancient times.

After Erichthonius became king, he established the worship of Athene in Athens.

**ERIGONE** *Greek* Daughter of King ICARIUS of ATTICA in ancient GREECE, the area of the southeastern mainland where modern ATHENS now stands. Drunken shepherds killed her father and buried him. Erigone and her faithful dog, Maera, set out in search of the vanished king. When Erigone discovered the tomb of Icarius, she was grief-stricken and hanged herself from a nearby tree. The gods transformed her into the constellation VIRGO, and Maera became Procyon, the brightest star in Canis Minor.

**ERINYES** *Greek* The three avengers of wrong, generally known by their Roman name, the FURIES. They were also called EUMENIDES (Good-Tempered Ones) by the wise and tactful Greeks, who feared their wrath.

**ERIPHYLE** *Greek* Wife of AMPHIARAUS mother of ALCMAEON, sister of ADRASTUS. Eriphyle was given the magic necklace of HARMONIA, a guarantee of unfading beauty, for persuading her husband, Amphiaraus, and her brother, Adrastus, to join in the disastrous rebellion known as the SEVEN AGAINST THEBES. Alcmaeon killed Eriphyle but his mother's dying curse was that no land would ever shelter her son.

**ERIS** (Discord) *Greek* The spirit or goddess of strife; the sister of ARES, Eris accompanied him into battle and helped to cause quarrels and lawlessness. In Hesiod's poems, she is the daughter of NYX (Night). Later legends say that Eris helped to cause the TROJAN WAR by flinging her "apple of discord" among the guests at the wedding of PELEUS and THETIS. Three jealous goddesses competed for the golden apple. PARIS awarded the prize to APHRODITE, goddess of love and beauty.

**EROS** (Erotic Love) *Greek* God of love and fertility, called CUPID by the Romans. In ancient times, Eros was a force to be feared. He represented the havoc and misery that could be brought about by love and desire. In later times, Eros was depicted as an overweight baby, winged, and carrying a bow and a quiver of arrows, which he would shoot off randomly. The parentage of Eros is confused and obscure. He is often thought of as the son of the goddess of love, APHRODITE. His father may have been the great god ZEUS; the god of war, ARES; or the god of fertility, HERMES. Older traditions say that he is the son of GAIA, and therefore almost as old as the Earth. Though he appeared in many legends, Eros was never considered important enough to be set among the 12 great OLYMPIAN GODS.

Eros, the winged god of love, pulls at the hair of an old centaur. This marble statue is a Roman copy made in the first century A.D. of an original from Greece made in the second century B.C. It stands in the Louvre in Paris. *(Photograph by Marie-Lan Nguyen.)*

Nevertheless he is depicted as the constant companion of Aphrodite. The most famous tale about Eros is *Eros (or Cupid) and Psyche.*

**Eros and Psyche** Eros was a Greek god of love, perhaps the son of Aphrodite, goddess of love. PSYCHE was a mortal princess. She was so beautiful that Aphrodite, in a jealous rage, ordered Eros to punish the maiden. Eros fell in love with Psyche and carried her off to a magnificent palace and married her. He did not reveal his identity to her and commanded her never to try to see his face. Psyche fell in love with the man she could not see and vowed never to look at him. Eventually, Psyche's sisters persuaded her to break her vow, and as Eros lay asleep next to her, Psyche lit a lamp and beheld her husband's beautiful face. Eros and all the beautiful surroundings immediately disappeared.

From then on, an angry Aphrodite pursued and tormented the maiden. She survived terrible ordeals, helped by a mysterious force, Eros. Finally Eros pleaded with Zeus to put an end to her suffering. Zeus consented and conferred immortality on Psyche. The wedding of Psyche and Eros was celebrated on OLYMPUS, and Aphrodite, it is said, joined in the festivities.

**ERYTHEIA** (ERYTHIA; Dazzling Light) *Greek* A DRYAD, or wood NYMPH; one of the sisters known as the HESPERIDES; either the daughters of EREBUS (Darkness) and NYX (Night) or the daughters of ATLAS and PLEIONE or Hesperis. Her sisters, those named by people writing during the classic age of Greek mythology, were AEGLE (2), ARETHUSA, and HESPERIA.

**ETHER** (AETHER; Bright upper air) *Greek* Son of NYX (Night) and EREBUS (Darkness); brother of HEMERA (Day).

Ether was the personification of the upper air, the pure, bright, and good realm where the gods dwelled. He stretched between the dome of the sky, which was the realm of URANUS, and the air close to the Earth that humans breathed. Each night, his mother blocked the mortal view of Ether, and each day Hemera revealed his brilliant blue to the people below. Some Greek poets and writers claimed that Ether was the source of all life, the soul of the universe.

Ether was said to be the father, with his sister Hemera, of the sea goddess THALASSA, and of many natural forces, such as anger, lies, sorrow, and pride.

**ETHIOPIA** A country in northeast Africa. In Greek mythology, ANDROMEDA was the daughter of CEPHEUS and CASSIOPEIA of Ethiopia. Memnon, a hero of the TROJAN WAR, was a king of Ethiopia.

**ETRURIA** *Roman* An ancient culture that thrived in west central Italy from as early as the eighth to the fourth centuries B.C. Etruria was northwest of ROME. Archaeologists and historians have concluded that Etruria was not a kingdom or nation as much as a people who shared a culture and a language and lived in what are now the regions of Tuscany and Umbria.

The history and development of the Etruscans, who joined their cities into a loose confederation or cooperative, overlaps with that of their neighbors, the people of the city of Rome. The last three kings of Rome, the Tarquins, were immigrants from Etruria. They ruled in the 500s B.C. Some scholars believe the stories of their reign are as much a part of legend and mythology as of history.

After expelling the last of these kings in about 509 B.C., the Romans formed their first republic and elected their first leaders. Eventually, the Romans conquered the cities of Etruria and absorbed that culture into their own.

The ancient gods of the Etruscans influenced the formation and development of the classical Roman religion. Many Roman gods and goddesses, such as SATURN and DIANA, were first Etruscan deities.

The Estruscans were highly regarded for the ability of some of their people to see into the future. This gift, known as divination or divining, involved elaborate ceremonies and rituals that enhanced their ability to read in the signs of the Earth the intentions of the gods. This knowledge helped the Roman leaders make major decisions. Divination was a key element in helping the Romans determine when to bring the power of a Greek god or goddess into their own culture.

**EUMENIDES** (Good-Tempered Ones) *Greek* The ironic name Greek people used for the ERINYES, fearsome creatures whose name means FURIES. Eumenides is the term writers and poets generally used for them in literature.

**EUNOMIA** (Order) *Greek* A goddess of order and lawful conduct and one of the three HORAE, guardians of the seasons, with her sisters DIKE (Justice) and EIRENE (Peace). She was the daughter of ZEUS and THEMIS.

Eunomia involved herself in the law-making process, helping mankind establish wise laws that allowed societies to prosper. Cities would lay claim to her, bragging that she chose to dwell within their walls. Eunomia had specific duties over springtime and the greening of nature.

**EURIPIDES** (480–406 B.C.) One of the great Greek tragedians, ranked with AESCHYLUS and SOPHOCLES, though his attitudes were very different from theirs. He found it hard to believe that the gods and goddesses, with their capricious, all-too-human ways, were the creators of the universe. To him, mortal men and women were more interesting and noble, and their triumphs and tragedies more worthy of notice and of compassion. Among his surviving plays are *Andromache, The Bacchae, Electra, Hecuba, Heracles, Medea,* and *The Trojan Women.*

**EUROPA** *Greek* Daughter of AGENOR, king of Tyre (a seaport in PHOENICIA) and Telephassa, and the sister of CADMUS, PHOENIX, and CILIX. Mother of MINOS, RHADAMANTHUS, and SARPEDON with ZEUS; and of Euphemus with POSEIDON; wife of ASTERION, king of CRETE.

Europa was famed for her beauty. Zeus fell in love with her and, knowing that the maiden liked to wander on the shore, devised a plan. He turned himself into a snow-white BULL and grazed peacefully on the grass near the shore. The beautiful animal enchanted Europa. She caressed him and twined garlands of flowers upon his horns. When the bull gracefully knelt before her, she climbed upon his back, whereupon the bull dashed into the sea and swam with Europa to the island of Crete, which lies south of GREECE. There he turned himself into an eagle and mated with Europa. She bore him three sons: Minos, Rhadamanthus, and Sarpedon. Later Europa married Asterion, the king of Crete, who adopted her sons. She was worshiped as a goddess after her death.

The story of Europa and the bull is very old. It probably refers back to a time when the bull, a symbol of strength and fertility, was the principal cult animal of the eastern Mediterranean. It seems possible that the figure of Zeus was grafted onto an ancient Cretan story.

Zeus's capture of Europa may refer to an early Hellenic raid on PHOENICIA by HELLENES from Crete, when Taurus, king of Crete, assaulted Tyre during the absence of Agenor and his sons. The Hellenes took the city and carried off many captives, including the king's daughter. The story also represents the contribution of Phoenician civilization to that of Crete, which is symbolized by the bull god.

**EURYALE** (Wide-Stepping) *Greek* One of the three GORGONS, female monsters; daughter of CETO, an ancient sea goddess, and PHORCYS; her sisters were STHENO and MEDUSA. Euryale and Stheno were immortal, while their sister, Medusa, was mortal. Euryale and Stheno shared with Medusa the power to turn people to stone when the mortals looked into a gorgon's eyes.

The hero PERSEUS was sent by POLYDECTES to retrieve the head of a gorgon; of course, he chose to cut off Medusa's because she was mortal. Euryale and Stheno chased Perseus after his theft, raking the air with their great claws. As she flew after Perseus, Euryale screamed an agonized shriek that echoed after him. The gods turned that shriek into lamenting music and gave the song to humans.

Euryale may also mean "the wide sea," which would fit her role as a daughter of sea gods.

**EURYBIA** *Greek* A TITAN; daughter of the EARTH MOTHER GAIA and her son PONTUS, an early sea god. This heritage gave Eurybia power over the seas, perhaps even over the tides and the rise and fall of the constellations. She married the Titan god CRIUS and with him had three children, ASTRAEUS, PALLAS, and PERSES.

**EURYDICE** *Greek* A beautiful DRYAD (tree NYMPH) who became the wife of ORPHEUS. While pursued by ARISTAEUR, she was bitten by a serpent and died. Stricken with grief, Orpheus charmed his way into the UNDERWORLD (1) and persuaded HADES to release his wife. Seduced by the beautiful music of Orpheus, Hades let Eurydice go, on the condition that Orpheus would not look back to see if she was following. The pair had almost reached the entrance to the world when Orpheus looked back. Eurydice disappeared instantly and he never saw her again. The tragic story of Orpheus and Eurydice is the subject of many plays and operas.

**EURYLOCHUS** *Greek* One of the crewmen on the journey of ODYSSEUS and, apart from Odysseus himself, the only one to escape the spell of CIRCE, the witch who turned men into swine. (See the *ODYSSEY*.) Eurylochus, who had been the head of the party exploring Circe's island, hid, saw what happened to his shipmates and fled to warn Odysseus. Later, when Odysseus and his crew had escaped both Circe and the UNDERWORLD, Eurylochus led the crew to feast on the sacred cattle of HYPERION, god of the Sun, thus bringing about the destruction of the entire crew, except for Odysseus.

**EURYNOME** *Greek* One of the eldest OCEANIDS, or ocean NYMPHS, daughters of OCEANUS. Counted among the TITANS. She became a sea goddess after falling from power on Mount OLYMPUS. Eurynome and Ophion, also a Titan, ruled the realm of these early gods after GAIA and URANUS until CRONUS and RHEA, the most powerful Titans, seized power and threw them into the sea. Eurynome's place in mythology diminished as people turned to the OLYMPIAN GODS.

Eurynome was also a love interest of ZEUS, the most powerful Olympian god. With him, she became the mother of the three graces and the river god Asopus.

Eurynome helped Thetis rescue and raise HEPHAESTUS, the Greek god of craftsmen, after one of his parents, Zeus or HERA, threw the infant into the ocean. Eurynome was portrayed in statues as a mermaid.

**EURYSTHEUS** *Greek* The king of ARGOS and MYCENAE who imposed the Twelve Labors upon his cousin, HERACLES. Eurystheus was the son of Sthenelus, a descendant of the hero PERSEUS, and Nicippe. Eurystheus became king because of the wiles of HERA, the angry and jealous wife of the god ZEUS. On the day that Heracles was to be born, Zeus proclaimed before the OLYMPIAN GODS that the descendant of Perseus born on that day would become ruler of GREECE. Zeus fully expected that his son with ALCMENE, to be named Heracles, would qualify for the role of ruler. But Hera, knowing that Nicippe was about to give birth, caused her child, Eurystheus, to be born ahead of Heracles. Thus it was Eurystheus, not Heracles, who became ruler of Greece.

The chagrined Zeus decreed that if Heracles could perform the Twelve Labors imposed by Eurystheus he would become a god.

**EURYTUS** *Greek* King of Oechalia, father of IOLE. Eurytus was a renowned archer. He promised his daughter IOLE, to anyone who could shoot better than he. The great hero HERACLES won the contest, but Eurytus accused Heracles of using poisoned arrows and furthermore of being a slave of EURYSTHEUS and therefore unworthy of a king's daughter. Eurytus refused to honor Heracles' right to the hand of Iole. For this Eurytus died at the hand of Heracles, but Heracles was also to die because of Iole.

**EVANDER** *Roman* Evander was the name of a minor Greek deity from ARCADIA whose history took on mortal details when he fled GREECE for Italy.

Evander was the son of the Greek god HERMES and the NYMPH CARMENTA. He and his mother were banished from Greece for killing his stepfather. They settled in Italy long before the Trojan hero AENEAS is believed to have arrived there. Evander built a palace on the hill on the Tiber River that would become the Palatine Hill. He was a kind ruler and taught the native people music, religion, and, most notably, writing.

Some scholars believe Roman poets of the second and first centuries B.C. invented Evander to create a link between Roman and Greek traditions.

**FAMA** *Roman* A minor goddess who spread rumors, mixing truth and lies, and who also spread strife and disagreement. She was perhaps only the personification of the human trait of spreading rumor and gossip. When Fama, speaking in many voices, spread her rumors in the realms of the gods, JUPITER cast her out, sending her to live among humans where she found it easy to spread harm and evil. The Greeks knew her as Ossa, or Pheme.

The Roman poet VIRGIL described Fama in great detail. He said she had thousands of eyes and mouths and that she could fly between the Earth and the heavens. Her palace had many openings through which the false messages she spoke could pass to be spread over the Earth. Scholars suggest that Virgil himself, or Greek poets too, may have created this goddess, basing her features on little more than their ideas for the forces that cause rumors.

**FAUNA** *Roman* An ancient goddess of healing and productivity of the Earth. Fauna was also a goddess of chastity and of fertility in women. Fauna was either the sister or the wife of FAUNUS, an equally old Roman god of nature and fertility.

As a prophetess, she was called Fatua, and as a goddess she was also known by some as BONA DEA, which means "good goddess." In some stories, Fauna and HERCULES, the Roman version of the Greek HERACLES, fall in love when the hero arrives in Italy. Together they are the parents of LATINUS, who becomes the king of the people of the LATIUM region of central Italy.

**FAUNUS** *Roman* One of the oldest gods; god of nature and fertility, protector of farmers and shepherds. He also had the gift of prophecy. Faunus probably evolved into a single deity from the original idea of the *fauni*, spirits of the countryside. He was usually depicted as a young man with the horns and legs of a goat, similar to the SATYR of Greek myth. His female counterpart was FLORA. Faunus was identified with the Greek god PAN.

In natural history, the word *fauna* is used to denote the animals of a region or specific area, as the word *flora* denotes vegetation.

**FAUSTULUS** (FAUSTUS) *Roman* The shepherd who found the twin infants ROMULUS AND REMUS being suckled by a wolf and took them to his home to give them shelter. His wife ACCA LARENTIA (1) nursed them and raised the boys as her own.

Faustulus was, according to some versions of the story of these twins, a shepherd to King Amulias, who had ordered that Romulus and Remus be put into the Tiber River to die just after they were born. Having overheard the king's plan, Faustulus followed the servants who were going to destroy the boys and rescued the infants. Later, Faustulus made the boys' parentage known to the kingdom and helped them restore their grandfather, Numitor, as king of ALBA LONGA, thus ensuring their inheritance.

Faustulus died trying to stop one of the many fights between the adult Romulus and Remus. He was known in classical Roman times to have been buried on the Aventine Hill.

**FAVONIUS** (Favorable) *Roman* The god of the gentle west WIND. Favonius announced the coming of spring and helped vegetation grow.

According to the Roman poet OVID, Favonius beheld FLORA, the goddess of flowers and plants, as she wandered in a field. He fell in love with her, carried her off, and married her.

**FEBRIS** (FEVER) *Roman* The goddess of fevers. The people of ancient ROME and the tribes and people who lived nearby feared fevers for they spread quickly and often caused epidemics. Writers during the age of the Roman Republic and Empire recognized that the people, fearing fevers, created a goddess to whom they could offer sacrifices in an attempt to ward off fevers and to protect loved ones from illness and death.

In honor of Febris, ancient Romans built three temples, all in heavily populated areas, where they could offer such sacrifices. One stood on the Palatine Hill, one on the Esqualine Hill, and one at the top of a valley near the Quirinal Hill, which was one of the most populated areas of Rome, and a part of the city most threatened by diseases.

**FERONIA** *Roman*  Ancient deity thought to be a goddess of fertility and childbirth. Although little is known about her, inscriptions show that Feronia was popular in central Italy. Her most famous shrine, near Terracina, was used for the ceremony of bestowing freedom on slaves. Terracina is an ancient town on the Tyrrhenian Sea, midway between modern ROME and Naples.

**FIDES** (FIDES PUBLICA) *Roman*  The goddess or personification of honor, honesty, and good faith, particularly as displayed publicly in support of ROME. People called upon Fides to protect contracts and commerce, in private lives as well as in affairs of the government. Her origins in Roman religion were ancient, and she was held by some to be older than the great god JUPITER. Fides was pictured as a white-haired old woman.

Fides was worshiped at a temple on the Capitoline Hill in Rome, built in 282 B.C., which was also a place where the Roman Senate met. Here, too, leaders of Rome welcomed emissaries from other countries.

**FLAMEN** *Roman*  In ancient ROME, a special priest ordained to offer daily tributes to particular gods in the Roman pantheon. The flamens were responsible for organizing daily sacrifices to the gods, and were exempt from taxation and military duty. It was a peculiarity of Roman dictators and emperors that they accepted deification during their lifetimes, and so were allowed to have their own flamens who would honor them. Thus Mark Antony was a flamen, or priest, of Julius Caesar.

The flamens are historical, rather than mythological people, but they carried on some of the traditions of ancient peoples, such as the ritual sacrifices to particular gods.

**FLORA** *Roman*  The ancient goddess of flowers and plants, budding fruit, youth, and springtime. Flora's worship may have begun among the Sabine people, one of the many central Italian cultures, who brought her cult to ROME when they settled on the Quirinal Hill, one of the city's seven famous hills.

Flora was often honored with CERES, goddess of corn and Earth, and TELLUS, a fertility goddess. Together, these three goddesses represented features of the more ancient EARTH MOTHER, creator and guardian of all on Earth.

Flora was also considered the female counterpart of FAUNUS, Roman god of fertility and nature. Her festival, the Floralia, arrived in the end of May in the Roman calendar. She was shown in statues and paintings wearing flowers.

The word *flora* refers to the vegetation native to a region or area.

**FONS** (FONTUS) *Roman*  The god of springs and fountains. Little is known today about this god, though an important festival, the Fontinalia, was celebrated on October 13 in the ancient Roman calendar. Archaeologists have uncovered several temples dedicated to Fons in ROME. JUTURNA, an ancient Roman goddess of springs and fountains, was Fons' mother, according to some Roman historians.

**FORNAX** (FURNACE) *Roman*  A goddess of baking, who oversaw the ovens used for baking so that they did not become too hot and burn the roasting corn or bread. She was the patroness of bakers.

Fornax presided over the festivals of the Fornacalia, which were celebrated in early February, certainly before the 17th. During these feasts, often celebrated in households or small groups, people toasted corn, preparing it to be ground into flour and used for bread. Some scholars suggest that the festival is older than the name of the goddess and that the story of her influence developed as a way to explain the festival.

The traditions of Fornax eventually merged with the stories and duties of VESTA, goddess of the hearth.

**FORS** *Roman*  The god of fortune. Fors was closely connected with FORTUNA, goddess of destiny and chance. The two were often considered a pair in religious practices and were frequently linked in one phrase as Fors Fortuna. Some scholars say that Fors and Fortuna merged into one god that incorporated both male and female characteristics.

**FORTUNA** (Fate) *Roman* Goddess of destiny and chance, of great antiquity. She was identified with the Greek TYCHE. Fortuna was represented with a horn of plenty (a horn or basket filled with fruit and flowers, a symbol of fruitfulness), and a rudder, because it is Fortune that "steers" people's lives as a rudder steers a boat. Fortuna's most important temple was at Praeneste Palestrina, where she was called Primigenia (Firstborn, possibly of the god JUPITER, though there is some confusion about this). The Praeneste Palestrina in Latium, founded about 800 B.C., was one of the largest sanctuaries in Italy. Crowned with the round temple of Fortuna, it was visible for miles around.

See also FORS.

**FURIES** (FURIAE) *Greek and Roman* The Roman common name, now used almost exclusively, for a group of Greek goddesses of vengence. The proper Greek name for these goddesses is ERINYES. They were said by the poet HESIOD to be the daughters of the EARTH MOTHER, GAIA. They sprang from the blood of URANUS. In other accounts, they were the daughters of NYX or of EREBUS. Their numbers varied but there were generally thought to be three Furies: Alecto (She Who Rests Not), Megaera (Jealous One), and Tisiphone (Avenger of Blood).

The Roman Furies were merciless avengers of any crimes committed, especially those that involved bloodshed in a family or among kin. It is said that their punishment continued even after death and descent into the UNDERWORLD.

**FURRINA** *Roman* A NYMPH, or an ancient goddess, about whom little is known, even though people celebrated a feast to her each year on July 25. As a nymph, or water spirit, Furrina is said to have lived in a woods near a stream that flowed into the Tiber River in ROME, a place known as the Grove of Furrina. By the first century B.C. her name was included in a list of the Roman FURIES, goddesses of vengeance and fate.

**GAIA** (GAEA, GE; EARTH) *Greek* The personification of the EARTH MOTHER in Greek mythology; known to the Romans as TELLUS. She was born out of CHAOS at the beginning of time and in turn bore URANUS, the starlit sky.

Gaia was the mother of the seas, the mountains and valleys, and all the other natural features of the Earth. Once the Earth formed, Gaia mated with her son Uranus and produced the TITANS, the first race on Earth. Then came the CYCLOPES and the HECATON-CHEIRES (Hundred-Handed Ones). Uranus was horrified by his monstrous offspring and banished them all to the UNDERWORLD. At first, Gaia mourned her children but then she became angry with Uranus. She fashioned a sharp sickle and gave it to CRONUS, her youngest and bravest Titan son, bidding him to attack Uranus. Cronus mutilated his father's body and cast its parts into the ocean. From the blood that dropped upon the Earth sprang the FURIES, the GIGANTES (Giants), and the ash NYMPHS (the Meliae).

According to the Greek poet HESIOD and others, the primitive Greeks worshiped the Earth, which they pictured as a bountiful mother. She was the supreme deity not only of humans but of gods. Later, when the OLYMPIAN GODS were established, people still held Gaia in reverence. She presided over marriages and was honored as a prophetess. They offered her gifts of fruits and grains at her many shrines. Gaia was represented as a gigantic, full-breasted woman.

**GALATEA (1)** (Milk White) The most famous Galatea in Greek mythology was a NEREID, or sea NYMPH, daughter of NEREUS and DORIS. This Galatea was a prominent character in the stories of Sicily, the huge island off the tip of the "boot" of Italy, which was home to early Greek colonies. The one-eyed giant sea monster, POLYPHEMUS, fell in love with this fair creature, but she did not return his love, for she loved Acis, son of the god PAN. One day, Polyphemus

discovered Galatea and Acis as they lay together on the banks of a river. In a fit of jealousy, the giant hurled a boulder at them. To protect Acis, Galatea turned him into a river. This story was told by the first-century Roman poet OVID and has been retold by poets and musicians. The English composer George Frederick Handel based his musical masque *Acis and Galatea* on this love story.

**GALATEA (2)** *Greek* In a story from CRETE, a young woman named Galatea was married to a good man from a poor family. When she became pregnant, he told her he wanted only a son, and if a daughter should be born, Galatea was to leave her out in the wilds to die. While her husband was away on a trip, Galatea gave birth to a girl, but the mother could not expose her daughter. Instead, Galatea sought the help of soothsayer, who told her to dress the girl as a boy. This trick worked until the daughter reached early womanhood. In great fear, Galatea prayed for help from LETO, a kind, gentle TITAN goddess who took pity on Galatea and changed her daughter into a son.

**GALATEA (3)** *Greek* The name given to the ivory statue of a maiden, loved by PYGMALION, a king of Cyprus, after the goddess of love, APHRODITE, brought the statue to life.

**GALLI** *Greek* Priests of the goddess CYBELE. They celebrated her with wild dances, loud music, and the clashing of shields and swords. These priests were akin to the CORYBANTES, who also worshipped Cybele, and were later identified with the CURETES of CRETE.

**GANYMEDE** *Greek* A Trojan prince, great-grandson of DARDANUS, the founder of TROY. The god ZEUS, enraptured by the beauty of young Ganymede, carried him off to OLYMPUS to be a cupbearer to the gods. Some say that Zeus took the form of an eagle for this exploit; others that the god came as a wind storm. There are many famed depictions of this event. Ganymede is also the name of a moon of the planet JUPITER.

**GENIUS** (plural: GENITI) (Creative Force, Guardian Spirit) *Roman* The spirit that attended a man from birth until death. (A JUNO spirit accompanied a woman.) The genius determined the person's character, happiness, and fortune.

The genius was the source of creativity; hence the word *genius* is used to describe an exceptionally talented person. In some accounts, each person was thought to have both a good and a bad genius. Bad luck was the work of the evil genius. The plural of *genius* is *genii*.

(The genie of Eastern mythology were jinns [fallen angels] and had nothing to do with the genii of Roman mythology.)

**GERYON** *Greek* A monster with three heads, three bodies, and six hands. Geryon owned red cattle, which were guarded by the two-headed dog, Orthrus, and the herdsman, Eurytion. In his Tenth Labor, the hero HERACLES slew the dog and the herdsman. After a fearsome battle, Heracles defeated Geryon.

From Geryon's blood sprang a tree that produced a stoneless, cherrylike fruit that yielded a blood-red dye.

**GIGANTES** (Giants) *Greek* The offspring of GAIA and the blood of the wounded URANUS. Gaia prompted the giants to attack the TITAN gods, and the War of the Giants began. The gods finally won, with the help of the hero HERACLES, who used his bow to good effect. ZEUS killed Porphyrion with a thunderbolt, ATHENE killed Enceladus, and HEPHAESTUS hurled red-hot iron. DIONYSUS tripped up the giants with his vines. APOLLO, HERMES, and POSEIDON also joined in. The giants were completely defeated. Scholars say that the battle represented the conflict either between barbarism and order, or between humans and the forces of nature.

**GLAUCUS (1)** *Greek* The most famous Glaucus was the grandson of BELLEROPHON, a hero in the *ILIAD*. Glaucus fought on the Trojan side during the TROJAN WAR. He and the Greek hero DIOMEDES (1) discovered that their grandparents had been friends, so the two exchanged armor and vows of friendship. Another of Glaucus's friends was SARPEDON. When Sarpedon was killed, Glaucus appealed to the god APOLLO to help him retrieve the body. This he did,

with the help of the hero HECTOR. AJAX (1) eventually killed Glaucus in battle.

**GLAUCUS (2)** *Greek* The son of SISYPHUS and father of BELLEROPHON and owner of a famous herd of mares. However, Glaucus refused to let them breed, thus incurring the anger of APHRODITE, goddess of love. Aphrodite drove the mares mad and they tore Glaucus to pieces in their frenzy.

**GLAUCUS (3)** *Greek* This Glaucus was born a human but by chance ate an herb that made him immortal. He became a prominent sea god, pictured as a merman, his top half human and his lower half a fish tail. Glaucus was a lesser god, but he had the power of seeing into the future, and this gift made him a favorite deity of sailors and fishermen, who paid him special attention. Glaucus is said to have traveled the entire coast of the Mediterranean Sea each year, visiting each of its ports on that journey. Glaucus was either the son of a fisherman from Anthedon or the son of the great sea god POSEIDON.

**GOLDEN BOUGH** *Roman* The SYBIL OF CUMAE sent the hero AENEAS to obtain the Golden Bough, which would give him safe passage to the UNDERWORLD. The Golden Bough is thought to be the MISTLETOE, a plant that appears in many mythologies.

**GOLDEN FLEECE** *Greek* This fabled fleece was worn on the back of an extraordinary ram. The ram could talk and think, it could move through the air as easily as on land, and it had a fleece of gold. The god HERMES sent the ram to rescue PHRIXUS and HELLE, children of ATHAMAS, king of BOEOTIA. The hero JASON and his companions, the ARGONAUTS, overcame enormous obstacles to capture the precious fleece and return it to King PELIAS of IOLCUS, in Boeotia.

Many scholars think that the "golden fleece" represented either gold amber or perhaps the alluvial gold found in riverbeds near the Black Sea and collected by the natives in fleeces laid on the river beds.

**GORDIAN KNOT** *Greek* A puzzling and intricate knot tied by Gordius, king of PHRYGIA, in ASIA MINOR, in a rope linking the yoke and the pole of the ox-cart that had carried him to the temple of ZEUS. Zeus, obeying the words of an ORACLE, made the peasant Gordius the new king of Phrygia. It is said that the ox-cart remained for centuries at Gordium, the capital city of Phrygia founded by Gordius.

A superstition grew up around the knot: whoever could untie the knot would become the ruler of Asia. No one ever untied the knot, but in legend, Alexander the Great slashed through the knot with his mighty sword and did indeed become the ruler of Asia. The legend of the Gordian knot seems to demonstrate that, in some cases, the power of the sword is greater than that of superstition. "To cut the Gordian knot" has come to mean resolving a difficult problem with one decisive, forceful step.

**GORGONS** (Grim Ones) *Greek* Three female monsters (the Euryae); daughters of CETO and PHORCYS; sisters of the GRAEA. Their names were EURYALE, STHENO, and MEDUSA. They had the bodies of women, brass claws for hands, and snakes for hair. Two were immortal, but Medusa was not. The hero PERSEUS killed her and cut off her head.

**GRACES, THE THREE** *Greek* Goddesses of beauty and charm, they were themselves embodiments of both. The Graces are usually thought to be the daughters of the god ZEUS and EURYNOME. The poet HESIOD named them: Thalia (Flowering), Euphrosyne (Joy), and Aglaia (Radiance). The Three Graces were the personification of joy and well being. They were present at human and divine marriages, and constantly attendant upon the goddess of love, APHRODITE. They were also associated with the god APOLLO.

The Three Graces are often depicted as mingling with nymphs in joyous dances celebrating the bounties of nature.

**GRAEA** (Gray Women) *Greek* Daughters of PHORCYS and CETO; sisters of the GORGONS. Their names were Dino, Enyo, and Pemphredo. The personification of old age, they had only one eye and one tooth to share among themselves. PERSEUS stole the eye as they passed it from one to another. He gave it back to them after they had told him the whereabouts of their sister, MEDUSA, and where to find the helmet, winged sandals, and magic wallet he needed to complete his quest.

**GREECE** Today, a nation in southeastern Europe, part of the Balkan Peninsula. This country's official name is the Hellenic Republic, and the people who live there call their country "Ellas" or "Hellas." These names reflect images of the ancient past of this part of the Mediterranean world. *Greek* comes from *Graeci*, the name the Latin-speaking people of Italy gave to colonists from across the Ionian Sea. The word *Hellenic* refers to the god HELLEN, ancestor of the ancient peoples of the southern Balkan Peninsula and the name the people of this land gave themselves from ancient times.

People have inhabited the land that is now Greece from prehistoric times. Archaeologists have discovered Stone Age farming settlements on this peninsula from as long ago as 6500 B.C. The ruins of towns and villages built during the early and middle Bronze Age (3000 to 1600 B.C.) are also quite common. Evidence from all of these sites shows that, during the Bronze Age, the people of Greece began trading extensively with neighbors on CRETE and in ASIA MINOR and the Middle East.

In the late Bronze Age (1600 to 1150 B.C.), the first true cities and small kingdoms appeared, many of them on the southern part of the peninsula, an area known as the PELOPONNESUS. Here and in this age, the first significant power centers of ancient Greece developed. The city of MYCENAE grew into a major trading and military center on the northeastern side of the Peloponnesus, not far from the Isthmus of CORINTH. AGAMEMNON, one of the great heroes of Greek legends, was king of this city, according to HOMER's *ILIAD* and other ancient sources. This city also gave its name to the first great age of Greece, the Mycenaean Age.

Homer, the Greek poet credited with writing the *Iliad* and the *ODYSSEY*, lived and wrote, according to the best scholarly evidence, around 1050 to 700 B.C., a time known as the Archaic Age of Greek history. His subject matter, though, was the Mycenaean Age and the heroes and warriors of that time. The first people who worshiped the gods and goddesses that Homer wrote about lived in a time that left few if any written records, but their stories were preserved by the developing Greek culture. More than a century of archaeology has revealed much about this mythology and about the lives of the people who believed in these gods.

The great Classical Age of Greece began about 490 B.C. It was separated from the Mycenaean Age by a dark age of conflict and by the Archaic Age, including the time of Homer, from 750 to 490 B.C. During the Classical age, people built great temples to the gods, poets and dramatists drew upon the myths of the Greek religion to write their great works, and artists carved statues and fashioned jewelry to commemorate the gods. The Classical Age was the height of cultural development.

During all of its history, Greece was a collection of city-states, or small communities, rather than a nation. These communities organized around individual political ideals, but the people of this peninsula shared a great deal of culture and trade. They shared a common language and common beliefs in the great pantheon of ZEUS and the OLYMPIAN GODS. Though city-states waged war with one another as well as the people of other lands around the Mediterranean, the people found it easy to travel between cities and towns to visit religious sites such as APOLLO'S ORACLE at DELPHI, and to conduct business.

The Hellenistic Age followed the Classical Age. It began with the conquests of Philip III and his son Alexander the Great. This age represented the spread of Greek culture from Spain in the west to Pakistan in the east. People living in Greek colonies around the Mediterranean Sea helped spread the concepts of civilization to other people, greatly influencing the lives of people of other cultures. By the end of this period, the Romans had spread their political and military influence to this neighboring peninsula and made Greece part of the Roman Empire.

## The Ages of Greece

| Name | Time period |
| --- | --- |
| Early and mid-Bronze Ages | 3000–1600 B.C. |
| Mycenaean Age | 1600–1150 B.C. |
| Dark Ages | 1150–750 B.C. |
| Archaic Age | 750–490 B.C. |
| Classical Age | 490–323 B.C. |
| Hellenistic Age | 323–30 B.C. |

**HADES** *Greek*  God of the UNDERWORLD, associated in Roman mythology with PLUTO, ORCUS, and DIS. Hades was the son of CRONUS and RHEA, and like his sisters, DEMETER, HERA, and HESTIA, and his brother POSEIDON, was swallowed by Cronus. His brother ZEUS escaped and eventually rescued his brothers and sisters from Cronus.

After the defeat of Cronus, Zeus, Poseidon, and Hades drew lots to see who should rule the various parts of the universe. To Hades fell the UNDERWORLD.

Hades seldom left his underground realm—or if he did, no one knew about it, for he had a helmet that made him invisible. When he fell in love with PERSEPHONE, however, Hades traveled above ground to pursue her as she gathered flowers in a field. He carried her off into the dark Earth, and there she lived for four months of the year.

On another occasion, Hades came above ground to woo the NYMPH, MINTHE. In a fit of anger, Persephone, or perhaps Demeter, trod the maiden underfoot. A sorrowful Hades transformed her into the fragrant mint plant.

As he was essentially a god of terror and inexorable death, there were few temples built to Hades and he had few worshippers. The cypress and the narcissus were sacred to Hades.

The word *Hades* is often used as a euphemism for Hell.

**HARMONIA** (Peace) *Greek*  Daughter of APHRODITE and ARES; wife of CADMUS, king of THEBES. All the OLYMPIAN GODS attended the wedding of Harmonia and Cadmus. The gods blessed Harmonia with many gifts, including a golden necklace from Aphrodite, made by the smith-god, HEPHAESTUS. The necklace had the power of giving unfading beauty to its wearer, but it would also bring misfortune in the later history of Thebes (see ERIPHYLE and SEVEN AGAINST THEBES).

While Harmonia, which means "peace," may seem a strange name for a daughter born of Aphrodite, the goddess of love, and ARES, the god of war, some scholars note that then, as now, more than usual affection and therefore harmony are generated among people in times of stress such as war.

The children of Cadmus and Harmonia were daughters INO, AGAVE, and SEMELE, and Polydorus, a son.

**HARPIES** (Swift Robbers) *Greek*  The storm WINDS; daughters of ELECTRA (3), a sea NYMPH, and an ancient sea god, THAUMUS; sisters of the goddess of rainbows, IRIS.

In early stories, the Harpies were shown as beautiful winged women. They were said to appear suddenly and snatch up people and objects and were blamed for sudden disappearances. The Harpies served the great god ZEUS, who wielded thunder and lightning as his weapons, and sent them along with storms to do his bidding.

The poet HESIOD wrote that there were two Harpies and that their names were Aello and Ocypete. HOMER names a third Harpy, Pordage, and says she was married to the western wind ZEPHYRUS, and gave birth to the two great horses of ACHILLES. In later mythology, particularly the stories of JASON and the ARGONAUTS, authors described the Harpies as vicious bird-like creatures with sharp talons that carried off food and precious treasures and gave off a terrible stench.

In Roman mythology, Harpies attack AENEAS and his Trojan crew in VIRGIL's *AENEID*. This poet names a yet another Harpy, Celaeno.

**HEBE** *Greek*  Daughter of the gods ZEUS and HERA and cupbearer to the gods. She became the wife of the hero HERACLES after he was deified and transported to Olympus. Later Hebe was represented as the goddess of youth, with the power to rejuvenate, that is, bring back youth. In Roman mythlogy she is called JUVENTAS (Youth).

**HECATE** *Greek* A goddess with ancient origins whose traits changed significantly over time; daughter of PERSES and ASTERIA. In her earliest form, Hecate was a goddess of goodwill who gave prosperity and victory to people. She was originally a TITAN. In her later forms, Hecate was a powerful goddess of magic and witches. She presided over sorcery and had the power to send spirits of the dead up to the human world. She was honored and summoned at crossroads, which were, in ancient times, believed to be the best places to perform witchcraft.

Hecate became associated with PERSEPHONE, the queen of the UNDERWORLD, and was often linked to SELENE, a Titan moon goddess, and ARTEMIS, an OLYMPIAN moon goddess. Hecate was often portrayed as a woman with either three heads or three bodies.

**HECATONCHEIRES** (HECATONCHIRES) *Greek* The hundred-handed giants, offspring of GAIA and URANUS. Their names were Briareus, Cottus, and Gyges. They helped ZEUS in the war against the TITANS. The Hundred-Handed Ones are thought to represent early bands of warriors, who were organized in groups of 100 men. In Latin poetry, their name is Centimani.

**HECTOR** *Greek* A great hero of the Trojans (see TROJAN WAR); eldest son of PRIAM, king of TROY, and of HECUBA; brother of PARIS, HELENUS, and CASSANDRA; husband of ANDROMACHE; father of Astyanax. Hector has very little mythology except in HOMER's *ILIAD*. His death, the violation of his body by ACHILLES, and his magnificent funeral bring the *Iliad* to an end. There are references to Hector in VIRGIL's *AENEID*, and OVID's *Metamorphoses*.

**HECUBA** *Greek* Wife of King PRIAM of TROY; daughter of the king of PHRYGIA; mother of many, among them HECTOR, leader of the Trojans in the TROJAN WAR, and PARIS, whose abduction of HELEN was a leading cause of the war. Hecuba was a character in HOMER's *ILIAD* and in EURIPIDES' tragedies *Hecuba* and *The Trojan Women*.

**HELEN** *Greek* Daughter of ZEUS and LEDA, said to have been born from an egg, since Zeus came to Leda and mated with her disguised as a swan. Often called Helen of TROY, Helen was in fact from SPARTA. She was the sister of the DIOSCURI (CASTOR and Polydeuces) and of CLYTEMNESTRA. She became the wife of MENELAUS, king of Troy. Helen was said to be the most beautiful woman in the world, a symbol of womanly beauty. Her abduction by the Trojan prince PARIS was a leading cause of the TROJAN WAR.

There are varying accounts of the end of Helen. Some say that after the fall of Troy she was reconciled with her husband, Menelaus. Others say that she married DEIPHOBUS, that she was hanged by a vengeful queen, or that she hanged herself from a tree. She was venerated as a goddess of beauty on the island of RHODES in the eastern Mediterranean under the name Dendritis (Tree).

It seems likely that Helen was an ancient goddess of fertility in LACONIA, which may account for the halfhuman, halfdivine stories that feature her.

**HELENUS** *Greek* Son of PRIAM and HECUBA; brother of PARIS, HECTOR, and CASSANDRA. With his sister, Helenus shared the gift of prophecy. In HOMER's *ILIAD*, Helenus gives good advice to Hector, leader of the Trojans in the TROJAN WAR. In the play *Andromache*, by EURIPIDES, Helenus weds his fellow captive ANDROMACHE after the fall of TROY. In some accounts, Helenus becomes king of EPIRUS. In VIRGIL's *AENEID*, he warns the Trojan hero of SCYLLA and CHARYBDIS and urges him to consult with the SIBYL OF CUMAE.

**HELICON, MOUNT** *Greek* The highest mountain in BOEOTIA, in the southern part of the Greek mainland. It was celebrated in Greek mythology as the haunt of the nine MUSES. The poet HESIOD lived on the slopes of Mount Helicon. In later mythology, the spring of Hippocrene, created when the winged horse PEGASUS stamped his hoof, flowed just below the summit.

**HELIOS** (HELIUS) (The sun god) *Greek* Helios was husband to Rhodos, the NYMPH of the island of RHODES, which he chose as his favored abode. Their children—CIRCE, ACETES, and PHAETON—were the first inhabitants of Rhodes. Helios is usually depicted as a charioteer who drove the Sun across the Earth from east to west each day. Helios was all-seeing and often called upon as a witness (see *Demeter and Persephone*, under DEMETER). Helios (called HYPERION by HOMER) appears in both the *ILIAD* and the *ODYSSEY*; in the latter, the cattle of Helios (Hyperion) are victims of ODYSSEUS and his crew of hungry mariners.

In later times, Helios was identified with APOLLO, and, in the late Roman empire, with SOL, one of the principal gods of the Romans.

The goddess Venus (reclining above) gives Helen, the most beautiful woman in the world, to Paris in this painting by Scottish artist Gavin Hamilton (1723-1798). The painting hangs in the Museum of Rome.

**HELLE** *Greek* Daughter of ATHAMAS and NEPH-ELE; sister of PHRIXUS. Helle and her brother fled from INO, their stepmother, on the back of the winged ram with the famed GOLDEN FLEECE, which HERMES sent to them. One story has it that Helle fell from the air and drowned at a place in the ocean that came to be called the HELLESPONT in her honor, but Phrixus was rescued by AEETES.

**HELLEN** *Greek* The son of DEUCALION and PYRRHA, survivors of the Flood. He was the father of AEOLUS, Dorus, and Xuthus and through them the patriarch of all the HELLENES, who were also known as Greeks.

**HELLENES** *Greek* The name given to the people now known as Greeks. The name was derived from HELLEN, the son of DEUCALION, who became, after the Flood, the ancestor of all the Greeks. There is no good explanation of why the people of ancient GREECE should be called Hellenes, rather than Achaeans, Argives, or Danaans. The word *Greek* comes from the Latin *Graecia*, the country from which many "Greek" settlers came to live in Italy.

**HELLENIZATION** *Greek* The processes of spreading the influence of Greek mythology, philosophy, language, and culture to societies and cultures that came in contact with the people of ancient GREECE. In Greek and Roman mythology, Hellenization refers to the process by which the people of ROME and central Europe, and eventually the Roman Empire, adapted and adopted the myths of Greece as their own, though often giving different names to the gods and goddesses and modifying the stories to meet Roman needs.

Greek colonists living in southern Italy and on the island of Sicily before 800 B.C. were the first to influence the younger civilizations developing in central Italy. A period of widespread exploration and colonization of Italy by the people of Greece took place from 800 to 650 B.C., beginning, according to archaeological and linguistic evidence, with the people of ETRURIA. By 650 B.C., Rome came under Greek influence through trade and through the arrival of Greeks as residents of Rome. By the first century B.C., Greek culture had deeply influenced the thought, culture, literature, and mythology of Rome.

The early people of central Italy believed in gods and spirits closely connected to the needs of everyday life, but those beings appear not to have developed stories of their own. The Romans, over time, applied the stories of Greek gods to the names of their gods. The Romans, however, did not simply adopt the Greek myths. They transformed the gods and their legends to meet the social, personal, historical, and religious needs of their own culture.

Ancient histories and poetry as well as archaeology suggest that APOLLO was the first Greek god to have a strong influence on Rome. A temple dedicated to him was built at Cumae, on the western shores of Italy in the Bay of Naples. Greeks settled this location, about 120 miles southeast of Rome, as early as 730 B.C. The neighboring people may have gone there, too, to worship the gods. (See SIBYL OF CUMAE.)

Roman religious and civic leaders introduced more Greek gods into Roman life during emergencies. For example, leaders brought to Rome in about 295 B.C. the cult of ASCLEPIUS, the Greek god of healing, to help stop a devastating plague.

Even after the Romans made Greece part of their empire in the first century B.C., the Greek religions continued to have a strong influence on the cultures of Rome. Scholars of Rome's religious history suggest this Hellenization period was, in large part, due to the Roman characteristic of incorporating the cultures of conquered lands into the Roman culture. Other experts suggest that the Romans, having never developed a full mythology of their own, sought out the myths of other lands, including those of the Far East as well as Greece, to meet cultural and personal needs.

**HELLESPONT** (Dardanelles) *Greek* The long narrow channel or strait leading from the Aegean Sea into the Sea of Marmara and the Black Sea. It was an important trade route for ships traveling between Asia and Europe. There were many battles and wars for control of this channel, the most famous of which was the TROJAN WAR.

The Hellespont got its name from legends that say HELLE, the sister of PHRIXUS, drowned there when she and her brother, who were fleeing from their stepmother, INO, flew over the water on the ram with the GOLDEN FLEECE.

**HEMERA** (Day, Daylight) *Greek* The daughter of NYX (Night) and EREBUS (Darkness); sister of ETHER (Air). Mother and daughter lived in the same dwelling. At sunset, Hemera met her mother in the distant West, the realm of ATLAS, where that god held up the Earth. There they exchanged places, Hemera entering the home they lived in and Nyx spreading her darkness over the world. At dawn they traded places once again.

**HEPHAESTUS** *Greek* The god of craftsmen, especially smiths, and of fire; called "the divine artificer." In some accounts, Hephaestus was the son of ZEUS and HERA, in some of Hera alone. The Romans gave his attributes and stories to VULCAN.

Hephaestus was lame from birth and not as handsome as the other gods on OLYMPUS. Some myths say Zeus or Hera flung him from Mount Olympus in anger. He landed on the island of Lemnos, where the sea goddesses THETIS and EURYNOME rescued him and looked after him until he was grown.

Although lame, Hephaetus had strong shoulders and was an excellent craftsman, the patron of all smiths, and perhaps something of a magician.

In HOMER'S *ODYSSEY*, Hephaestus was married to the beautiful goddess of love, APHRODITE, but she was unfaithful to him, and had many lovers, including ARES, the god of war. Hephaestus used his craftsmanship to get the better of Ares.

Another story has it that Hephaestus cracked open the head of Zeus in order to release the goddess ATHENE.

In other accounts (including Homer's *ILIAD*) Aglaeia, one of the three graces, is the wife of Hephaestus.

Hephaestus is an ancient god whose origins are probably in ASIA MINOR, and who was kindly and peace-loving. His smoky, flaming workshop was supposed to be located beneath Mount Etna, the volcano in Sicily, an idea that the Romans adapted for Vulcan. With ATHENE, the cult of Hephaestus was important in the life of the city of ATHENS.

Some scholars say that every Bronze Age (c. 3000 B.C.) tool, weapon, or utensil was believed to have magical properties and that the smith who made them was thought to be a sorcerer.

**HERA** (Lady) *Greek* Queen of OLYMPUS, sister and wife of ZEUS, daughter of CRONUS and RHEA. Known as JUNO by the Romans. Mother of ARES, HEBE, HEPHAESTUS, and EILEITHYA. The patroness of marriage, Hera was the goddess most concerned with the welfare of women and children.

Hera was an ancient goddess, existing long before the new gods, including Zeus. Her original name is unknown: *Hera* is a title, meaning "Lady." Her original cult was so strong that the newcomers to the Greek peninsula from the North had to acknowledge it and absorb it into their own religion by making Hera the consort of Zeus, the king of the OLYMPIAN GODS.

Hera was depicted as a young woman, fully clad and of regal beauty, sometimes wearing a high, cylindrical crown. Her emblems include a scepter topped with a cuckoo and a pomegranate, symbol of married love and fruitfulness. The peacock is sacred to Hera, testifying to the services of the hundred-eyed ARGUS (1).

The marriage of Hera and Zeus was not a happy one, because Zeus was unfaithful to his wife and Hera was angry and jealous. She sought to avenge herself on Zeus and his loves in various ways. The many quarrels between Hera and Zeus may reflect the conflicts between the old gods, where woman was the EARTH MOTHER and Queen, and the new male-dominated religion of Zeus and the Olympians.

**Hera and the Cuckoo** There are several legends about how the marriage of Zeus, chief god of the Olympians, and Hera, queen of Olympus, came about. The writer Pausanius tells the most famous one. In this story, Zeus appears before Hera in the shape of a cuckoo, a small, shivering bird, drenched with rain. Tenderhearted Hera takes the poor creature to her bosom to warm it. Zeus at once resumes his normal form and Hera finally agrees to become his wife. The gods solemnly celebrated the marriage on Olympus, but the ceremony did not put an end to the amorous adventures of Zeus. With Zeus, Hera had two sons, Ares and Hephaestus, and a daughter, Hebe. Some legends say that Hera conceived and gave birth to Hephaestus without any help from Zeus. Some say that she was also the mother of Eileithya, about whom little is known.

**Hera and Ixion** Hera was ever faithful to her fickle husband, Zeus. However, she was very beautiful and men found her desirable. Ephialtes, one of the ALOEIDS, was determined to capture Hera and make her his wife. Thus he and his brother started a war with the Olympians. Another admirer, King IXION of Lapith, fell in love with Hera at a banquet at Olympus. When Zeus found out about Ixion's advances, he was angry and jealous and used his magic to shape a cloud in the likeness of Hera. Ixion made love to the cloud, whose name was NEPHELE, and from this union was born CENTAURUS, father of the CENTAURS. Ixion was bound to a fiery wheel and doomed to whirl perpetually through the sky.

**Hera and Io** One of the loves of Zeus was the maiden Io. Zeus turned Io into a beautiful white cow to protect her from Hera, but Hera was not deceived. She demanded to be given the heifer and Zeus could not refuse her. Hera then tied up the heifer and the hundred-eyed Argus guarded her. The god HERMES rescued Io by using songs and stories to close all the eyes of Argus in sleep, and then killing him. But Io remained a heifer, relentlessly pursued by a gadfly sent by Hera, until she reached Egypt. Hera transferred the eyes of Argus onto the magnificent tail of the peacock, where, legend has it, they remain to this day. Some scholars believe that Io was a form of Hera as an ancient goddess dispossessed by the Olympians. In HOMER's work, the goddess Hera is often described as "ox-eyed."

**HERACLES** (HERAKLES; Glory of Hera) *Greek* The greatest hero of Greek mythology, he was called HERCULES by the Romans. Heracles was the son of the god ZEUS and of a mortal, ALCMENE, who was the wife of AMPHITRYON of THEBES. Both Alcmene and Amphitryon were descendants of the hero PERSEUS. Heracles was a superman and demigod and a supreme athlete but at the same time a man of many human weaknesses. He performed seemingly impossible tasks, fought in battle, loved many women including DEIANIRA who would eventually cause his death, and was afflicted by murderous madness and sudden rages. Zeus snatched Heracles from his funeral pyre and took him to Olympus, where Heracles was worshiped like a god, became immortal, and married HEBE.

Heracles' name, Glory of Hera, suggests an origin among ancient people who worshiped the goddess HERA, wife of Zeus. The myth of Heracles is based perhaps on a historical figure, possibly a lord of TIRYNS (in ARGOS) whose military prowess led to the Homeric legend of his having met and conquered death. Later, invaders of the PELOPONNESUS, the southern peninsula of what is now called GREECE, adapted the cycle of the Heracles hero myths to fit their own ancestry.

**The Childhood of Heracles** Heracles' mother, Alcmene, was married to Amphitryon, also a descendant of Perseus. While Amphitryon was at war, Zeus visited Alcmene disguised as her husband. He wished to father a son that would be a champion of both humans and gods. This son was Heracles. When Amphitryon came back the next evening, he, too, fathered a son with Alcmene. His name was IPHICLES.

Hera, the wife of Zeus, was, as usual, jealous and angry at the dalliance of her husband. Using her magic arts, she contrived the premature birth of EURYSTHEUS, another descendant of Perseus. Eurystheus was born a few minutes before Heracles and therefore became ruler of Argos. Heracles was obliged to serve him, and this he did most heroically.

One legend has it that Hera sent two serpents to the cradle of the infant Heracles to kill him, but the baby managed to strangle both serpents with his supernormal strength. Another legend holds that Amphitryon sent the serpents, knowing that one of the twins belonged to Zeus. Thus, while his own son, Iphicles, cried pitifully, the son of the god was able to vanquish the serpents.

Amphitryon made sure that his godlike stepson was trained in all the arts of fighting, wrestling, and boxing. Heracles became a supreme athlete.

**Heracles, The Young Hero** Heracles was the greatest of the Greek heroes. When Heracles was a boy, his stepfather sent him to tend his cattle in the mountains and to develop athletic skills. A ferocious lion came from Mount Kithaeron to devour Amphitryon's cattle. Heracles killed the lion and ever after wore its pelt (though some say that the pelt worn by Heracles was that of the Nemean lion; see *The Twelve Labors of Heracles*, right).

Heracles then did battle with Erginus, King of Orchomenos, who attacked Thebes. Amphitryon died in this struggle. The victorious Heracles became the idol of Thebes. Creon, the new king of Thebes, gave his daughter MEGARA (2) to Heracles in marriage. The marriage was not a happy one, and in later years, in a fit of madness sent upon him by the goddess Hera, Heracles killed his children and possibly his wife as well. He went to the ORACLE at DELPHI for advice. As atonement for the dreadful killings, the oracle put Heracles into the servitude of his cousin, King EURYSTHEUS, who would impose upon the young hero the Twelve Labors, seemingly impossible tasks.

**The Twelve Labors of Heracles** Like many a hero in mythologies from all over the world, Heracles, the greatest Greek hero, fought and won battles with extraordinary creatures that represented man's ancient strife with evil and the forces of darkness. Because of a fit of madness, in which he killed his children and his brother's children, Heracles, son of the god Zeus and the mortal Alcmene, was put into the service of King Eurystheus, a descendant of Perseus and ruler of Argos. To atone for his sins, Heracles had to perform 12 almost impossible tasks over the course of 12 years. In all of them, he emerged as a victorious hero against unbelievable odds. The order of the Twelve Labors varies in some sources but they are thought to begin with the killing of the ferocious Nemean lion and end with either the stealing of the apples of the HESPERIDES or the vanquishing of the dog CERBERUS.

1. *The Nemean Lion* The lion was gigantic, an offspring of SELENE. It lived in a cave with two entrances. After many futile battles, Heracles sealed off one mouth of the cave and strangled the trapped lion with his bare hands. Ever afterward, he wore the pelt and head of the lion. The two mouths of the lion's cave perhaps symbolize the entry of Heracles into the battles (the Twelve Labors) from which he would eventually escape, after death, into rebirth and immortality.

2. *The Hydra of Lernaea* The HYDRA was a many-headed monster who grew a new head each time Heracles lopped off the previous one. With the help of his companion IOLAUS, who burned the stumps of the heads and prevented them from growing again, Heracles vanquished the monster. He dipped his arrows in the blood of the Hydra, which contained a deadly poison. Most mythographers are

still puzzled as to the exact meaning of the Lernaean Hydra.

3. *The Wild Boar of Erymanthus* The boar was a huge beast that Heracles hunted through deep fields of snow. He captured the boar and delivered it to Eurystheus. The king was so terrified at the sight of the beast that he hid himself in his bronze jar.

4. *The Hind of Ceryneia* This beautiful Arcadian deer had feet of bronze and antlers (surprising for a hind) that shone like gold, and ran so swiftly that it took Heracles a year to capture it. He carried it unharmed to King Eurystheus.

5. *The Stymphalian Birds* These monstrous birds had wings, beaks, and claws of bronze. They fed on human flesh and were so numerous that when they took flight their hordes blotted out the Sun. Heracles terrified them with the shattering noise from a bronze rattle that the goddess ATHENE helped him make. The birds flew away and were never seen again.

This legend may refer to Heracles' reputation as a healer, expert at getting rid of fever demons. In ancient times, fevers were little understood and often proved fatal. Since they occurred frequently in marshy places, they were identified with marsh birds such as cranes and ibises, large birds on which the Stymphalian birds may have been modeled.

6. *The Augean Stables* The Sixth Labor of Heracles was to clean, in one day, the pestilent, dung-filled stables of the cattle of King Elis of Augeus. Heracles did this by diverting the courses of two nearby rivers and sending their cleansing waters rushing through the stables. "Cleaning the Augean stables" has come to mean getting rid of noxious rubbish in any area, whether physical, moral, religious, or legal.

7. *The Cretan Bull* Heracles captured the BULL that had been terrorizing the island of CRETE and returned with it to Greece. THESEUS later killed the bull. The combat of a man with a bull was one of the ritual tasks imposed on heroes (see the stories of Theseus and JASON).

8. *The Horses of Diomedes* Heracles captured the horses (some say they were wild mares) of DIOMEDES (2) of Thrace. It was said that Diomedes fed the horses on human flesh Heracles killed Diomedes and gave his flesh to the horses, after which, it is said, the beasts became quite tame. The taming of wild horses was an important rite in many ancient cultures.

9. *The Girdle of the Amazon* Eurystheus asked Heracles to obtain the girdle of Queen HIPPOLYTA of the AMAZONS, for his daughter. Some versions of the legend say that Hippolyta fell in love with Heracles and gave him her girdle. Other versions say that Hippolyta was later abducted by Theseus.

10. *The Cattle of Geryon* GERYON was a three-headed monster whose fine red cattle were the envy of everyone, including Eurystheus, who ordered Heracles to capture them. Heracles did this on the way erecting the Pillars of Hercules (now known as the Straits of Gibraltar), where Africa and Europe face each other at the western end of the Mediterranean Sea. Stealing another man's cattle was an ancient custom; a prospective husband bought his bride from the proceeds of a successful cattle raid.

11. *The Stealing of Cerberus* Cerberus, the fearsome three-headed dog, guarded the gates of the UNDERWORLD. Eurystheus ordered Heracles to bring him the monster, never expecting the hero to return to the land of the living. However, with the help of the gods HERMES and Athene, Heracles overcame both HADES, god of the UNDERWORLD, and the monstrous dog. When Eurystheus saw the huge creature, he jumped into his bronze jar in terror.

The three heads of Cerberus may have represented the three seasons vanquished by the demigod who became immortal.

12. *The Apples of the Hesperides* Heracles' final task was to bring some of the golden apples of the HESPERIDES (daughters of ATLAS) to Eurystheus. The apples belonged to Hera who set the dragon LADON to guard them. Only the TITAN Atlas, who carried the sky on his shoulders, knew where the apple orchard was. Heracles took the sky from Atlas and persuaded him to fetch some apples. He then tricked the Titan into taking back the weight of the sky.

The explanation for this labor may lie in the primitive ritual in which the candidate for a kingship or immortality (Heracles) had to overcome a monster (Ladon) and rob it of its treasure (the golden apples).

**The Exploits of Heracles** There is no clear chronology for the exploits of Heracles, but rather a patchwork of events, with some confusion about the order in which they took place. For example, it is not clear at what point the goddess Hera, wife of Zeus, angry at the dalliance of her husband with Alcmene, took revenge upon Heracles by sending him fits of murderous madness. Among his crimes were the killing of his own children and, some say, his wife Megara, and the killing of Iphitus, a guest in his house. Such deeds were unforgivable. Even the oracle at Delphi refused to help Heracles after the killing of Iphitus. In another fit of madness, Heracles ravaged the oracle's shrine and attacked his halfbrother, the god Apollo. As a result of this outrage, Heracles became a slave to Omphale, queen of Lydia.

Among his exploits for Omphale was the capture of the clever thieves called the Cercopes. Heracles also killed Syleus, the king of Aulis, who had forced strangers to work in his vineyards and then, instead of paying them, cut their throats. Heracles rid the banks of the Sagaris from a gigantic serpent and then killed Lityerses, another evil man who forced people to work for him and then killed them. Omphale so admired Heracles that she set him free.

After his servitude to Omphale, Heracles offered his services to Laomedon, king of Troy. Laomedon had incurred the wrath of the sea god, Poseidon, who sent a monster to ravage Troy. The oracle told Laomedon that only the sacrifice of his beautiful daughter, Hesione, would appease the monster and save Troy. Laomedon chained the girl to a rock to await her fate. Heracles agreed to rescue the maiden in return for two magical horses that had been a gift from Zeus to Laomedon. But Laomedon, his daughter now safe, reneged on his agreement and Heracles killed him. Heracles then gave Hesione to his friend Telamon in marriage. Priam, now king of Troy, demanded the return of his sister, Hesione. The Greeks refused to return her. The subsequent ill-feeling between the nations of Troy and Greece was one cause of the Trojan War.

**Heracles, Deianira, and the Centaur**  Heracles, the mortal hero, spent his life engaging in one heroic exploit after another. Sometimes Heracles sought adventure, sometimes he sought revenge for injustice, and sometimes he had to flee from the punishment due him for acts committed in madness.

After many bold deeds, Heracles came to Calydon, in Aetolia, whose king, Oeneus, had a beautiful daughter, Deianira. Deianira was constantly plagued by the attentions of Achelous, who appeared to her in the form of a river, a dragon, and a bull. After a furious contest, Heracles vanquished Achelous and

won the hand of the beautiful Deianira, with whom he bore a son, Hyllus.

Heracles, Deianira, and Hyllus fled from Calydon after Heracles, again afflicted by rage, killed an innocent cupbearer, Eunomus.

When they came to the river Evenus, a Centaur, Nessus, offered to carry Deianira on his back, while Heracles swam across. When they reached the other side, the centaur tried to carry Deianira off. Heracles shot him with his arrow. As he lay dying, Nessus told Deianira to collect some of his blood and use it as a love potion if she ever thought that her husband was straying. Deianira respected the wishes of the dying beast and took his blood in a vial that she carried. This potion would eventually cause the death of Heracles.

**The Death of Heracles**  The last expedition of Heracles was against his old enemy Eurytus. Heracles slew Eurytus and carried off his daughter, Iole, with whom he had been in love before he had met his present wife, Deianira. When Deianira heard about the beautiful maiden, she remembered the vial of blood that she had taken from Nessus. Innocently thinking that the potion would bring Heracles back to her, she soaked a shirt in a liquid made from the blood in the vial and sent it to her husband with his messenger, Lichas.

As soon as Heracles put on the fateful shirt, he began to writhe with pain, for the potion was a deadly one, and proved fatal to Heracles. He commanded a funeral pyre to be built and laid himself upon it. His son, Hyllus, told him that Deianira had not intended his death and had killed herself in despair. Heracles, in his last throes of agony, gave Iole to his son in marriage. No one wanted to light the funeral pyre, but at last, Philoctetes (or his father, Poeas) set the wood on fire. Immediately, a cloud descended from the sky, and in a display of thunder and lightning, Zeus snatched his son from death and bore him to Olympus, where he would become immortal.

**HERBS** *Greek*  The mythic power of herbs to transform people and to restore life to the dead features prominently in several Greek myths. Gaia, the Earth Mother, the oldest goddess in Greek mythology, found an herb that would protect the Gigantes (Giants), some of her children, in their war with the Olympian gods. Zeus, the supreme god among the Olympians, who were themselves descendants of Gaia, obtained that herb and used it to help him defeat the giants in their war against the gods.

The herb *moly* helped Odysseus resist the efforts of the goddess-sorceress Circe to turn him into a swine when he landed on the island of Achaea. The heroine MORIA used an herb known as balis to restore her brother to life after he had been bitten by a snake.

Dittany, a creeping herb of the mint family that is native to GREECE, was known as the herb of VENUS and was also the sacred herb of ARTEMIS, goddess of childbirth and chastity. Some historians suggest that women in ancient Greece used dittany, also known as ditamy, to bring on menstruation.

## HERCULES *Roman*

A god, closely associated with the Greek hero HERACLES. Ancient Romans also saw Hercules as the patron and guardian of merchants and soldiers. He was a helper to those in need and protected men at sea from danger and disease.

A shrine to Hercules stood on the edge of the Palatine Hill in ROME. He was honored in the Roman festival calendar on August 12, when men held a great celebration that included slaughtering oxen. Women were not allowed at this festival.

The cult of Hercules arrived early in Italy from GREECE, about the second century B.C. and soon developed a very strong following. Greek colonists who settled in communities on the eastern shores of Italy brought the stories of this much-loved deity with them when they traveled across the Ionian Sea. Hercules' cult grew until he commanded a wide following throughout the Italian peninsula.

Many of the stories of Hercules traveled across the seas with his religious celebrations, but Roman poets shared details their own people added to the mythology.

**Hercules and Cacus** According to LIVY, a Roman historian of the first century B.C., Hercules arrived at the Tiber River in central Italy on his way back to Greece after capturing the cattle of GERYON, which was the 10th labor he undertook for King EURYSTHEUS. The hero stopped to rest by the river. As he slept, a strong, fierce local shepherd named CACUS (2) stole the finest cattle in the herd. Cacus tried to disguise his theft by dragging the cattle by their tails. He hid his treasure in a nearby cave.

When Hercules awoke, he was confused at the disappearance of so many cattle. Unable to find the missing animals, he began to drive the remaining cattle on their journey. As these cows bellowed, the cows hidden in the caves began to moo in reply. Hercules, hearing this evidence, discovered the cave, killed Cacus with a club, and continued on his journey.

VIRGIL, a Roman poet who lived at the same time as Livy, told a much more dramatic version of this story in the *AENEID*.

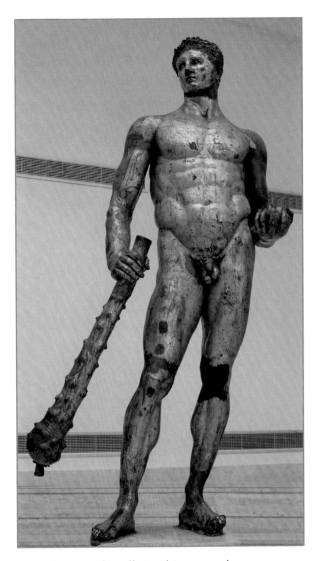

Hercules stands tall in this second century B.C. bronze statue, which was found in the Roman forum in the 15th century. It now stands in the Musei Capitolini in Rome.

In astronomy, Hercules is a large constellation in the northern celestial hemisphere. It is also the name of a large crater on the Moon.

## HERMAPHRODITUS *Greek*

The son of APHRODITE and HERMES, brought up by NYMPHS on Mount IDA (2), in CRETE. One of the nymphs, Salmacis, fell in love with Hermaphroditus but he scorned her. Salmacis prayed to be joined with him forever in one body. The gods answered her prayers, for when she finally clasped him to her their two bodies became one.

In terms of mythological and religious concepts, a young man with womanish breasts and long hair may represent the transition from matriarchy (the EARTH MOTHER) to patriarchy (the rule of males).

**HERMES** *Greek* The winged messenger of the Greek gods; son of ZEUS and MAIA (1). Hermes is also associated with fertility, and is god of flocks, roads, trading, and thieves. Hermes was the inventor of the lyre and the guide of souls on the way to HADES. He was the father of many, including AUTOLYCUS, DAPHNIS, and HERMAPHRODITUS. In Roman mythology, he is known as MERCURY.

Archaic artists portrayed Hermes as a bearded man wearing a broad-brimmed hat and winged sandals, and carrying a herald's staff. From the fifth century B.C. on, artisans showed him as a nude and beardless young man, typical of an accomplished athlete.

The earliest center of Hermes' cult was ARCADIA, where he was worshiped as a god of fertility with phallic images called *hermae (hermai)*. These were heaps of stones set up by the ancient Greeks to mark boundaries or distances along roads. With the development of artistic taste, in the fifth century B.C. these crude piles became pillars crowned with the head of Hermes. In cities the hermae were erected at street corners and at the doors of houses.

**The Childhood of Hermes** Hermes, son of Zeus and Maia, was born in a cave in Mount Cyllene, in Arcadia. He grew miraculously fast, and soon after his birth he was able to walk out of the cave, kill a tortoise, and make the first lyre from its shell.

To complete the lyre, Hermes needed strings. He stole a herd of cows belonging to APOLLO by making them walk backward so that their tracks would lead Apollo in the wrong direction. He killed the cows and made strings for the lyre from their guts.

When Apollo finally discovered the thief (now back in his cradle), he brought Hermes before his father, Zeus. Zeus was more amused than angry at his infant son, and when Hermes produced the lyre and played it, even Apollo was charmed and offered the rest of his flock to Hermes in return for it.

Apollo also gave Hermes his CADUCEUS, a herald's staff of gold. Hades instructed Hermes to lay the golden staff on the eyes of the dying and lead them gently to the realm of the dead.

Some accounts say that Apollo taught Hermes how to prophesy, ARTEMIS taught him to hunt, and PAN taught him to play the pipes. Hermes was undoubtedly a favorite with the gods.

**HERO AND LEANDER** *Greek* The subjects of a tragic love story. Hero was a priestess of APHRODITE. Leander, a young man from Abydos, Mysia, in ASIA MINOR, was her lover. He swam across the HEL-LESPONT every night, guided by her light. One stormy night, the flame blew out and Leander drowned. In her grief, Hero cast herself into the waves to be with him and perished. The story has been the subject of many literary works, including a long poem, *Hero and Leander*, by Christopher Marlowe (1564–1593).

**HESIOD** *Greek* Poet whose work is usually dated between 800 and 700 B.C. Hesiod was a poor farmer. His poem *Works and Days* gives us a vivid picture of everyday life in ancient GREECE as it was lived by ordinary people, as opposed to the adventurers and courtiers of HOMER's *ILIAD* and *ODYSSEY*. Hesiod's *Theogony* is concerned with mythology; it describes the Greeks' beliefs about creation, the universe, and the genealogy of the gods and goddesses. Hesiod also tells about sinister aspects of religion, such as witchcraft and human sacrifices. Both poems are invaluable sources for the study of Greek religion and mythology.

**HESIONE** *Greek* Daughter of LAOMEDON, king of TROY; sister of PRIAM. Laomedon offered Hesione as sacrifice to a sea monster to appease the gods POSEIDON and APOLLO. HERACLES slew the monster and gave Hesione in marriage to TELAMON, with whom she bore a son, TEUCER. Hesione's brother, Priam, now king of Troy, demanded her return. The refusal of the Greeks to return Hesione to her Trojan home was said to have caused some of the ill feeling that eventually led to the war between GREECE and Troy (see the TROJAN WAR).

**HESPERIA** *Greek* A DRYAD, or wood NYMPH; one of the sisters known as the HESPERIDES; either the daughters of EREBUS (Darkness) and NYX (Night) or the daughters of ATLAS and PLEIONE or Hesperis. Her sisters, those named by people writing during the classic age of Greek mythology, were AEGLE (2), ARETHUSA, and ERYTHEIA.

**HESPERIDES** (Daughters of the West) *Greek* The DRYADS, or wood NYMPHS; sisters, who lived in the beautiful garden on the western edge of the world and helped guard the tree that grew the golden apples of the goddess HERA. They were the daughters of EREBUS (Darkness) and NYX (Night) or the daughters of ATLAS and PLEIONE or Hesperis. Some sources say there were seven sisters, others three or four. Those who are named in Greek poetry are AEGLE (2), ERYTHEIA, HESPERIA, and ARETHUSA.

Hera suspected the Hesperides of being as likely to steal the apples as guard them, so she also put the dragon LADON in the garden to guard her treasure.

In his 12th labor, the hero HERACLES stole the apples either himself or by sending ATLAS to do the work.

**HESTIA** (HEARTH) *Greek*  Goddess of the hearth and fire; eldest daughter of CRONUS and RHEA; sister of ZEUS and HERA; one of the 12 OLYMPIAN GODS. Gentle, peace-loving, and pure, Hestia kept away from all disputes. She was the embodiment of a sacred principle—the household fire—and much honored as such, though there are few surviving stories about her.

**Hestia and the Hearth**  It was a difficult task for primitive people to make and preserve fire. They tended the hearth with care and honored it as a source of power. When a member of the family left home, he or she carried a glowing ember from the hearth, thus symbolizing the continuity of the family. When groups of people began to form villages and then towns, each community had a public hearth (*prytaneum*) where the fire was maintained. In later days, the fire of the public hearth was used

in religious sacrifices and took on a sacred character. Eventually, the character of the *hestia* was personified as the deity Hestia.

**Hestia and Priapus**  The hearth was the center of domestic life in early GREECE. Hestia represented personal security and happiness and the sacred duty of hospitality. One story emphasizes the importance of the hearth as a symbol of hospitality and protection.

One day, at a rustic feast, the drunken god PRIAPUS assaulted Hestia. The guests were extremely angry and drove Priapus away. This anecdote represents a warning against the ill-treatment of guests, particularly women, who are under the protection of the domestic or public hearth.

**HIPPODAMEIA** *Greek*  The daughter of King OENOMAUS, who lost her in a chariot race to PELOPS. Hippodameia and Pelops became the parents of ATREUS and THYESTES.

**HIPPOLYTA** *Greek*  Queen of the AMAZONS; daughter of ARES; wife of THESEUS; mother of Hippolytus.

A centaur, a creature that was half horse and half human, tries to carry off Hippodameia, who was also known as Laodamia, at her wedding party. The scene is painted on ancient Greek red-figure pottery. This piece is in the British Museum in London. *(Photograph © Marie-Lan Nguyen.)*

The hero HERACLES stole her girdle as part of his ninth great labor. Heracles had been accompanied on this exploit by Theseus, king of ATHENS. Hippolyta and the Amazons attacked Athens, but Theseus defeated them and made Hippolyta his wife. She bore him a son, Hippolytus. According to some legends, however, Heracles murdered Hippolyta.

**HOMER** *Greek* The great poet of ancient GREECE to whom the epic poems the *ILIAD* and the *ODYSSEY* are usually attributed. Although he is Greece's most famous name, hardly anything is known about Homer. His birthdate is estimated between 1050 and 750 B.C. His birthplace is not known, though the island of Chios, off the coast of Ionia, in ASIA MINOR, is a likely location according to references in the poems. Some say that the work of Homer may have been a kind of anthology of ancient writings that Homer gathered together with great genius and poetical unity. Other scholars say that the *Iliad* and the *Odyssey* were the work of a single poet, developed from older legendary material.

A second century B.C. Greek artist sculpted a bust of a man believed to be Homer, and a Roman artist copied the bust in the second century A.D. It stands in the Louvre in Paris. *(Photograph by Hay Kranen.)*

Whatever the origins of the poet, the poems had a tremendous influence on the Greeks, providing them with an elementary education in their mythology. Homer's works have been of enormous value to historians, archaeologists, and students of comparative religion. His stories preserve the social and religious customs of the late Bronze Age Achaeans who invaded TROY (3000 B.C.). After the fall of the Achaeans, there were three or four centuries of "darkness" until the great flowering of culture in the fifth century B.C. known as Classical Greece.

**HONOS** *Roman* God of honor, chivalry, and justice, particularly as displayed by soldiers. Honos was often called upon for support in military conflicts, often in prayers also offered to the goddess VIRTUS.

Temples were built in his honor by leaders after successful battles against enemies. One stood in the city of Pompeii. On coins, Honos was often pictured as a young man carrying a spear and a CORNUCOPIA.

**HORAE** *Greek* Daughters of ZEUS and THEMIS; goddesses of the seasons. According to HESIOD, there were three Horae: EIRENE (Peace), DIKE (Justice), and EUNOMIA (Order). The names and numbers of the Horae differed from place to place in ancient GREECE. The Horae, goddesses of flowers and fruits, controlled the four seasons, watched over agriculture, and had many names, including Thallo (flowers) and Carpo (fruits). Artwork showed them as beautiful maidens, often in the company of the graces in the retinue of the love goddess APHRODITE. They were especially tender toward children.

**HOUSEHOLD GODS** *Roman* Throughout ancient ROME, people believed in a variety of gods that influenced their home lives. In their homes were small altars to these gods. They performed small rituals to honor the household gods. In fact, some modern scholars suggest that the Roman cultures maintained familiar rituals from generation to generation without remembering their origins and in later times developed myths to explain these practices. The stories of these lesser gods may have been borrowed from nearby cultures to explain these Roman domestic rituals.

The most prominent among the household gods were the LARES and the PENATES. Each home had its own Lar, a spirit, originally a revered ancestor, that watched over the house and brought prosperity to the family. Homes typically had small shrines in them which included a statue that represented the

Lar. Family members placed a portion of each meal on this shrine, a token of thanks for the protection the Lar brought.

Two Penates dwelled in each home, protecting the storeroom or food cupboard from pests, molds, and thieves. Families recognized a certain spot on the hearth, near the family's fire, where the Penates lived, and believed that these two spirits joined them at their table for every meal.

Doorways were particularly important to Roman citizens. The comings and goings of the family and the community represented opportunities for both success and danger. The greatest god of the doorway was Janus, the two-faced god who could see forward and backward, in toward the home and out toward the community. He eventually became a prominent god in Roman society. Janus was joined in his service to the threshold by Limentinus, Lima, Cardea, and Forculus.

Vesta, the goddess of the hearth and protector of the fire, like Janus, became a prominent Roman deity. In the home, Vesta watched over baking and food preparation. Here it was the younger daughters' responsibility to watch over the fire. A portion of each meal was also dedicated to Vesta.

Even the tools of the household had forces protecting them and watching over their users. Devera, for example, was the goddess of brooms, who was called upon to help clean the home for rituals and for welcoming a new child.

**HYACINTHUS** *Greek* A young man loved by the Greek god Apollo; son of Amyclas, a Spartan king, and Diomede, or of Pierus and Clio, the Muse. Zephyrus, the West Wind, killed him with a flying disc. Apollo created a fragrant flower, the hyacinth, in honor of his friend.

Hyacinthus was an ancient, pre-Hellenic fertility god, whose worship was absorbed by Apollo's cult in later years when the Hellenes were invaded by migratory tribes. Followers held a three-day festival, the Hyacinthia, at Sparta in honor of the god, where boys and girls participated in games, competitions, sacrifices, and various entertainments.

**HYDRA** (Water Creature) *Greek* A many-headed serpent, the offspring of Echidna and Typhon. When one head was chopped off, another grew in its place. The second labor of Heracles was to kill the dreaded serpent. Hydra's blood was venomous. Arrows or garments dipped in it killed Chiron, the centaur; Nessus; and Philoctetes.

**HYGEIA** (Hygieia; Health) *Greek* Goddess of physical and mental health. According to some legends, Hygeia is a daughter of Asclepius, god of medicine, and granddaughter of Apollo. Her sisters were Aegle (1) (Brightness), Panacea (All-healing), and Iaso (Healthy). Her brothers were Machaon, a surgeon, and Podalirius, a general practitioner. Hygeia is most often portrayed in the company of her father or her sisters. Sculptors show her wearing a long robe and feeding a huge snake from a cup. The word *hygiene* derives from this goddess's name, and the symbol of Hygeia's snake combined with her father's scepter form the modern symbol of the medical profession, the caduceus.

See also Salus.

**HYPERION** (The One Above) *Greek* One of the Titans; son of Uranus and Gaia; father with Theia of Helios, Selene, and Eos (the Sun, the Moon, and Dawn). Hyperion is sometimes used as the name for the Sun itself. Earlier mythologies name Helios as the Sun. In some accounts, Hyperion, like Helios, is identified with Apollo.

See also Eurylochus and Odysseus.

**HYPNOS** (Sleep) *Greek* The personification of sleep and the twin brother of Thanatos (Death); the son of Nyx (Night) and Erebus (Darkness).

Hypnos had power over mortals and gods and put them to sleep by sprinkling over them water from a twig or juice from a horn. Poets, such as the Greek Homer and the Roman Virgil, gave him more characteristics than he has in records of religious practices.

The Romans gave Hypnos the name Somnus as Greek mythology influenced Roman religion.

**IAPETUS** *Greek* A first generation TITAN; son of URANUS and GAIA. Iapetus married CLYMENE, a daughter of his brother OCEANUS, and with her was father of four brothers, second-generation Titans: ATLAS, PROMETHEUS, EPIMETHEUS, and a lesser known son, MENOETIUS. The Greeks considered Iapetus the primary ancestor of the human race since it was his son, Prometheus, who was the primary supporter of humans.

When the OLYMPIAN GODS fought the Titans, ZEUS threw Iapetus down to TARTARUS, a realm even deeper down and farther away from the Earth than was HADES, the realm of the dead. According to one Greek poet, the gods put an island on top of Iapetus to keep him from escaping.

**ICARUS** *Greek* Son of the great inventor DAEDALUS. When Daedalus wanted to escape from the island of CRETE, where he was being held prisoner by King MINOS, he invented and crafted wings from the feathers of birds, held together by wax. He and Icarus took flight, but Icarus ignored the warnings of his father and flew too near the Sun. The heat of the Sun melted the wax, and Icarus's wings fell apart. Icarus plummeted into the sea and drowned.

The Icarian Sea, a part of the Aegean Sea between Turkey and the Greek islands of Patmos and Leros, is named after him.

**IDA (1)** *Greek* The NYMPH who with her sister, ADRASTIA, and the goat-nymph, AMALTHEA, tended the infant god ZEUS on Mount IDA (2) in CRETE.

**IDA (2)** *Greek* Mountain in the center of CRETE, associated with the childhood of ZEUS.

**IDA (3)** *Greek* A mountain range in Mysia, northwest ASIA MINOR. It was from here that ZEUS seized the beautiful youth GANYMEDE and took him to OLYMPUS

to be a cupbearer to the gods. It was the scene of the *Judgment of Paris* (see under PARIS). From here, the gods watched the battles of TROY during the TROJAN WAR.

**ILIAD** *Greek* The name of the epic poem by HOMER, who is thought to have lived during the eighth century B.C. The name derives from Ilion, one of the names for TROY, an ancient city on the northwestern tip of ASIA MINOR.

The 24 books of the *Iliad* tell of the last few days of the TROJAN WAR, focusing especially on the Greek hero ACHILLES, who withdrew from the conflict, causing severe setbacks to the Greeks. However, Achilles rejoined the war, and slew HECTOR, the hero of the Trojans. The *Iliad* also tells of other leaders of the Greeks, such as ODYSSEUS, DIOMEDES (1), AJAX (1), and MENELAUS, who was the leader of the Achaeans. It does not tell of the beginning of the Trojan War, which was supposed to have been caused by the abduction of HELEN, a Spartan princess, by the Trojan PARIS. Homer never calls the victors of the Trojan war "Greeks." That was a name the Romans later gave to the people of the peninsula in southern Europe that would eventually become the nation of GREECE.

The *Iliad* tells not only of the war but of the peaceful lives of shepherds, fishermen, and woodcutters of an era that is now supposed by historians and archaeologists to have been between 1200 and 1300 B.C.

According to many scholars, the *Iliad* is one of the greatest works of literature, and certainly the earliest. Achilles is the first hero of Western literature. The poem tells of petty rages and jealousies, but also speaks of heroism and nobility in a memorable narrative.

**ILIUM (ILIA)** *Greek* Another name for TROY. In Greek legend, Ilus, son of Tros by CALLIRHOË, was the founder of Ilium, which was also called Tros or

Nymphs mourn over the fallen body of Icarus, whose great wings melted when he flew too close to the sun. British artist Herbert James Draper (1863-1920) created this *Lament for Icarus*, an award-winning painting, in 1898. It hangs in the Tate Britain in London.

Troy after his father. The *ILIAD* by HOMER, means "about Troy."

**INCUBUS** *Roman*  In folklore and very early religious beliefs, an evil spirit or devil that came out at night and sat on the chests of sleeping people. People believed an incubus caused nightmares and had intercourse with sleeping women.

**INDIGETES** (DII INDIGITES) *Roman*  Apparently, lesser gods of the many people who inhabited Central Italy in the seventh and early sixth centuries B.C. These gods were numerous and responsible for specific aspects of life, some governing the individual, some the household, some the land and farming, and some the city of ROME itself. Many of these deities received names that indicated their functions, usually verbs in the original languages of the people who first worshipped them. Others were referred to on monuments by group names or functions, but these collective gods appear to have been as important to the early Romans as the gods who received names.

The worship of these gods continued for centuries, their names and functions carried on as cultures merged. Centuries after the earliest surviving mentions of them were created, Roman historians, such as VIRGIL, who lived from 70-19 B.C., early Christian writers, such as Augustus of Hippo (Saint Augustine), who lived from A.D. 354-430, and writers from Near East cultures, mention them, by name or as indigetes, but in ways that do not make their origins or functions clear to modern audiences. That references to so many of these minor gods survived indicates to many experts the importance of the roles these gods played in daily life and the development of the Roman society.

Modern scholars have worked to sort out the origins of these gods. They disagree over the meaning of the term *indigete* as it would have been used in the sixth century B.C. That disagreement has been taking place since at least the 1920s. Using linguistics and language studies, some scholars have tried to decipher the meaning of the word *indigete* itself. Other scholars have used the works of the poets and historians and carvings on monuments and markers from across the Roman Empire to decipher just who these gods were and the roles they played in people's lives.

Today, scholars seem to agree that too little is known to state absolutely who the indigetes were. Beyond that agreement, though, there are differing opinions. Some experts say the indigetes were ancestors that people worshipped after their deaths. Others modify that and say that the indigetes were the great heroes who people later deified, or worshipped as gods, such as AENEAS, the hero from TROY, who settled in Italy.

Others argue that the indigetes were HOUSEHOLD GODS or PERSONAL GODS who directed the daily lives of individuals. In this view, even the greater Roman gods, such as JANUS and CERES, began as personal gods. As the Roman society grew and merged with other cultures, many, but not all, of these gods took on more roles and prominence and moved from their influence on individuals to influence on all of society.

Still others argue that classical Roman authors used the term *dii indigites* to distinguish the many personal gods from the *dii novensiles*, or newcomer gods, particularly those brought to the Italian peninsula by Greek colonists. Some argue more specifically that the indigetes were the group of gods named in one of the oldest recovered calendars of Roman festivals, inscribed in a stucco wall sometime in the sixth century B.C. and discovered by archaeologists in the early 20th century.

See also AGRICULTURAL GODS; HOUSEHOLD GODS; PERSONAL GODS; STATE GODS.

**INO** *Greek*  Daughter of CADMUS and HARMONIA; sister of Agave, Antonoë, and SEMELE; wife of ATHAMAS. Ino was a moon goddess and a corn goddess. She is important in the legend of JASON and the ARGONAUTS as the second wife of ATHAMAS.

Ino hated her stepson PHRIXUS, the firstborn of Athamas and NEPHELE. Ino, as a corn goddess, persuaded the women of BOEOTIA to roast the corn seeds secretly before sowing them, so that no new corn would grow from the dead seeds. She then bribed an ORACLE to tell Athamas that Phrixus must be sacrificed to the corn goddess to make the barren fields fertile. Terrified, Athamas agreed to the sacrifice. The winged ram that wore a GOLDEN FLEECE rescued Phrixus.

Ino and her husband, Athamas, took care of the infant DIONYSUS (son of Ino's sister Semele), which earned them the gratitude of ZEUS (father of Dionysus) but the wrath of HERA (wife of Zeus), who visited madness on both Ino and Athamas.

**IO** *Greek*  The beautiful daughter of the river god Inachus, and a priestess of HERA. Hera's husband, the great god ZEUS, fell in love with Io. To protect Io from the wrath and jealousy of Hera, Zeus changed Io into a pretty white heifer (a young cow). Hera was not deceived. She asked Zeus for the heifer and Zeus was forced to hand over Io. Hera put Io under the care of the hundred-eyed Argus (1), who watched her night and day, for his eyes never closed.

Stricken with remorse, Zeus sent the god Hermes to rescue Io. Hermes told long stories and sang songs until all the eyes of Argus closed in sleep. Then Hermes cut off the monster's head and released Io. Io fled, but Hera, still jealous, sent a gadfly to torment her. Io eventually reached Egypt, where at last she became a woman again and bore Zeus a son, Epaphus.

It is said that the Ionian Sea is named after Io, for she swam across it. The Bosporus, a narrow strait between the Black Sea and the Sea of Marmara, is also named after her. (Bosporus means "cow ford," a crossing for cows.)

Some say that the strange story of Io had its origin in pre-Hellenic religion, when perhaps Io was a moon goddess. It is said that moon goddesses wore horns, as Io did as a heifer. Some accounts say that Io was but one aspect of the goddess Hera, ancient Earth Mother, often described as "ox-eyed."

**IOLAUS** *Greek*  The son of Iphicles (halfbrother of Heracles). Iolaus was the constant companion of Heracles and also his charioteer. Iolaus helped Heracles slay the Hydra.

**IOLCUS** *Greek*  A town in Magnesia, a region of Thessaly. In Greek mythology, it was the home of Pelias and Jason, and the starting point for the expedition of the Argonauts in search of the Golden Fleece.

**IOLE** *Greek*  Daughter of Eurytus, king of Oechalia. Heracles loved Iole. It was because of this love affair that Deianira, Heracles' wife, unwittingly caused her husband's death by administering to him what she thought was a love potion but which was actually poison. After Heracles' death, Iole married his son, Hyllus.

**IPHICLES** *Greek*  Halfbrother of the hero Heracles; son of Amphitryon, a prince of Tiryns, and his wife, Alcmene, who was a daughter of the king of Mycenae; husband to Automedusa, and later, to the youngest daughter of King Creon of Thebes.

Heracles' mother was also Alcmene but his father was the great god Zeus. The brothers were born on the same day, leading some writers to call them twins.

However, the boys were conceived a night apart, after Zeus disguised himself as Amphitryon and slept with their mother, the night before Amphitryon returned from war and conceived Iphicles.

Iphicles proved himself mortal when, in his first test in life as an infant, he was frightened, unlike his brother. One night, as the two babies slept, Hera, wife of Zeus, or according to some, Amphitryon himself, put a snake in their room. Iphicles cowered in terror and Heracles fought and killed the snake.

Iphicles was with Heracles when the hero went mad and began killing family members. Iphicles managed to save his eldest son, Iolaus, and Heracle's wife, Megara (2), but two of Iolaus's children and two of Heracle's children died at Heracle's hands. Iphicles accompanied his brother on several of his 12 great labors. He also fought in the Calydonian Boar Hunt and at Heracle's side in Troy, when the hero rescued King Laomedon's daughter, whom the ocean god Poseidon had demanded as a sacrifice. Iphicles died in Troy.

**IPHIGENIA** *Greek*  Daughter of Clytemnestra and Agamemnon, king of Mycenae and leader of the Greek forces in the Trojan War; sister of Electra and Orestes. Agamemnon sacrificed Iphigenia to placate the goddess Artemis, whom he had offended, and to ensure by this sacrifice fair winds on the voyage to Troy. Greek tragedians, notably Sophocles and Euripides, cited the death of Iphigenia as as motive for the murder of Agamemnon by Clytemnestra.

**IRIS** *Greek*  Messenger of the gods, especially of Zeus, and a devoted attendant of Hera. Iris personifies the rainbow, a path, it was said, that she often traveled. Daughter of the Titan Thaumus; sister of the Harpies.

**IXION** *Greek*  King of the Lapiths in Thessaly, the largest ancient region of north-central Greece. Ixion fell in love with Hera, wife of the god Zeus. Angry at the advances of Ixion to his wife, Zeus tricked Ixion by creating a cloud, Nephele, in the likeness of Hera. Ixion made love to the cloud and from the union was born Centaurus, the ancestor of the Centaurs. Zeus then hurled a thunderbolt at Ixion and had him tied to a fiery wheel, condemned to whirl forever through the heavens.

The poet Ovid saw Ixion as symbolic of sensuality.

**JANUS** (IANUS) *Roman*  One of the principal Roman gods and one of the oldest. Janus was the guardian of gates and doors, and as such his name is used in the name of the month of January, the gateway to the year. He is depicted as being two-faced or two-headed: One of his faces looks forward, into the future; the other looks backward, into the past. Janus was the opener and closer of all things. His name was mentioned in prayers even before that of JUPITER.

The people of ROME dedicated a shrine to Janus in the Forum. The doors to this shrine were opened only in time of war to allow the warriors to march forward into battle.

The chief festival of Janus was on New Year's Day.

**JASON** (IASON) *Greek*  The hero of one of the most famous Greek legends, often known as "Jason and the GOLDEN FLEECE," or "Jason and the ARGONAUTS." Jason was the son of AESON, king of IOLCUS, in THESSALY, and of Queen Alcimede. When PELIAS, the half-brother of Aeson, deposed Aeson and claimed the throne of Iolcus, threatening to kill any who disputed his claim, Jason, the heir to the throne, was smuggled away from the kingdom and put into the care of CHIRON, the gentle CENTAUR.

After many years, Jason made his way back to Iolcus to regain his kingdom. On his way, he helped an old woman by carrying her across a river. He lost one of his sandals in the stream but earned the gratitude of the woman, who was the goddess HERA in disguise. Hera would always be an ally of Jason.

Pelias had been warned by an ORACLE to beware of a man wearing one sandal. When Jason appeared with one bare foot, Pelias sent him on an expedition to find the Golden Fleece, knowing it was unlikely that Jason would ever return. However, Jason came back triumphant. As well as the fleece, Jason also brought with him the sorceress-queen MEDEA, who brought him disaster after he deserted her for Glauca.

Jason lived a lonely and unhappy life, wandering about from place to place, until he finally died under the prow of his ship, the *ARGO*.

**Jason and the Argonauts**  Jason was the hero of this, one of the most famous Greek myths. Pelias, who had usurped the kingdom of Iolcus, sent Jason to capture the Golden Fleece, a quest from which he thought Jason would never return.

However, Jason had won the favor of the goddesses Hera and ATHENE. With their help, Jason built the fabled ship *Argo*, which had 50 oars. He recruited 50 remarkable people called the Argonauts. They included one woman, ATALANTA; HERACLES, the strongest man who ever lived; ORPHEUS, the poet from THRACE who could sing more sweetly than the SIRENS; and CASTOR AND POLLUX, brothers of HELEN. They set sail for the Black Sea where legend said the Golden Fleece was hidden.

After many adventures, the Argonauts reached the kingdom ruled by AEETES. The king, whose help the Argonauts needed, imposed seemingly impossible tasks upon Jason. One was to harness fire-breathing BULLS with brazen feet and plow a field. Then he was to sow the plowed field with dragons' teeth, from which would spring fully armed warriors. Fortunately for Jason, Medea, daughter of Aeetes, had fallen in love with him. She used her powers as a sorceress to help him. Jason mastered the bulls, and when the armed men sprang from the dragons' teeth, Jason did what CADMUS had done before him: he threw a stone into the midst of the warriors, who accused each other of throwing the stone. They fought among themselves until all were dead.

Medea then led Jason to the place where the Golden Fleece hung, guarded by a terrible dragon. Using a magic potion, Medea put the dragon to sleep, allowing Jason to secure the precious trophy.

Jason and the Argonauts went to sea, accompanied by Medea, and pursued by King Aeetes. Medea slew her brother, ABSYRTUS, who had accompanied them.

She cut his body into pieces and flung them into the sea and onto the surrounding land, knowing that Aeetes would gather up the dismembered pieces of his son's body to give them a ceremonial burial. Thus the Argonauts escaped with the Golden Fleece, and returned it to Iolcus.

**JUNO** (IUNO) *Roman*  An old goddess among the Roman people who became one of the principal deities of ancient ROME. In her earliest traditions, Juno was a goddess of the Moon and seen as the queen of the heavens. She was very important to women and protected them during childbirth. Married and unmarried women celebrated her great festival, the Matronalia, on March 1. Juno developed great status in Roman society and, with JUPITER and MINERVA, became part of the supreme trio of the state religions. (Juno and Minerva replaced MARS and QUIRINUS, who were part of an older supreme trio with Jupiter.) In 509 B.C., the people of Rome dedicated a great temple to Jupiter, Juno, and Minerva on the Capitoline Hill. As the empire grew, people built temples to them throughout the conquered territories.

Juno developed great cult status in Rome. Her name is joined with a variety of titles that show her special functions in society. Juno Lucina was the bringer of light. Juno Moneta was the goddess of helpful counsel to whom the Romans dedicated a mint; the word *money* comes from this name for Juno. Rome's leaders turned to her to support their wars and to help them on diplomatic missions. Juno accompanied colonists as they moved into new lands behind the Roman armies.

The month of June is named after Juno.

**JUPITER** (IUPITER; JOVE) (Jove) *Roman*  The supreme god of the Roman PANTHEON; son of SATURN and OPS; husband of JUNO. Jupiter was an ancient sky god of LATIUM, in central Italy, before the rise of Roman power. He was master of thunder, lightning, rain, and light, and also the giver of victory and peace. Jupiter was the special protector of ROME. Eventually, he became the supreme god of the Romans.

Jupiter was the principal god of the two divine trios worshiped by the Romans. The older trio, Jupiter, MARS, and QUIRINUS, were worshiped in the early years of Rome as a regional power. As Rome grew to a republic and a great military power in the Mediterranean, the religion changed and people worshiped Jupiter as the most powerful member of the supreme trio that included Juno and MINERVA.

Romans built great temples to Jupiter on the Capitoline Hill.

Jupiter is also the name of the largest planet in our SOLAR SYSTEM.

**JUSTITIA** (IUSTITIA; Justice) *Roman*  The goddess of justice; some say a mere personification of the legal concept of fairness. Justitia was often portrayed as blindfolded so that she was not swayed by what she saw, and carrying scales in her hands to weigh each side of a disagreement.

Some sources say that the Roman emperor Augustus introduced a cult to Justitia in ROME in 13 B.C., at the same time that he introduced the goddesses SALUS (Public Welfare), CONCORDIA (Harmony), and PAX (Peace), to inspire in his people the traits he wanted society to have. Other sources say that Justitia, like the Greek goddess ASTRAEA, was the last of the great gods to dwell among humans, but when their conflicts became too fierce and her influence too weak, Justitia fled to the heavens where she became the constellation VIRGO.

**JUTURNA** (IUTURNA) *Roman*  An ancient goddess of springs and fountains. In her earliest forms, Juturna was worshiped most notably on the banks of the river Numicius, which flowed near the city of Lavinium, founded by the Trojan hero AENEAS after he settled in Italy. She also provided protection against fire.

According to some legends, Juturna was the sister of TURNUS, king of the RUTULI people, and fought with her brother against Aeneas for the love of LAVINIA. In her own story, Juturna became the love interest of JUPITER, supreme Roman god, who granted her immortality and reign over small bodies of water.

Some early historians say Juturna was the wife of JANUS, one of the oldest Roman gods, and by him the mother of FONS, the Roman god of springs. Juturna's cult moved to Rome as the city became an urban center. A famous spring dedicated to her flowed in the Roman Forum near the temples to VESTA and the divine twins, CASTOR AND POLLUX.

**JUVENTAS** (JUVENTUS, IUVENTUS) *Roman*  The goddess of youth, especially of youths who had reached the age of wearing adult clothing, which usually began at age 14. Juventas also protected young men who had reached the age of preparing for active military duty, which was typically 17. Juventas appears to be a very old deity in Rome's religions, for hers is one of the oldest temples built on the Capitoline Hill, a center for religious activities in the oldest part of the city.

In this portion of a huge mural painted by Luca Giordano (1634-1795) in the Palazzo Medici Riccardi in Florence, Italy, the Roman goddess Justitia (with scales) reaches toward the heavens.

**KER** (plural: KERES) *Greek* Female spirits that represented a person's death or perhaps destiny. Each person had one ker as a companion through life. The keres were portrayed as black, winged beings with long, pointed tails. According to stories, they tore at dead bodies to drink the blood. HOMER, the great Greek poet credited with writing the *ILIAD*, indicated that the keres accompanied heroes and determined not only their deaths but the ways in which their lives would unfold. According to HESIOD, a Greek poet who wrote in the 800s B.C., the keres were the daughters of NYX (Night) and the sisters of THANATOS (Death) and the Fates.

**LABYRINTH** *Greek* The word *labyrinth* means any intricate building full of chambers and passages, or a maze of paths bordered by high hedges. In Greek mythology, the labyrinth designed by DAEDALUS for King MINOS to house the MINOTAUR may have been patterned on the design of the palace itself, which had a complex of rooms.

**LACONIA** *Greek* A region in the southeast PELOPONNESUS whose capital was SPARTA. In Greek mythology, HELEN, wife of MENELAUS and legendary cause of the TROJAN WAR, was sometimes said to have been an ancient goddess of fertility in Laconia. She was worshiped there as a goddess of beauty.

**LADON** *Greek* The dragon who guarded the garden where the apples of the HESPERIDES were kept. In this garden, on Mount ATLAS, there was a tree that bore golden fruit. The tree was a present from GAIA to HERA on her marriage to ZEUS. No mortals knew the whereabouts of this sacred tree. It was the last task of the hero HERACLES to find and collect some of the apples. This Heracles did with the help of Atlas, a TITAN. Heracles then killed the dragon, incurring the wrath of Hera.

**LAELAPS** (LELAPS, LALAPS) *Greek* A hound that could catch whatever he chased. The god ZEUS gave the dog to the NYMPH Procris, who then gave him to her husband, CEPHALUS, the hunter. Cephalus inadvertently killed Procris. Laelaps lay forlorn at the feet of the slain nymph. Laelaps was later sent out to hunt the Teumessian fox, which had been destined by the goddess HERA never to be caught. To end the seemingly impossible, unsolvable chase, Zeus turned both animals to stone.

**LAERTES** *Greek* King of Ithaca husband of ANTICLEA, father of the hero ODYSSEUS. Laertes was one of the ARGONAUTS, the gallant crew who helped JASON find the GOLDEN FLEECE. He was also present at the CALYDONIAN BOAR HUNT. Laertes was still alive when his son, Odysseus, returned from the TROJAN WAR.

**LAESTRYGONIANS** *Greek* A race of giant cannibals who devoured many of the crewmen of the ships of ODYSSEUS when the hero anchored near their island. Only Odysseus's own ship escaped this terrible fate, since Odysseus had the foresight to anchor his vessel outside the harbor. In Book 10 of the *ODYSSEY*, HOMER describes how the giants threw rocks on the ships from the top of the cliffs and then harpooned the screaming men as if they were fish, and carried them off to be eaten.

**LAOCOÖN** *Greek* A priest of APOLLO and POSEIDON; son of PRIAM, king of TROY, and of HECUBA. Laocoön made Apollo angry by marrying and begetting children, breaking his priestly vow of celibacy. The Trojans had chosen Laocoön to make sacrifices to Poseidon, whose priest they had murdered nine years earlier. Before he went to the altar with his two sons, Laocoön warned Priam to beware of the Trojan horse. (See *The Wooden Horse of Troy*, under TROJAN WAR.) Laocoön said that he feared the Greeks, especially when they brought gifts. From this, "a Greek gift" has come to mean a treacherous gift. As Laocoön and his twin sons, Antiphas and Thymbreus, stood at the altar of Poseidon, two gigantic serpents, sent by a vengeful Apollo, coiled about them and crushed them to death.

A famous statue of Laocoön and the serpents was discovered in Rome in 1506. It is believed to date from the second century B.C., and now stands in the Vatican Museum.

The story of Laocoön is told in VIRGIL's *AENEID*.

The Trojan hero Laocoön (center) and his two sons struggle against the giant serpents sent by the Greeks in this Roman marble sculpture, a copy of a Greek original from the second century B.C. *(Photograph by Jean-Christophe Benoist. Used under a Creative Commons license.)*

**LAOMEDON** *Greek*  First king of TROY; father of PRIAM, HESIONE, and others. He was slain by the hero HERACLES.

The gods APOLLO and POSEIDON had displeased ZEUS. As punishment, he sent them to work for Laomedon for wages. Poseidon built the walls of Troy, while Apollo tended the king's flocks on Mount IDA (2). After the two gods had completed their tasks, Laomedon refused to pay them. In revenge, the gods sent a sea monster to ravage Troy. Only the sacrifice of a maiden would appease the monster. One of the maidens chosen was Hesione, the daughter of the king, but Heracles rescued her. Again Laomedon refused to pay his debt, and Heracles killed him.

**LAPITHS** (plural: LAPITHAE) *Greek*  Mythical people of THESSALY, in north-central GREECE. Their king, IXION, fathered with NEPHELE (a cloud that ZEUS had formed in the likeness of HERA) the half-human, half-horse creatures called CENTAURS. PIRITHOÜS, half-brother of the Centaurs, became the ruler of the Lapiths.

**LAR** (plural: LARES) *Roman*  Ancient Roman spirits of the dead. A guardian spirit who in its earliest form seems to have watched over the places where roads met. Over time, the Lares became associated with the home and each household had its own Lar Familiaris. A home featured a shrine to its Lar, which stood near the hearth, the center of family life, and included a statue of this spirit. Families trusted their Lares to provide for their posterity. Eventually, cities, too, had their own watchful spirits.

The Lares are closely related to the PENATES, spirits of the storeroom, and the goddess VESTA, the Roman goddess of the hearth. AENEAS, the Trojan hero who settled in Italy, was sometimes known as Lars Aeneas, a title that meant honored ancestor.

**LARA** (LALA; LARUNDA; The talker) *Roman* Originally, a SABINE goddess who presided over houses. Later a NYMPH, a daughter of the river Tiber or the river Almo, known for her inability to keep a secret. Little information remains about the Sabine goddess, but her story as a nymph lives on in the works of Roman poets.

Lara suffered a price for her chatter. When JUPITER, who was married to JUNO, wanted the help of the nymphs to seduce the goddess JUTERNA, he swore them all to silence then told them of their roles in his plans to capture Juterna, who kept avoiding him. Since childhood, Lara had been unable to keep a secret, so she spread word of the great god's plans. She told Juno and Juterna. Some sources say that telling both the wife and the love interest was a sign of Lara's great disapproval of Jupiter's actions. Others say she was essentially a gossip.

Jupiter avenged himself against Lara by pulling out her tongue and sentencing her to life in the silence of the UNDERWORLD. He charged his son MERCURY with delivering the nymph, but Mercury fell in love with her on the way and made love to her—some sources say he raped her—and hid her in a grove of trees where she bore him twin sons.

**LATINUS** *Roman* A legendary, perhaps historical, king of the Latini or Latins, an original people of central Italy, and the hero from whom that people got their name.

Several traditions surround Latinus and the role he played in the history of ROME. In one tradition, he was the son of the god FAUNUS and the NYMPH Marica. In another, he was the grandson of HERCULES. Over the centuries, as the influence of Greek mythology over Roman religion grew, the story of Latinus changed and he was seen as the son of the Greek goddess CIRCE and the hero ODYSSEUS. Scholars believe that Latinus was an actual person, but most of his history is lost within the myths of the founding of Rome. He is prominent in the poet VIRGIL's story of the *AENEID*, which tells of the arrival of AENEAS in Italy.

According to different versions of Latinus's story, he had consulted an ORACLE and learned that his daughter, LAVINIA, would marry a foreigner. When Aeneas arrived in Italy, he fell in love with Lavinia, and Latinus and his wife, Amata, agreed to a marriage. In another version, Latinus formed an alliance with Aeneas to defend against the RUTULI people, with whom the Latins were at war. Both stories end with Aeneas going to war with and defeating TURNUS, prince of the Rutuli, who claimed Lavinia in marriage, and Aeneas winning the hand of Lavinia and naming the city of Lavinium after her.

**LATIUM** *Roman* In ancient times, a region in west-central Italy, south and east of the Tiber River on the shores of the Tyrrhenian Sea. The people of this region were known as Latins. Archaeological evidence shows that Latin communities first developed around 1200 B.C. in the Alban Hills, 12 miles southeast of the hills of modern ROME. As communities grew and shifted from herding flocks of animals to farming, they eventually spread as far north as the Tiber River, by 850 B.C. Latium's largest city was Lavinium, but by the 700s B.C., Rome became the principal city of Latium.

In ancient Roman and Greek writing, authors sometimes refer to the people who would become Latins as "Aborigines," which modern scholars understand to mean "mountain people." Scholars also agree that the Latin people came originally from east central Europe.

Because Rome is located in this ancient region, all of the myths of the founding of this great city tell either of the founding of Latium or of the conquest of the Latin people by newcomers. Early myths say that it was in Latium that SATURN hid after his son JUPITER attacked him in the Roman version of the Greek story about the overthrow of the TITANS by the OLYMPIAN GODS. Here Saturn established a society and reigned over a Golden Age of the people.

Here, too, ROMULUS AND REMUS found land suitable for establishing their own kingdom and on the great seven hills on the east banks of the Tiber, 18 miles north of Lavinium, they founded Rome. Romulus, after killing Remus and declaring himself king, made war on the people of Latium to find wives and to grow his kingdom.

Greek colonists who had settled on the Italian peninsula as early as 1000 B.C. also developed stories of the founding of Rome and the role the Latins played in the development of the early city. Their stories were centered on Greek myth. The first of the Greeks to build a community on what would become Rome was the hero EVANDER, who fled Greece and settled with his mother on the Palatine Hill. Sixty years later, the TROJAN WAR hero AENEAS arrived in Italy. With the help of LATINUS, king of Latium, Aeneas defeated the nearby RUTULI people and established the neighboring city of Lavinium, which he named after his wife, LAVINIA, daughter of Latinus. Thus Evander and Aeneas united the Latin people as one great community over which Rome ruled.

**LAVERNA** *Roman*   A goddess of the UNDERWORLD of ancient Italian origins. Laverna was known as a goddess to whom thieves, cheats, imposters, and frauds would pray when they were trying to hide. They would ask Laverna to make them look innocent and law abiding. Near a temple to Laverna on the Aventine Hill grew a grove of trees in which thieves would hide and ask for her help. She became known through Roman poets as the goddess of trickery.

**LAVINIA** *Roman*   The daughter of LATINUS and Amata. She had been betrothed to her relative TURNUS, but Latinus gave her instead to the hero AENEAS, who founded a city and named it Lavinium in her honor. Her story is told in VIRGIL's *AENEID*.

**LEDA** *Greek*   The daughter of King Thestius of AETOLIA; wife of Tyndareus, king of SPARTA. She was the mother of the twin brothers Castor and Polydeuces (Pollux in Latin; see CASTOR AND POLLUX), known by the joint name of the DIOSCURI; and of HELEN and CLYTEMNESTRA. According to one myth, Leda mated with the god ZEUS, who had disguised himself as a swan. Leda then laid an egg from which Helen and Polydeuces emerged. Castor and Clytemnestra arrived by normal delivery and were said to be the children of Tyndareus.

**LEMURES** *Roman*   Ghosts of the dead, malignant or mischievous spirits who returned to Earth to terrify the living. People rid themselves of these spirits during the Lemuria, a feast held on three nights in May with odd numbers, the 9th, 11th and 13th. Families went through an extraordinary ritual at the Lemuria: Every father rose from his bed at midnight, snapped his fingers to scare away the spirits, then washed his hands three times. Next he filled his mouth with black beans, then tossed the beans behind him, chanting words of atonement. He repeated this performance nine times. Finally he washed his hands again, struck a gong and bade the evil spirits to depart. After that he could safely go back to bed.

See also MANES.

**LETHE** (Forgetfulness, Oblivion) *Greek*   One of the rivers of HADES. The souls of the dead were obliged to drink the waters of Lethe so that they could forget everything they had said or done when they were alive. Lethe is sometimes associated with DIONYSUS, god of the wine that encourages forgetfulness.

**LETO** *Greek*   A TITAN; daughter of COEUS and PHOEBE; mother, by ZEUS, of the twin deities, ARTEMIS and APOLLO. The Romans called her Latona.

According to HESIOD, Leto was noted for her gentleness. HERA, the jealous wife of Zeus, relentlessly pursued Leto, who wandered from place to place, finally resting at DELOS, where she gave birth to the divine twins. It is said that Artemis was born first and immediately became mature enough to help her mother with the birth of Apollo. At one time, Delos was a floating island in the Aegean Sea. In recognition of its being a haven for Leto and the children, Zeus made the island immovable and decreed that no one should be born or die there.

**LIBER** (Free) *Roman*   An ancient god of fertility and procreation, particularly of seeds and plants. Liber was the husband or perhaps brother of LIBERA, an ancient fertility goddess, and closely connected with her to CERES, the Roman goddess of plants and grains.

Romans prayed to Liber and Libera to bring them many children and good crops. They celebrated a festival in Liber's honor, the Liberalia, on March 17.

By the first century B.C., Liber was closely identified with the Greek god DIONYSUS at which point he became a protector of grapevines. Then vintners prayed to him for good wine.

**LIBERA** *Roman*   An ancient goddess of fertility, especially of grape vines; wife or sister of LIBER.

In most surviving information, her name is tied to Liber and CERES, the goddess of grains and cereals. Together this trio signified food and drink, as well as liberty and law. Some suggest that Liber and Libera also presided over the selection of brides for young men, a symbol of their connection with fertility.

Early in Roman history, Libera was connected with the Greek goddess PERSEPHONE, who was also known as Kore.

**LIBERTAS** *Roman* The personification of liberty, considered by some a goddess who protected the freedom and liberty of Roman citizens, even from despots and dictators, and who granted liberty to freed slaves.

A temple in honor of Libertas, built in the third century B.C., stood on the Aventine Hill. Her profile, with the goddess wearing a cap that signified this freedom, was commonly featured on Roman coins during the Roman Empire to commemorate conquests by the Roman army and by the Roman emperors.

**LIBITINA** *Roman* Ancient goddess who presided over funerals. Her name is often synonymous with death. Originally she was an Earth goddess or agricultural deity.

Undertakers in ancient Rome were called *libitinarii*. They had their places of work within Libitina's temple. Here deaths were registered and the bereaved paid money to honor the goddess.

Libitina was sometimes identified with the Greek goddess PERSEPHONE.

**LIBYA (1)** *Greek* Mother, with sea god POSEIDON, of AGENOR, king of Tyre.

See also EUROPA.

**LIBYA (2)** The Greek name for North Africa, excluding Egypt and ETHIOPIA. In HOMER's *ODYSSEY*, ODYSSEUS and his crew make landfall in Libya in the land of the LOTUS-EATERS. In VIRGIL's *AENEID*, AENEAS and his crew reach the coast of Libya, where Aeneas is visited by his mother, the goddess VENUS.

**LITYERSES** *Greek* Son of King MIDAS of PHRYGIA. Lityerses prided himself on his skill in the harvest. He challenged all to compete with him and was brutal to those who lost in the contest. In some legends, the hero HERACLES defeated Lityerses, cut off his head with a sickle, and threw his body into the Meander River.

**LIVY** (59 B.C.–A.D. 17) *Roman* A Roman historian born as Titus Livius, in Padua, Italy. Livy is best remembered for his 142 books on the history of ROME. Livy was most concerned with showing Rome's destiny as the greatest power in the Mediterranean world. Modern scholars point out Livy's reliance on legend to tell the earliest histories and the inaccuracies in his works. However, Livy's histories, of which only 36 complete volumes have survived, were highly regarded during his time and by medieval European scholars.

**LOTUS-EATERS** (LOTOPHAGI) *Greek* In HOMER's *ODYSSEY*, people who lived on the fruit or the roots of the lotus plant. The food made them forget their pasts, their families, and their futures, so that they lived in a state of dreamy bliss. ODYSSEUS and his crew made landfall in the land of the Lotus-Eaters on their way home to Ithaca. Several of the crew became addicted to the food of the lotus plant. They had to be dragged back to the ship by force.

"Lotus Land" was probably LIBYA (2), in North Africa.

**LUA** (LUA MATER) *Roman* An old goddess who was called upon in war to destroy the enemy's weapons. At the end of a victorious battle, early Roman soldiers gathered the swords and shields of the enemy in a pile and dedicated those spoils to Lua.

She also had the task of protecting the city of ROME, but people were not allowed to speak Lua's name, and she is known as the "ineffable" or unnamable patron goddess of that city and kingdom. One of Lua's responsibilities was to protect people from plagues and to bring to enemies illnesses that might destroy them.

Lua was sometimes known as the wife of SATURN, the ruler of a golden age said to have existed long before the beginning of Rome. In that role, she was known as Lua Saturni.

**LUCINA** *Roman* An ancient Italian goddess of light and childbirth. Poets tell of Lucina presiding over the birth of animals and plants as well as humans. Women called upon her while struggling through labor pains.

The stories of EILEITHYA, the Greek goddess of childbirth, were attributed to Lucina. Her traits and responsibilities in Roman religion were eventually blended into the goddess JUNO, who was also associated with light and childbirth.

**LUNA** (Moon) *Roman* An ancient Italian goddess of the Moon, probably of a lesser rank than the great Roman goddesses, such as MINERVA and JUNO. Very early in Roman religion, Luna took on the stories and myths of the ancient Greek moon goddess, SELENE, and even some of the mythology of the Roman goddess DIANA, the huntress. A temple to Luna stood on the Aventine Hill in ROME.

**LYDIA** *Greek* A wealthy kingdom of western ASIA MINOR (now northwestern Turkey). In Greek mythology, Lydia was the home of ARACHNE, the skillful weaver who rashly pitted her talents against those of the goddess ATHENE.

**MAENADS** *Greek* The crazed women who followed the god DIONYSUS. (See also BACCHANTS, which was their Latin name.)

**MAGNA GRAECIA** (Great Greece) *Greek* The collective name given to Greek colonies founded by settlers in southern Italy and the island of Sicily. The cult of the Greek hero HERACLES, and of other personages in Greek mythology, found their way into Roman mythology through the Greek colonists of Magna Graecia. This influence of Greek culture on other cultures is called HELLENIZATION.

**MAIA (1)** *Greek* Daughter of ATLAS and PLEIONE, the eldest and most beautiful of the PLEIADES (the Seven Sisters). Maia was the mother of HERMES, whose father was ZEUS. She bore Hermes in a grotto on Mount Cyllene in ARCADIA. Maia's only appearance in Greek mythological writings is in the works of HESIOD.

**MAIA (2)** (MAIESTA) *Roman* A very early and now little-known Roman goddess of agriculture and fertility. People made sacrifices to her to ensure the fertility of their crops. Maia was a supporter of and perhaps assistant to VULCAN, the Roman god of fire.

**MANES** (Good Ones) *Roman* The spirits of the dead. They were greatly feared and were called "Good Ones" to placate their anger. (Similarly, the Greek FURIES were called the EUMENIDES, "good ones" or "good-tempered ones.")

Whenever a town was founded, people first dug a pit at the site and then covered the pit with a stone. The hole represented a gateway to the UNDERWORLD (2) through which the Manes could pass when the citizens removed the stone, which they did three times a year.

**MARS** *Roman* The god of war who, in his earliest forms, was a god of agriculture and prosperity. Mars was the second most powerful god in early Roman mythology, after JUPITER. With Jupiter and the god QUIRINUS, Mars shared a position of prominence in the religious lives of the people of ROME. While Mars remained a prominent god, he and Quirinus were replaced as part of the supreme trio by JUNO and MINERVA.

Mars has old origins. Some suggest he was an agricultural god of the SABINE people. As a god who watched over their food supply, Mars was seen as the primary protector of their society. Mars was also known as the father of ROMULUS AND REMUS, the twin brothers, who according to some legends, founded the city of Rome. He was referred to as "Father Mars" and Romans believed themselves to be his descendants.

As Rome expanded from a city into an empire through military power, Mars evolved into the god who protected the nation by protecting its army. In that way, he became the god of war. When Roman armies conquered peoples and lands across Europe and the Mediterranean, the soldiers and colonists who followed them built temples to Mars to thank him for their success. They built most of their temples outside of cities, where Mars could watch over the land.

In time, Mars became associated with ARES, the Greek god of war, and took on some of his attributes. Unlike many other Roman gods, however, Mars retained most of his ancient reputation and mythology despite the influence of Greek culture.

The month of March, the first in the Roman calendar, received its name from Mars, for that was the beginning of the growing season and the beginning of the season to wage war. He was often portrayed carrying a shield and spears or lances. The oak and fig trees and the woodpecker were sacred to Mars.

In astronomy, Mars is the fourth planet from the Sun in the SOLAR SYSTEM. It was well known to the ancient Romans as the star that shone red in the sky. Its color, the color of blood, strengthened the connection between Mars and war.

**MEDEA** *Greek* A sorceress; daughter of King Aeetes of Colchis (Asia Minor); niece of Circe, the witch of the *Odyssey*. In his quest for the Golden Fleece, Jason fell in love with Medea, who helped him capture the precious fleece.

As Jason and Medea fled with the prize, they were pursued by Aeetes, the father of Medea and her brother, Absyrtus. In one version of the story, Medea killed her brother and threw pieces of him behind them on the road, knowing that Aeetes would stop to pick up his dismembered son. Thus she and Jason escaped from the angry king.

Medea returned to Iolcus (Thessaly) with Jason. Her first deed was to destroy Pelias, the king who had taken over the throne of Iolcus from Jason's father. Medea suggested to the daughters of Pelias that, if they killed him, cut him up into small pieces, and cooked him in a stew, he would then be rejuvenated. She demonstrated her idea by cutting and cooking a ram and, by the use of magic, making a lamb spring forth from the pot. The daughters did as she suggested but, of course, Pelias did not survive. The people were so horrified at this deed that Jason and Medea had to flee the country.

Jason and Medea settled for a while in Corinth. Jason deserted Medea for Glauca, daughter of the Corinthian king Creon. Medea killed Glauca by sending her a wedding dress saturated with poison. Medea also killed the two sons she had borne with Jason, then fled to the court of King Aegeus of Athens.

When the hero Theseus arrived at his father's court, Medea tried to murder him with a goblet of poisoned wine. Just in time, Aegeus recognized his son and dashed the cup from his hands.

Medea fled from Athens and there is no record of where she went next. Some legends say that her son, Medus, was the ancestor of the Medes, an ancient people of Asia Minor.

The poet Euripides wrote a famous tragedy about Medea, first produced in 431 b.c. Medea has been the subject of numerous plays and operas.

**MEDUSA** *Greek* One of the three Gorgons, the only one who was not immortal; her sisters were Stheno and Euryale. Medusa was once a beautiful maiden, wooed by the sea god, Poseidon, in a temple of Athene. The goddess was angry at the violation of her shrine and turned Medusa into a monster so hideous that anyone who looked upon her was turned to stone. Perseus cut off Medusa's head and used it to turn his enemies into stone. From the

Italian artist Gian Lorenzo Bernini (1598-1680) created this bust of the witch Medusa and the snakes that form her hair. It is in the Musei Capitolini in Rome. *(Photograph by Marie-Lan Nguyen.)*

blood of Medusa sprang the children of her union with Poseidon: Pegasus, the winged horse, and Chrysaor, father of the monster Geryon (see *The Twelve Labors of Heracles*, 10. The Cattle of Geryon, under Heracles).

**MEGARA (1)** *Greek* A Greek city-state on the Greek mainland, between Attica and Corinth.

**MEGARA (2)** *Greek* Daughter of King Creon of Thebes; first wife of the hero Heracles.

**MELAMPUS** *Greek* A descendant of Aeolis and a cousin of Jason. Melampus was a seer, taught by the god Apollo, and perhaps the first mortal in Greek mythology to possess prophetic powers.

One story has it that Melampus saved the lives of a nest of young snakes. In gratitude they "cleaned out his ears" with their forked tongues so that he could hear and understand the languages of birds and other animals. Melampus used this special knowledge to win a bride for his brother, Bias. The desired maiden was Pero, daughter of King Neleus of Pylos, in the kingdom of Messene on the west-central coast of the PELOPONNESUS. Neleus asked as bride-price, or dowry, the cattle of a neighboring king, Phylacus. The cattle were guarded by a dog that never slept. Melampus was caught trying to steal them and thrown into a prison cell. During the night, he heard worms gnawing at a beam and saying that the beam would fall by dawn. Melampus demanded a new cell. When the roof of his old cell crashed down, Phylacus was so impressed that he released Melampus.

Phylacus then begged Melampus to cure the sickness of his son, Iphiclus, with his magic powers. Melampus heard two birds talking to each other about a knife that had been stuck into an oak tree for many years. By finding the knife and scraping its rust onto Iphiclus, Melampus cured the boy's affliction. As a reward, Melampus was given the cattle and his brother Bias got the bride.

In ARGOS, another kingdom of the Peloponnesus, Melampus helped rid the king's daughters of madness by immersing them in a holy well. As a reward, he won part of the kingdom of King Proetus and took one of the now sane daughters as his bride.

**MELANION** *Greek* A prince of ARCADIA who won the hand of the renowned virgin huntress ATALANTA. Atalanta did not want to get married, but she could not disobey the command of her father, Iasus, king of Arcadia, in the central PELOPONNESUS. A great athlete, Atalanta put a condition on her acceptance of a suitor: he must beat her in a footrace, or die. Many died before Melanion sought the help of APHRODITE, goddess of love. She gave him three golden apples. These he dropped, one at a time, throughout the race. Atalanta could not resist stopping to pick up the beautiful apples, and so she lost the race and married Melanion. The two had a son, Parthenopaeus. In some versions, it is said that Aphrodite turned the couple into lions who were forced to pull the chariot of CYBELE, a goddess of Earth and nature.

**MELEAGER** *Greek* Son of King OENEUS of CALY-DON, and of Althea. A great javelin thrower, Meleager is most famous for killing the Calydonian Boar (see under CALYDONIAN BOAR HUNT).

A few days after his birth, the three FATES appeared before Althea. They told her that the child would die when a certain log in the fireplace burned. Althea at once snatched the wood from the fire, quenched its flame, and hid it away.

When Meleager was a young man, he was sent to kill the Calydonian Boar that was ravaging the countryside. Heroes and princes came from all parts of GREECE to hunt the boar. Among them was one woman, ATALANTA, the great huntress. She scored the first thrust at the boar. Meleager dealt the death blow and awarded the coveted pelt and tusks to Atalanta, with whom he had fallen in love. The other men were jealous and angry, and fighting ensued, during which Meleager killed both his uncles, brothers of Althea.

When Althea saw the corpses of her brothers and learned that Meleager had killed them, she retrieved the wood from its hiding place and angrily cast it into the fire. Meleager died soon thereafter.

**MENELAUS** *Greek* King of SPARTA; brother of AGAMEMNON; husband of HELEN. The Trojan prince PARIS stole the beautiful Helen from Menelaus. This act was a leading cause of the TROJAN WAR. In some accounts, Menelaus and Helen were happily reunited after the fall of TROY.

**MENOETIUS** *Greek* A second-generation TITAN; son of IAPETUS and CLYMENE, who was a daughter of OCEANUS; brother of ATLAS, PROMETHEUS, and EPIMETHEUS.

Menoetius was said to be the god of anger and harshness and was himself said to be brutal and arrogant. During the battle between the Titans and the OLYMPIAN GODS, ZEUS hurled a lightning bolt at Menoetius. Some sources say he was killed, others that he was just stricken and then sent with most of the other Titans into TARTARUS, the deepest pit in the UNDERWORLD.

**MEPHITIS** (MEFITIS) *Roman* A goddess who protected the people of ROME and surrounding cities in Italy from the dangerous fumes of sulphur that spewed from the many volcanoes and the gaseous vents surrounding them. People believed that these fumes caused illness and plagues, as well as damage to their homes and cities, and called upon Mephitis to protect them from these evils. She became more commonly known as the goddess of plagues. A temple in her honor stood on the Esquiline Hill in Rome.

Volcanic eruptions were, and still are, a prominent threat to the people of Italy. Mount Vesuvius, which overlooks the Bay of Naples, erupted in a famous explosion in A.D. 79, destroying Pompeii and

Herculaneum. It had been more mildly active for hundreds of years before then, frequently spewing sulfur and other gases into the atmosphere. Mount Etna (Aetna), on the island of Sicily off the tip of the Italian peninsula, was very active during the classical era of Rome. Mount Stromboli, on an island north of Sicily, has been active for more than 2,000 years, spewing forth gases in frequent explosions.

**MERCURY** (MERCURIUS) *Roman*   The god of trade and commerce and the supporter of success. Evidence of a cult to Mercury in ROME goes back to the sixth century B.C., and there is some evidence that he was a figure in early Etruscan mythology. According to Italian myth, Mercury was the father of FAUNUS, one of the oldest Roman gods. However, Mercury was one of the earliest Roman gods to come under the influence of Greek mythology (see

The god Hermes—Mercury in Roman myths—gives an apple to the Greek hero Paris, the gift that eventually led to the Trojan war. The painting is by Italian artist Donato Creti (1671-1749).

HELLENIZATION) and very little information on him survives from before the 400s B.C.

As Rome grew and became prosperous, the people needed a god for the merchants and business class in their growing society. They knew of the Greeks' HERMES, who, with many other responsibilities, was the god of trade and commerce, of travelers, and of the marketplace. The Romans gave Mercury these traits and adapted for him many of the stories about Hermes. Mercury, however, was given no responsibility over fertility.

Mercury was the god of travelers by land and sea and of good luck, music, astronomy, weights and measures, and trade. He was also the god of thieving. Merchants honored Mercury more than any other Romans did and celebrated a festival to him at his temple on the Aventine Hill. The word *Mercury* comes from the Latin word for "merchandise."

Mercury, as he took on the details of the stories of the Greek Hermes, became known as the son of MAIA (1) and JUPITER, whom he served as a messenger. He was also known as the father of EVANDER, an early king in central Italy, and of the Lares, who were lesser gods of crossroads. (See LAR.) Artists portrayed Mercury wearing a broad-brimmed hat and winged sandals and carrying a purse, the symbol of profit.

In astronomy, Mercury is the closest planet to the Sun in the SOLAR SYSTEM. Visible to the ancients as a rapidly moving star, it received its name for the speed with which it traveled around the Sun.

**MEROPE** *Greek*   Daughter of ATLAS and PLEIONE; wife of SISYPHUS; one of the "Seven Sisters" called the PLEIADES. Merope was sometimes named "the lost star," the one invisible to the naked eye. It is said that she hid her light in shame for having married a mortal, and a disreputable one at that.

**METIS** (Wisdom) *Greek*   A TITAN, daughter of OCEANUS and TETHYS, an OCEANID, or ocean NYMPH, who was counted among the Titans. According to HESIOD, Metis was the first wife of the god ZEUS. She was the wisest of all among both mortals and gods. It was Metis who advised Zeus to give his father, CRONUS, a drink that would make him cough up the siblings of Zeus that Cronus had swallowed.

When Metis became pregnant by Zeus, URANUS and GAIA advised Zeus to swallow Metis, lest her offspring overthrow him. This Zeus did, thus uniting his power with her wisdom. In due time his daughter ATHENE was born from his head, fully grown and clad in armor.

**MIDAS** *Greek* A mythical king of PHRYGIA, an ancient region of central ASIA MINOR; son of the goddess CYBELE and Gordius, from whom he inherited the throne. In Greek mythology, there are two well-known stories about Midas: one in which everything he touches turns to gold and another in which an angry god gives King Midas donkey's ears.

**Midas and the Golden Touch** Midas, king of Phrygia, was a devotee of the god DIONYSUS. The followers of Dionysus were well known for their wild behavior. One of them, an old man called SILENUS, could not keep up with the revelers. Some peasants captured him, tied him up with garlanded ropes, and presented him to their king. Midas knew at once that Silenus was a follower of Dionysus and treated him with respect. When Midas returned Silenus to Dionysus, the grateful god offered Midas any gift he wished.

Midas asked that everything he touched should turn to gold. Dionysus granted the wish and Midas became very rich. However, he almost died of hunger, for who can eat gold? He begged to have his gift taken away. Dionysus answered his desperate prayer, bidding the king to bathe in the river Pactolus, in LYDIA, ASIA MINOR. This Midas did. He lost the "golden touch" in the river, where legends say that gold was found in historical times.

**Midas and the Donkey's Ears** Midas lost his taste for riches and luxury after his unfortunate experience with "the golden touch," in which everything he touched, including food, turned to gold. Now Midas preferred the simple life, spending more time in the woods and fields, listening to the pipes of PAN, an ancient deity. One day, Pan boasted that he could make better music than the god APOLLO, great OLYMPIAN GOD of music. The mountain trembled and Apollo appeared. After Pan had played on his pipes, Apollo played the lyre. The assembled NYMPHS and mountain spirits declared Apollo the winner, but King Midas declared for Pan. Apollo promptly conferred on Midas a pair of donkey ears as punishment.

Midas covered his embarrassing ears with a turban of royal Phrygian purple. Only his barber knew his secret. The barber whispered the secret into a hole in the Earth. This spot of Earth immediately became covered with reeds that are said to whisper the secret whenever the wind blows.

**MINERVA** *Roman* A Goddess of Etruscan or perhaps SABINE origins. Over time, the Romans elevated Minerva to a high-ranking position and she joined with JUPITER and JUNO to form the main triad of Roman worship, replacing an earlier triad of Jupiter, MARS, and QUIRINUS.

In her earliest form, Minerva was a goddess of education and business worshiped by the Etruscans and neighboring peoples of central Italy. She then developed into a goddess of war, battle, death, and sexuality. NUMA POMPILLIUS, the second king of ROME, who ruled from 715 to 673 B.C., introduced the worship of Minerva to the citizens of that city-state. Artisans and well-educated people paid special honor to Minerva.

In about 509 B.C., the Romans built a majestic temple on the Capitoline Hill to honor Jupiter, Juno, and Minerva. The chamber to Jupiter, the supreme god, stood in the middle, with smaller chambers to the two goddesses on either side. As the Roman Empire grew in the first and second centuries B.C., people built temples to Minerva across the conquered lands.

Minerva lost many of her warlike, savage attributes as Greek influence on Roman culture increased (see HELLENIZATION), and she became the goddess of domestic skills, industry, culture, and arts and sciences. Though her name was used in place of ATHENE in the Greek stories of that goddess, some scholars believe Minerva was a much more warlike goddess than her Greek counterpart.

Minerva wore a helmet and held an owl, her sacred animal, in most images of her, including statues and coins. Romans celebrated her during the Quinquatria festival on March 19.

**MINOS** *Greek* Son of ZEUS and EUROPA. When Europa arrived in CRETE, she married the King ASTERION, who adopted her children, including Minos, RHADAMANTHUS, and SARPEDON. With PASIPHAË, Minos was the father of ANDROGEUS, ARIADNE, and PHAEDRA.

Minos succeeded Asterion to the throne of Crete. He became so well known for his wisdom and sense of justice that after his death he was made a judge in the UNDERWORLD (1).

Minos was eventually drowned in a bathtub of boiling water at the court of King Cocalus of Sicily.

The adjective *minoan*, means "pertaining to Crete." The Minoan period is the Cretan Bronze Age, roughly 2500 to 1200 B.C.

**Minos and the Minotaur** Minos, king of Crete, was married to Pasiphaë. Minos incurred the wrath of the sea god, POSEIDON, by refusing to sacrifice a magnificent BULL to the gods. Poseidon took cruel revenge on Minos by making Pasiphaë fall in love with the bull, with whom she bore a strange offspring—half human, half bull. This monster was called the MINOTAUR.

American artist Elihu Vedder (1836-1923) portrayed the Greek goddess Minerva in this mosaic at the landing of one of the staircases in the Thomas Jefferson Building at the Library of Congress in Washington D.C. *(Photograph by Carol M. Highsmith, from the Library of Congress.)*

Wishing to hide the Minotaur from the eyes of the world, Minos asked the renowned inventor, DAEDALUS, to construct a prison that no one could penetrate. The ingenious Daedalus designed the LABYRINTH, a tortuous maze. Once inside the labyrinth, no one could find a way out. Only Daedalus knew how to escape.

Minos made war on ATHENS, where his son, Androgeus, was killed. The people of Athens were made to pay for this crime by sending an annual tribute of seven men and seven maids to Crete. It would fall to the hero THESEUS, with help from Minos's daughter, Ariadne, to put an end to the Minotaur and the yearly sacrifice.

Meanwhile, Daedalus made his escape from Crete, where Minos had wished to hold him prisoner. Minos pursued him and eventually found him at the court of King Cocalus of Sicily, an island in the Mediterranean off the coast of Italy. Here the great King Minos died an undignified death in a bathtub of boiling water.

**Minos and Scylla**   Scylla was the daughter of Nisus, the king of MEGARA (1) (southeastern Greek mainland). Nisus had a lock of hair that made him invulnerable and thus protected him and his city from enemies. Scylla fell in love with Minos, who was laying siege to the city. She cut off the magic lock of Nisus while he slept, thus enabling Minos to capture Megara. Minos had promised Scylla love in return for her deed but he despised her for her treachery to her father and reneged on his promise. He allowed Scylla to drown as she swam after his ship.

**MINOTAUR** *Greek*   A mythical monster, half-human, half-BULL, the offspring of PASIPHAË and a bull. Pasiphaë was the wife of King MINOS of CRETE. Minos wanted to keep the Minotaur hidden from the world. He asked DAEDALUS, the great inventor, to design a hiding place that would remain forever secret. Daedalus designed the LABYRINTH, a maze so full of tortuous passages that no one who entered could find a way out. Here the Minotaur lived, feeding on the flesh of young men and girls sent to him as sacrifices from ATHENS. At last, the hero THESEUS, with the help of ARIADNE, found his way into the center of the labyrinth, where he slew the Minotaur and emerged to tell the tale.

**MINTHE** (MENTHE) *Greek*   A NAIAD, or river NYMPH of the Cocytus, a river that flowed to the UNDERWORLD. She was beloved by HADES (or PLUTO). In jealous rage, the wife of Hades, PERSEPHONE (or perhaps her mother, DEMETER), stamped the nymph into the ground. Hades then transformed her into a fragrant herb, mint.

The legend of Minthe was probably the result of the use of herbs, especially mint, rosemary, and myrtle, to sweeten the air during funeral rites in ancient times.

**MNEMOSYNE** (Memory) *Greek*   A TITAN, daughter of GAIA and URANUS; with ZEUS, mother of the MUSES.

**MOIRAE** (MOIRAI) *Greek*   Greek spirits; personification of fate and destiny in an individual's life. Each person had his or her own Moirae. The spirits represented a law of nature, a sense of determination. No mortal human could overcome their power. Even the gods could not break the ruling of the Moirae without seriously jeopardizing all of existence. In Roman mythology, these spirits were known as the PARCAE.

Eventually, the concept of a spirit ruling over life evolved from individual fate to influence all of humanity. After the time of HOMER in the ninth century B.C., the Moirae took on personalities and were seen as three daughters of ZEUS and THEMIS who regulated birth, life, and death.

**MORIA** (Folly) *Greek*   The heroine of a story of overcoming death. Moria was a woman from LYDIA, a kingdom in ASIA MINOR. One day, as her brother, Tylus, was walking along a river bank, a snake bit him. Tylus died instantly. Moria, seeing the tragedy, called upon the powers of the giant Danasen, a son of GAIA, an ancient Greek EARTH MOTHER. The giant answered Moria's plea. He pulled up a huge tree and crushed the snake with this club. The snake's mate had been nearby and, seeing her mate dead, hurried away but quickly returned carrying an herb in her mouth. She put the herb in the dead snake's mouth, he revived immediately, and both slithered away to safety. Moria hurried to where the female snake had plucked the herb, took some herself, and put it in the mouth of her dead brother. Tylus, too, revived immediately. The herb, some experts say, was known as balis.

**MORS** (Death) *Roman*   The goddess or personification of death. Little is known about this goddess, and scholars suspect that she was more an idea than a personality. The Greek equivalent was the god THANATOS.

**MUSES** *Greek*   Originally deities of springs, later designated as goddesses of various human inspirations. In later mythologies, the Muses were the daughters of the god ZEUS and MNEMOSYNE (Memory).

The nine Greek muses decorate the sides of a sarcophagus found in excavations of an ancient site near Rome. The muses are (left to right): Calliope, Thalia, Terpsichore, Euterpe, Polyhymnia, Clio, Erato, Urania, and Melpomene. The ancient coffin is now in the Louvre in Paris. *(Photograph by Marie-Lan Nguyen.)*

The Muses sang and danced, led by the god APOLLO, at celebrations given by the gods and heroes. They were the personifications of the highest aspirations and intellectual minds and represented a remarkable and attractive conception in Greek mythology. Their separation into fields of inspiration was a Roman fancy of a later date. The word *museum* denotes a place of education and research, named after them.

The Muses and their various attributes are listed below.

CALLIOPE: Muse of epic poetry. She carried a stylus and tablet and sometimes a trumpet.

Clio: Muse of history. She carried a trumpet and scrolls.

Erato: Muse of lyric poetry, or love poetry, and hymns. She carried a lyre.

Euterpe: Muse of flute-playing.

Melpomene: Muse of tragedy. She carried the mask of tragedy.

Polyhymnia: Muse of mime. She had a pensive attitude.

Terpsichore: Muse of dance. She carried a lyre and plectrum.

Thalia: Muse of comedy. She carried the smiling mask and a shepherd's crook.

Urania: Muse of astronomy. She carried a globe and compass.

**MYCENAE** *Greek* An ancient city of GREECE situated in ARGOS, in the northern PELOPONNESUS. It was the center of the important Mycenaean civilization, which was roughly contemporary with that of the Minoan civilization of CRETE. In mythology, Mycenae was the royal city of AGAMEMNON.

**MYRMIDONS** *Greek* Warlike people of ancient THESSALY, in the eastern part of the Greek mainland, who accompanied the hero ACHILLES into battle in the TROJAN WAR. According to some legends, the Myrmidons were ants turned into people by ZEUS to increase the population of Thessaly after a plague sent by his wife, HERA, had killed thousands.

**MYRTILUS** *Greek* Son of the god HERMES and a mortal woman. He was the charioteer of King OENOMAUS of Pisa in Elis, in northeast PELOPONNESUS. When PELOPS came to compete in a chariot race with Oenomaus for the hand of the king's daughter HIPPODAMEIA, Pelops persuaded Myrtilus to fix Oenomaus's chariot so that it would overturn. Myrtilus did as Pelops asked; Pelops won the race and the hand of Hippodameia. Oenomaus was killed when his chariot overturned. Pelops then killed Myrtilus. With his dying breath Myrtilus placed a curse upon Pelops and all his descendants.

# N

**NAIADS** (NAIADES) *Greek* NYMPHS of fresh bodies of water, such as springs, wells, brooks, streams, lakes, and marshes. One of the three classifications of water nymphs. The others were the OCEANIDS, nymphs of the oceans, and the NEREIDS, nymphs of the Mediterranean Sea. The Naiads were daughters of the Greek river gods.

Each Naiad presided over her own body of water and was worshiped for her ability to help and protect people with her water. The Naiads had the power of

Naiads of all ages play among river rocks in this portrayal of the Greek water nymphs by Swiss painter Arnold Bökclin (1827-1901). He called the painting "Game of the Naiads" or "Naiads at Play" and gave his nymphs mermaids' tails. It is in Kunstmuseum in Bonn, Germany.

prophecy, to be able to see into the future. Because of this, the Naiads were said to inspire people who drank from their fountains or streams. They were also the protectors of young girls as they became women.

Naiads were very popular with both gods and humans. Many had affairs with the Olympians. Many married human kings and rulers and became mothers to the heroes of mythology.

Some of the more prominent of the thousands of Naiads were MINTHE, who was loved by HADES, god of the UNDERWORLD; STYX, loved by the TITAN PALLAS; and ARETHUSA, whom ARTEMIS turned into a fountain.

Narcissus stares at his reflection in a pool of water in this painting by Michelangelo Merisi da Caravaggio (1571-1610). The painting hangs in the Palazzo Barberini in the National Gallery of Ancient Art in Rome.

**NARCISSUS** *Greek* The son of the river god Cephissus and Liriope. He was a beautiful man. When he rejected the love of ECHO, a NYMPH, NEMESIS, the goddess of vegeance, condemned Narcissus to reject all love except that of his own image reflected in a pool. Narcissus pined away and changed into a beautiful flower that bears his name. The story of Echo and Narcissus is told by OVID in *Metamorphoses*. It belongs to later Greek mythology.

**NAUSICAA** *Greek* Daughter of ALCINOUS, king of the Phaecians. It was she who discovered ODYSSEUS when he was shipwrecked on the island of Scheria on his way back to Ithaca after the TROJAN WAR. She took him as a guest to her father's court, a place of peace and luxury. The location of Scheria and the Phaecian kingdom is unknown.

**NAXOS** *Greek* An island in the Aegean Sea southeast of GREECE. It is famous in Greek mythology as the place where THESEUS abandoned ARIADNE, daughter of King MINOS, after she helped him find his way out of the LABYRINTH. Naxos was a center for the worship of DIONYSUS.

**NECESSITAS** *Roman* A goddess of destiny or fate, of that which is necessary; or perhaps merely the personification of necessity. With the goddess FORTUNA, Necessitas ruled over or influenced the future of men and women. The two are often pictured together, with Necessitas, carrying nails and wedges, walking before Fortuna. Necessitas was equated with ANANKE, the Greek personification of absolute destiny.

**NEDA** *Greek* One of the oldest of the OCEANIDS, sea NYMPH daughters of the TITAN gods, OCEANUS and TETHYS; considered by many Greek writers to be a second-generation Titan. With help from her younger sisters, Theisoa and Hagno, Neda nursed the infant ZEUS.

According to ancient stories, the Titan goddess RHEA found no water with which to cleanse herself and her son after giving birth to her youngest child, ZEUS. In frustration, she struck her scepter against a boulder, or a mountain, and called on her mother, GAIA, to bring forth water. A spring gushed forth and Rhea named the spring Neda, after the nymph, her niece, who would soon help keep this son safe from the anger of his father, the Titan god CRONUS.

**NEMESIS** *Greek* Goddess of vengeance; personification of the wrath of the gods toward those who had *hubris*, a Greek word meaning exaggerated pride in one's achievements or good fortune. Nemesis rewarded virtue and punished wickedness. At first, Nemesis was an abstract concept. In later mythology she was personified as a daughter of NYX (Night) and EREBUS (Darkness), a powerful force.

**NEOPTOLEMUS** (Pyrrhus) *Greek* Son of ACHILLES and DEIDAMIA. Neoptolemus played no great part in HOMER's epics, except as one of the heroic Greek warriors who brought about the fall of TROY. He was hidden with the others inside the cunning wooden horse (see *The Wooden Horse of Troy*, under TROJAN WAR). However, as the son of the great hero, Achilles, Neoptolemus is mentioned in many myths. Some say that it was he who killed PRIAM, the vanquished king of Troy; others say that he won the Trojan princess, ANDROMACHE, as one of the prizes of victory. One tradition has it that he was killed at DELPHI by ORESTES. For many years there was a hero-cult dedicated to Neoptolemus at Delphi.

**NEPHELE** *Greek* Wife of ATHAMAS; mother of PHRIXUS, Leucon, and HELLE. Nephele had started her life as a cloudlike form created by the god ZEUS to trick IXION, who was making advances to Zeus's wife, HERA.

**NEPTUNE** (NEPTUNUS) *Roman* Originally, a Roman god of freshwater. Neptune became associated with the Greek sea god POSEIDON early in Roman history.

Unlike the people of GREECE, the people of ROME were not seafarers, so Neptune played only a small role in their lives. He did, however, keep many of his freshwater characteristics as he took on the stories of Poseidon, who inhabited the saltwater seas around Greece. The Romans celebrated the festival of the Neptunalia on July 23, the height of summer, when freshwater often was scarce. They would make sacrifices to Neptune in hopes of easing those water shortages.

A sanctuary to Neptune stood between the Aventine and Palatine hills in Rome on the spot where a stream once flowed.

Neptune, like Poseidon, is often portrayed carrying a trident and riding a dolphin.

The eighth planet in the SOLAR SYSTEM was named Neptune after its discovery in 1846.

**NEREIDS** *Greek* The NYMPHS of the sea, specifically the Mediterranean Sea; the daughters of NEREUS, an ancient sea god, and DORIS, a daughter of OCEANUS. The Nereids lived in their father's palace at the bottom of the sea and came up often to play in the waves. They rode dolphins and other sea creatures and gathered on shore to play games and dry their long hair. Greek legends consistently report that there were 50 of these lesser goddesses and name all of them. These sisters had the power to change their shape, and some of them could see into the future. They aided sailors in distress and were generally friendly to mortals.

The Nereids take the role of observers in many Greek legends and myths, but several of them played prominent roles. THETIS was the mother of the hero ACHILLES. AMPHITRITE was the wife of POSEIDON. GALATEA fatefully rejected the love of the sea monster POLYPHEMUS.

**NEREUS** (Old Man of the Sea) *Greek* A sea god depicted as a very old man. His special dominion was the Aegean Sea. Nereus had 50 daughters, the NEREIDS, or sea NYMPHS.

**NERIO** (NERINE; NERIENE; NERIENIS; Valor) *Roman* A traditional and legendary wife of the war god MARS. She personified valor and bravery in life and in war. Nerio's name seems to come from the SABINES,

Neptune rides four horses on the left of this grand mythological painting by French artist Nicholas Poussin (1594-1665). Art experts debate whether the woman in the middle is supposed to be Venus or Galatea. The painting is in the Philadelphia Museum of Art.

and there is disagreement among Roman historians and modern scholars of how to spell her name.

The fragments of her stories that remain suggest Nerio was a goddess connected with war and with taking prisoners and confiscating their weapons. This was the feature that survived into the Roman Empire, when the goddess took on many of the traits of MINERVA, who was a prominent goddess of war.

**NESSUS** *Greek* The CENTAUR who caused the death of the hero HERACLES. Nessus carried DEIANIRA, the wife of Heracles, across the river Evenus when the couple were escaping from CALYDON. Nessus tried to force his attentions on Deianira, and Heracles shot him with an arrow. As he was dying, the centaur told Deianira to take some of his blood and use it as a love potion if Heracles ever seemed to be straying from her. Deianira used the potion when Heracles became interested in IOLE, not knowing that the centaur's blood would poison and kill Heracles.

**NESTOR** *Greek* King of Pylos (on the west coast of Messenia, in the PELOPONNESUS) and, at 60 years old, the oldest and most experienced of the chieftains who fought in the TROJAN WAR. Nestor was greatly respected for his strength and wisdom. He was also famous for being garrulous. He was one of the few heroes of TROY who returned safely to his kingdom in GREECE. In HOMER's *ODYSSEY*, Nestor tells TELEMACHUS, son of ODYSSEUS, of some of the adventures of the Greek leaders.

**NIKE** (NICE; Victory) *Greek* The spirit of victory; a demigod or lesser goddess; daughter of the TITAN PALLAS and the water NYMPH STYX; sister of BIA (Force), CRATUS (Strength), and ZELUS (Zeal). Nike had wings and flew very quickly.

When Styx sided with ZEUS in his great battle with his father, CRONUS, and the Titans, she brought her children into service with her, though their father was a Titan. After that war, as a reward for their loyalty, Nike, Bia, Cratus, and Zelus lived with Zeus and stood beside his throne, carrying out his commands.

When Zeus granted victory to a warrior, he sent Nike to deliver the message and bestow the honor. She also awarded victory to winning athletes. Nike is often portrayed on Greek pottery holding a wreath over the victor's head.

Nike's Roman counterpart was VICTORIA. The most celebrated statue of Nike is called The Nike (or Victory) of Samothrace and is in the Louvre in Paris.

**NIOBE** *Greek* The daughter of TANTALUS; wife of AMPHION, king of THEBES. She was the mother of 12 children and the personification of maternal sorrow. She was unwise enough to boast about her numerous children and was heard by the goddess LETO, who had only two children. Those children were the formidable twins APOLLO and ARTEMIS, however, and they punished Niobe by slaying all of her children. Niobe wept herself to death and was subsequently changed into a rock, from which water eternally flowed, symbolizing Niobe's tears. This story is told in HOMER's *ILIAD*.

**NUMA POMPILLIUS** *Roman* The legendary second king of ROME, who succeeded ROMULUS to the throne; eventually seen as an agricultural deity.

Upon the death of Romulus, the legendary founder of the city of Rome, the citizens and senate of the city invited Numa to be their king. At that time, Numa, who was about 40 years old, was living a life of seclusion in a SABINE town, mourning the death of his wife. He had established himself as a man of peace, fairness, and justice. After the warlike beginning of their city under the powerful and military influence of Romulus, and a year of oppression under the alternating rule of the senators, the people sought a leader to establish order and justice. Numa, legend tells, had the traits they needed. In addition, his birth as a Sabine would help unite the different peoples living in the expanding city at that time.

Numa's first objective was to establish order in Rome. He divided conquered lands equitably among people and established boundaries. He introduced the people to the god TERMINUS, who helped them learn to respect borders and property lines.

Then Numa turned his attention to establishing religious rites. In this work Numa received magical help from the NYMPH EGERIA, with whom he had a close relationship. Egeria was his teacher and mentor. She provided Numa with the ceremonies he would need to give to his people and taught him how to properly worship the gods and goddesses.

Numa also had magical powers. He could summon gods, contain them at his feasts and festivals and coerce them into helping him. At one feast, he mixed wine with water and used it to summon and trap FAUNUS and PICUS, two rural gods, who then taught him how to summon the great god JUPITER. Once Numa had Jupiter in his grasp, the king persuaded the god to stop requiring human sacrifices.

A water nymph dips a shell into a pool in this statue made in 1685 by French sculptor Antoine Coysevox (1640-1720). He based his work on classic Roman marble sculptures. The statue is in the Louvre, Paris. *(Photograph by Marie-Lan Nguyen.)*

The influence of these powers and his role in establishing formalized religion itself eventually led to Romans regarding Numa Pompillius as even greater than a king. They came to regard and worship him as the foundation of their society, the primary guiding principle of all they stood for.

**NYMPHS** (young maidens) *Greek* Minor female spirits who were supposed to inhabit various places in the natural world. They were beautiful, and while not immortal, they lived for a few thousand years and thus were supposed to have certain magical and oracular powers. Among them were

DRYADS (tree nymphs and forest nymphs);
NAIADS (nymphs of freshwater springs and lakes);
Napaeae (nymphs of glens and valleys);
NEREIDS (nymphs of the Mediterranean, or inner sea);

OCEANIDS (nymphs of the great ocean);
OREADS (nymphs of mountains).

Among the best-known nymphs were AMPHITRITE, ARETHUSA, CALYPSO, ECHO, OENONE, and THETIS.

The name *nymphs* was also given to the companions of certain goddesses such as ARTEMIS.

**NYX** (NOX; Night) *Greek* The goddess of night, daughter of CHAOS and sister of EREBUS (Darkness). Nyx was the mother of ETHER (Air), HEMERA (Day), and a series of abstract forces such as destiny, sarcasm, and deceit. She lived in a realm far to the west, beyond the setting Sun and beyond the lands of ATLAS. Nyx rode in a chariot pulled by two horses. People saw in her both good and bad. She was the bringer of rest from the worries of the day and the bringer of death and darkness.

**OCEANIDS** (OCEANIDES) *Greek* The many daughters of the two TITAN deities, OCEANUS, the ancient god of water, and his wife and sister, TETHYS. The Oceanids were the female personalities given to the rivers and streams of the lands of ancient GREECE. They were also known as NYMPHS or lesser goddesses. HESIOD, the Greek poet whose works date to about 800 B.C., wrote that there were more than 3,000 Oceanids, but he named only 41, among them STYX, ELECTRA, and CALYPSO. The Oceanids were very closely related to the NEREIDS, nymphs of the Mediterranean Sea. They were also sisters to the lesser gods of the rivers, after whom many rivers themselves were named: the Nile, the Eridanus, and the Sangarius.

**OCEANUS** *Greek* The TITAN son of GAIA and URANUS and the brother and husband of the Titan TETHYS; father of all the OCEANIDS and all the rivers and seas of the world. Like many ancient peoples, the Greeks believed that water encircled the world. They called this water Oceanus. Oceanus was represented sometimes as a serpent encircling the Earth, its tail in its mouth, or as an old man with a long beard and with a BULL's horns upon his head. With the ascendancy of worship of the OLYMPIAN GODS, POSEIDON became the lord of the seas and rivers while Oceanus retired into oblivion, though his name was still used to denote the vast waters that stretched beyond the known world of the ancients.

**ODYSSEUS** *Greek* Son of LAERTES, king of ITHACA, and ANTICLEA. Husband of PENELOPE; father of TELEMACHUS. The Romans knew him as ULYSSES. Odysseus is one of the most famous characters in literature. His adventures on his homeward journey to Ithaca after the TROJAN WAR are recounted in HOMER's *ODYSSEY*.

**ODYSSEY** *Greek* The epic poem by HOMER that describes the adventures of ODYSSEUS on his homeward voyage to Ithaca after the TROJAN WAR. The action of the *Odyssey* occurs in no more than six weeks, but 20 years' adventures are related by means of flashback episodes told by Odysseus to the people he encounters.

Scholars see the *Odyssey*, divided into 24 books, as a collection of folktales to which Homer gave continuity and coherence by attributing the adventures to a single hero (Odysseus) and by reworking each incident so that it contributes to a consistent picture of the hero.

Some scholars say that the *Odyssey* is the first novel, a fictional story with fictional characters, to be read and enjoyed. Homer wrote the *Odyssey* in about the eighth century B.C. after he wrote the *ILIAD*, according to most modern scholars.

**Odysseus and Polyphemus** On his way home from the Trojan War, Odysseus and his crew landed on an island that had rich pastures and great flocks of sheep. The shepherd turned out to be POLYPHEMUS, one of the CYCLOPES, one-eyed giants. When he discovered Odysseus's men in his cave, Polyphemus immediately killed and ate two of them, then closed off the entrance to the cave with a huge rock. While the giant slept after his meal, Odysseus and his men devised a plan. They made a sharp spear from olive wood. After the giant awoke, they gave him some very sweet and potent wine that they had brought with them from Ismarus. After the giant had killed and eaten another two crewmen and fallen into a drunken stupor, Odysseus gouged out his one eye, leaving the Cyclops blind. The men knew that they could never move the rock that closed the entrance. They waited anxiously for the giant to awaken. Meanwhile the cunning Odysseus helped his men to tie themselves under the bellies of the sheep. When the giant awoke,

Odysseus (helmet) and his men are discovered by the giant cyclops Polyphemus who is driving his sheep into his cave for the night. Flemish artist Jacob Jordaens (1593-1678) captured the moment in this painting, which now hangs in the Pushkin Museum of Fine Arts in Moscow.

he moved the rock to let out the sheep to their pasture. He never suspected that Odysseus's men were leaving at the same time. It was not until the men were safe aboard their ship that they learned that POLYPHEMUS was the name of the monster. Polyphemus hurled rocks after the ship and vowed that his protector, POSEIDON, the sea god, would avenge him, and that the sea would always be Odysseus's enemy.

**Odysseus and Circe** On their way back to Ithaca after the Trojan War, Odysseus and his crew made landfall on the island of Aeaea, on which dwelled the witch-goddess CIRCE. Circe turned all the men into swine, except for Odysseus and EURY-LOCHUS. Eventually Odysseus persuaded Circe to turn his men back into their human forms. Under her spell, he dallied for a year on the island of the sorceress, who gave him warnings about the perils he would encounter on his way home.

**Odysseus in the Underworld** After suffering under the spell of the witch-goddess Circe for a year,

Odysseus and his crew grew restless and wanted to leave. On the advice of Circe, Odysseus and his crew visited the UNDERWORLD (1) to consult the ghost of the blind seer TIRESIAS. Tiresias had many warnings for Odysseus and his men, particularly about the danger of offending the gods on Thrinacie, the Island of the Sun.

Terrified by the ghosts and the gloom of the Underworld, Odysseus and his crew fled.

**Odysseus and the Sirens** Circe had warned Odysseus about the SIRENS, beautiful NYMPHS who lured sailors to their destruction by singing so sweetly that the men would be driven mad and would be shipwrecked on the rocky coast where the Sirens lived. Always resourceful, Odysseus plugged the ears of his men with wax so that they would not hear the singing. Then, because he himself wanted to hear the songs, Odysseus had himself tied to the mast of the ship while the men rowed on. They could hear neither the singing nor the pleas of their captain to be released so that he might join the Sirens.

**Odysseus and Scylla and Charybdis**  One of the many dangers Odysseus encountered on his way home after the Trojan War was the narrow strait guarded by the monsters SCYLLA AND CHARYBDIS. Odysseus steered his ship close to Scylla to avoid being sucked into the boiling whirlpool of Charybdis. He lost six men to Scylla, the many-headed monster who lived high up on a cliff and sent down six long necks armed with ferocious teeth to devour any who came close.

**Odysseus on the Island of the Sun**  Both Circe, the witch-goddess, and Tiresias, the blind seer, had warned Odysseus about the Island of the Sun, which belonged to the sun god, HYPERION; but in a state of despair and exhaustion, Odysseus and his crew went there. While Odysseus rested, his crew disobeyed his orders and killed and ate the cattle of Hyperion. Odysseus was horrified when he awoke to the smell of roasting meat, but it was too late. Hyperion was furious and asked ZEUS to punish the men. This Zeus did, by causing the wreck of Odysseus's ship in a terrifying storm. Only Odysseus escaped alive. He was cast up on the island of the nymph CALYPSO, where the hero stayed for seven years.

**Odysseus Returns to Ithaca**  Odysseus and his men struggled for 10 years and through many adventures before they got back to their kingdom of Ithaca. By this time Odysseus, who had been shipwrecked many times, looked like a poor old man rather than a king. Only his old dog, ARGUS (3), and his loving old nurse, Eurycleia, recognized him. Odysseus chose to remain silent as he observed what was happening at his court. His wife, Penelope, who had waited for him faithfully for 20 years (10 years for the war, and 10 years for the return), was besieged by a host of aggressive suitors who wanted to rule Odysseus's kingdom. The son of Odysseus and Penelope, Telemachus, guided by the goddess ATHENE, had gone off in search of his father and come back to Ithaca convinced that he was still alive and was nearby. At last Penelope, in desperation, put her suitors to the test by asking them to string the magnificent bow of Odysseus and shoot an arrow straight through a double row of axes. The suitors failed. The old man took up the challenge. He strung the bow with ease and shot it straight and true. After that, with the help of his son, Odysseus slew all the greedy suitors and reclaimed his wife and his throne.

**OEDIPUS** (Swollen Foot) *Greek*  Son of Laius, king of THEBES, and of Jocasta. Father of Polynices, Eteocles, ANTIGONE, and Ismene.

An ORACLE had warned King Laius that Oedipus would kill him, so Laius abandoned his infant son on a hillside (a fate common to many unwanted children in ancient times), having first pierced the child's feet and bound them together (hence the name Oedipus, meaning "Swollen Foot," or, some say "Clubfoot").

A shepherd rescued Oedipus and took him to the king of CORINTH, who raised Oedipus. Years later another oracle told Oedipus, now a young man, that he would kill his father and marry his mother. Believing that his foster parents were his real parents, Oedipus fled from them.

On his journey, he met Laius, his real father. The two had a skirmish at a crossroads and Oedipus killed Laius. In Thebes, Oedipus correctly answered a riddle set by the SPHINX and in so doing won the hand of Jocasta, whom he married not knowing she was his mother. Thus the oracles' prophecies were fulfilled.

When Oedipus learned the truth about his parents and his relationships with them, he blinded himself in agony and was either killed in battle or exiled to Colonus in ATTICA, while his sons battled for the throne of Thebes (see SEVEN AGAINST THEBES). His loving daughter, Antigone, guided Oedipus in his blind wanderings.

SOPHOCLES, AESCHYLUS, and EURIPIDES all wrote plays based on the story of Oedipus. The one by Sophocles, known as *Oedipus Rex*, has been called the greatest and most powerful of the Greek tragedies.

**OENEUS** (OENEOUS; Vintner) *Greek*  King of CALYDON; husband of Althea, father of MELEAGER, Tydeus, Gorge, and the beautiful DEIANIRA, who eventually married HERACLES. Oeneus was deprived of his kingdom by his nephews, and though his grandson, DIOMEDES, avenged him, two remaining nephews, who hid in ARGOS when he went there with Diomedes, killed the old king.

**OENOMAUS** *Greek*  King of Pisa in Elis, in northeast PELOPONNESUS; father of HIPPODAMEIA. Many suitors contended for the hand of Hippodameia in chariot races with Oenomaus. The penalty for losing was death, and Oenomaus made sure that they all lost. Thirteen suitors had died by the time PELOPS came along and won the race. Oenomaus died in a final chariot race with Pelops, who won Hippodameia and Pisa itself.

**OENONE** *Greek*  A NYMPH, daughter of the river god Cebren. She was loved by PARIS when he lived among the shepherds on Mount IDA (2). Paris deserted Oenone when the goddess APHRODITE promised him the love of the most beautiful woman in the world,

HELEN. Oenone prophesied that this voyage to GREECE to claim Helen would only bring ruin for him and his country, TROY. Her prophecy came true.

**OLYMPIAN GODS** *Greek*   The 12 (sometimes 13) major deities who lived atop Mount OLYMPUS; the primary gods of the Greek PANTHEON of classical GREECE. Here they are listed in alphabetical order, with their attributes, and their Roman names opposite.

| Greek names | Roman names |
| --- | --- |
| APHRODITE (love and beauty) | VENUS |
| APOLLO (music; poetry) | APOLLO |
| ARES (war) | MARS |
| ARTEMIS (Moon and hunting) | DIANA |
| ATHENE (wisdom) | MINERVA |
| DEMETER (fertility; corn goddess) | CERES |
| HADES* (underworld) | PLUTO |
| HEPHAESTUS (fire; blacksmith) | VULCAN |
| HERA (marriage; women) | JUNO |
| HERMES (messenger; commerce; travelers; rogues) | MERCURY |
| HESTIA (hearth) | VESTA |
| POSEIDON (ocean; earthquakes) | NEPTUNE |
| ZEUS (light; the heavens) | JUPITER |

* Since Hades did not live on Mount Olympus, he is not always counted as an Olympian.

**OLYMPIC GAMES** *Greek*   The principal athletic meeting of the ancient Greeks held every four years. In mythology, it is said to have been instituted by PELOPS to honor the god ZEUS. According to tradition, the first games were held in 776 B.C.

Only Greek men were allowed to compete and the rivalry was ferocious, for while no gold medals were awarded, the winners received great honor and prestige.

The site of the games, on a flat plain at the meeting of two rivers, is in northwest PELOPONNESUS, part of the territory of Elis.

**OLYMPUS** *Greek*   A mountain range in northern Greece. Its highest peak is Mount Olympus (about 9,600 feet high). The Olympic range stretches along the border between THESSALY and Macedonia, near the Aegean coast. The range overlooks the Vale of TEMPE, a valley in northern Thessaly famous for its beauty.

In mythology, Mount Olympus was regarded as the home of the OLYMPIAN GODS. Within its mysterious heights, higher even than the visible mountain, were the abodes of the gods; there lived ZEUS, HERA, and all members of the Greek PANTHEON. They feasted on ambrosia and nectar and listened to sweet music. No harsh winds, rain, or snow disturbed their heavenly peace.

**OMPHALE** *Greek*   The queen of LYDIA who took the hero HERACLES as her slave after he had desecrated the temple of APOLLO. Heracles performed many services for the queen, including ridding her kingdom of the two mischievous CERCOPES.

**OMPHALOS** (NAVEL) *Greek*   The stone swallowed by CRONUS, one of the TITANS, thinking that it was his son ZEUS. The stone was set up at DELPHI and people came to worship it as the center, or navel, of the Earth.

**OPS** (OPIS: Abundance) *Roman*   Goddess of plenty, of the harvest, and of wealth. Her name refers to the bounty of the Earth and the riches of a plentiful harvest.

Surviving evidence suggests to scholars that the people of ROME worshiped Ops as the consort or wife of CONSUS, the god of storage, or as the cult partner of SATURN, the Roman god of agriculture. Ops was, perhaps, the mother of JUNO, Roman goddess of childbirth and queen of the heavens.

Ops was honored with Consus in the harvest festivals of August 21 and 25 and in a celebration on December 19. Eventually, Ops took on the characteristics and stories of the Greek goddess RHEA.

**ORACLE** *Greek*   The spokesperson of the ruling deity of a shrine. The oracle answered people's questions about the future or the past. These utterances were regarded as profoundly wise and authoritative, since they were supposed to come from the gods. The answers of the oracles were often obscure, ambiguous, and misleading, yet kings and peasants alike eagerly sought their advice. Priests, who were paid for their services, tended the shrine. It was in their interests to make sure that the words of the oracle were vague. In this way, the priests would not be blamed for disastrous events that occurred from following the advice of the oracles.

There were many oracles in ancient GREECE. The most famous was the oracle at DELPHI, who spoke the words of the god APOLLO through the mouth of

PYTHON. The ORACLE at DODONA spoke the words of ZEUS.

Other oracles include those of ARTEMIS at Colchis, ASCLEPIUS at EPIDAURUS, HERACLES at ATHENS, ARES in Thrace, ATHENE at MYCENAE, PAN in ARCADIA, and APHRODITE at Paphos, in CRETE.

## ORCUS *Roman*

Either an ancient Roman god of the UNDERWORLD (2) or an alternative name for DIS, the primary Roman god of this land of the dead.

Some scholars believe that Orcus had no individual identity. Others argue from existing evidence that Orcus was the bringer of death, rather than a king of the dead, as was Dis. Orcus was sometimes shown as a reaper, cutting down the corn with his scythe, in sculptures and paintings on pottery.

PLUTO was a euphemism, or name that was safe to speak, that was sometimes used to refer to Orcus and Dis in ROME and to HADES in GREECE.

## OREADS (OREIADES) *Greek*

Mountain NYMPHS; like most nymphs, daughters of ZEUS.

Some sources say the Oreads were, specifically, the nymphs of mountain conifers, since nymphs were often associated with specific trees. The Oreads were the special companions of the goddess ARTEMIS, who liked to go hunting in mountains. Other sources, however, associate them with specific mountains: for example, the Idae were nymphs of Mount IDA.

The most famous Oread was ECHO, who was punished by the goddess HERA for helping her sister nymphs, who were dallying with Zeus, to escape from the great god's wife. Hera made Echo fade away, except for her voice.

Cynosure, an Oread of Mount Ida, nursed the infant Zeus when his mother, RHEA, hid him from his father CRONUS. Pitys, an Oread who vowed never to marry, was loved by PAN, who pursued her relentlessly though she discouraged him. The gods turned her into a pine tree to help her escape. BRITOMARTIS, a guardian of fishermen, was also said to be an Oread, but only in later Greek stories; in earlier stories, she was a Cretan goddess.

## ORESTES *Greek*

The only son of AGAMEMNON and CLYTEMNESTRA; brother of ELECTRA, Iphigenia, and Chrysothemis. Orestes killed his mother, who had killed her husband, Agamemnon. According to some accounts, the FURIES drove Orestes mad for the unforgivable crime of matricide. He took refuge in ATHENS. He was tried and acquitted at the court of Areopagus, a tribunal of Athenian judges. He then took possession of his dead father's kingdom and married Hermione, the daughter of MENELAUS and HELEN.

Matricide had always been regarded as a terrible crime, but in this myth, a court finds the son, Orestes, innocent. ZEUS, APOLLO, and ATHENE had championed his cause in this trial. Orestes absolution represents the final triumph of patriarchy over the old pre-Hellenic religions and customs.

## ORION *Greek*

Best known as a mighty hunter and as a constellation of stars. Orion was the son of POSEIDON and EURYALE. He was a Boeotian giant, with the power to walk on the seas. Orion loved MEROPE, daughter of King Oenopion of Chios, an island off the coast of ASIA MINOR. In a fit of anger, the king made Orion blind and left him to die on the seashore. Orion met a boy, Cedalion, who guided him east toward the Sun, where he found Eos, goddess of the dawn. She restored Orion's sight. Many women and goddesses loved Orion, including the goddess of the hunt, ARTEMIS, and Eos.

In one story, APOLLO, brother of Artemis, was jealous of his sister's affection for Orion. He sent a giant scorpion to sting Orion to death. In another story, Apollo had a fight with Orion and flung him into the sea. Orion swam away. Apollo asked Artemis to shoot the object in the sea with her arrow. This Artemis did and unknowingly killed her lover. She set the constellation Orion in the heavens, with the scorpion (Scorpio) at its feet. His faithful hunting dog, Sirius, is part of the constellation, seen high in the winter sky in the Northern Hemisphere.

## ORPHEUS *Greek*

A famous poet and singer; son of Oeagrus, king of Thrace, and of CALLIOPE, the MUSE; husband of EURYDICE.

The god APOLLO (some say he was the father of Orpheus) gave Orpheus a lyre, which he played so beautifully that even the rocks were moved to tears, trees bent to listen, flowers bloomed, and rivers changed their courses.

As an ARGONAUT, Orpheus distracted the crewmen from the sweet singing of the SIRENS (see *Jason and the Argonauts*, under JASON).

When Eurydice died from a serpent bite, Orpheus charmed his way into the UNDERWORLD and persuaded HADES to release her. Hades did so, on the condition that Orpheus would not look back until he had reached Earth. Orpheus failed in his promise and Eurydice disappeared instantly.

**O**VID (43 B.C.–A.D. 17) *Roman* Poet. According to some literary historians, Ovid was the most popular Roman poet. Ovid was born Publius Ovidius Naso near ROME to a middle-class family. He studied in ATHENS and traveled widely in Asia and Sicily. Ovid, as he was commonly known, began writing poetry as a young man and soon developed a strong following and reputation among the citizens of the Roman Empire. Ovid's greatest work is *Metamorphoses*, a collection of 15 books that used Greek and Roman mythology, particularly those stories of lovers who are transformed into other objects, to trace the history from the beginnings of CHAOS to the rule of Julius Caesar. He also wrote *Fasti*, a poetic description of the Roman religious calendar and the myths and legends behind each festival. Rome's first emperor, Augustus, banished Ovid from Rome in A.D. 8. The poet died in exile in Tomi, a city on the Black Sea.

In Europe's Middle Ages, Ovid's poetry was a primary source of knowledge of Greek and Roman mythology. It is still a prominent source of the stories of these ancient cultures.

**PALAMEDES** *Greek* Son of Nauplius, a king of Euboea, and his wife CLYMENE, a granddaughter of King MINOS of CRETE. One of the Greek heroes who fought against TROY in the TROJAN WAR. When ODYSSEUS feigned idiocy, in his attempt to avoid joining the Greek army on its way to Troy, Palamedes put TELEMACHUS, son of Odysseus, in the path of his father's plow. Odysseus avoided running down his infant son, showing that he was sane, and was forced to join the army. In revenge, Odysseus concocted a plot against Palamedes, accusing him of treachery against the Greeks. The army stoned Palamedes to death.

Palamedes is described as a sage, and he is credited with inventing certain letters of the Greek alphabet and for inventing dice, measures and scales, lighthouses, and the discus.

**PALES** *Roman* An ancient spirit of agriculture and of flocks and herds. Pales is sometimes referred to as a god, sometimes as a goddess. Belief in this spirit existed in central Italy even before 752 B.C., when ROMULUS is said to have founded the city of ROME. The festival of Parilia on April 21 honors Pales. This celebration by shepherds exists in the oldest records of Roman religious festivals. It fell on the same day in later years when people celebrated the founding of Rome.

**PALLADIUM** *Greek* The sacred statue of PALLAS ATHENE that was said to have fallen from heaven. It stood in the temple of ATHENE in TROY. According to legend, ZEUS sent the statue to DARDANUS, the founder of Troy. Trojans believed that the preservation of the city depended on possession of the Palladium. During the TROJAN WAR, two Greeks, DIOMEDES (1) and ODYSSEUS, stole it, and Troy fell to the Greeks. In another legend, AJAX (2) the Lesser carried it off. The Romans said that AENEAS took the statue to Italy. In fact, many cities claimed to own the statue, among them ATHENS, ARGOS, and Luceria.

A rare metallic element is called palladium. It was named after an asteroid, Pallas, discovered in 1803 at about the same time the element was found.

**PALLAS** (Warrior) *Greek* A second generation TITAN; considered by some to be the god of warfare and of the springtime battle season.

Pallas was the son of CRIUS and EURYBIA and the brother of ASTRAEUS and PERSES; He married STYX, a daughter of OCEANUS; and with her had four children, ZELUS, NIKE, CRATUS, and BIA, whose names meant, respectively, zeal, victory, strength, and force, all terms of warfare.

His children and wife fought against him when they joined the great OLYMPIAN GOD Zeus in his battle against the Titans.

**PALLAS ATHENE** *Greek* One of the many names of the goddess ATHENE. In some traditions, Pallas was the name of a youthful playmate of the goddess.

**PAN** *Greek* An ancient deity from the mountainous region of ARCADIA, in GREECE. Pan was a deity of herds and flocks, fertility, forests, and wildlife. He is usually depicted as half man, half goat. The Romans called him FAUNUS.

Pan was a notable musician, playing the SYRINX (panpipes, or Pipes of Pan), a seven-reed flute still played by Arcadian shepherds. In one myth, Pan challenged the god APOLLO to a musical contest (see *Midas and the Donkey's Ears*, under MIDAS). Some sources say Pan is the son of the god HERMES and of the NYMPH PENELOPE. People worshiped Pan as a fertility symbol and thought of him as lusty and playful, though at times a little sinister. They believed Pan was the cause of a sudden, terrifying, unreasoning fear in humans and beasts, a feeling given the name *panic*, from Pan.

Almost every region in Greece had its own Pan, a primitive, ancient deity. (See ARISTAEUS and PRIAPUS.)

**PANACEA** (PANACEIA; All-healing) *Greek* A daughter of the god of medicine, ASCLEPIUS. Panacea symbolizes universal healing, particularly through the power of HERBS. A temple to her stood at Oropus, in the region of Oropia, north of ATTICA. Panacea's sisters were HYGIEA and Iaso, and her brothers, both doctors, were Machaon and Podalirius.

**PANDORA** (All-giving) *Greek* The first woman to appear on Earth, according to Greek mythology. The gods created her and sent her down to release upon the world all the misfortunes that could occur. At the command of the great god ZEUS, the smith-god HEPHAESTUS crafted her out of clay and the other gods and goddesses breathed into her surpassing beauty, charm, graciousness, and cunning. They also gave her a vase to take with her to Earth and told her never to open it.

PROMETHEUS (Forethought) resisted the beauty of Pandora, but his brother, EPIMETHEUS (Afterthought) at once took the beautiful creature to be his bride. After the wedding, Pandora opened the sacred vase, sometimes called Pandora's Box, and released upon the world all the ailments that it contained. Only Hope remained inside the vase, and it was Hope who enabled humankind to go on living despite all adversity.

Some legends say that Zeus released Pandora upon the Earth because he was angry with Prometheus, champion of humankind. Pandora was to be humankind's punishment for having learned the use of fire from Prometheus.

"Pandora's Box" has come to mean a gift or opportunity that at first seems valuable but turns out to be a source of troubles.

**PANTHEON** *Greek and Roman* In mythology, *pantheon* refers to all the gods of a people, particularly those considered to be the most prominent or most powerful. The Romans used different names for many of the Greek OLYMPIAN GODS whose cults they brought to Italy, but the stories of the gods and goddesses, as told by the poets and historians, are very similar.

| Greek gods/ goddesses | Roman gods/ goddesses |
| --- | --- |
| ZEUS | JUPITER |
| HERA | JUNO |
| APOLLO | APOLLO |
| ARES | MARS |
| ARTEMIS | DIANA |
| APHRODITE | VENUS |
| POSEIDON | NEPTUNE |
| HERMES | MERCURY |
| ATHENE | MINERVA |
| HESTIA | VESTA |
| DEMETER | CERES |
| HEPHAESTUS | VULCAN |

**PARCAE** *Roman* The origins of the Parcae in Roman mythology are unclear. By the time the influence of Greek mythology on Rome's religions reached its strongest, the Parcae had become the equivalent of the Greek Fates, three women who watched over a person's destiny. Their Roman names at this time were Nona, Decuma, and Morta. One presided over birth, one over marriage, and one over death. Scholars see some evidence that these three may have been part of a larger group of Roman goddesses, perhaps as many as nine, who watched over and guided many phases of a person's life.

**PARIS** *Greek* Son of PRIAM, the king of TROY, and of HECUBA. Before he was born, soothsayers prophesied that Paris would cause death and destruction. Accordingly, his parents placed him upon a mountainside (Mount IDA [2]) and left the infant to die. Shepherds rescued and raised Paris. He fell in love with OENONE but was later to abandon the NYMPH in favor of HELEN. He became a fine athlete and a very handsome man. Paris competed at the games at Troy and won many prizes, gaining the attention of King Priam, who recognized him as his son. In spite of the soothsayers' warnings, Priam welcomed Paris back into the household. The prophecies came true. Paris's abduction of Helen became one of the leading causes of the TROJAN WAR.

In some versions of the story, Paris kills the hero ACHILLES, and is himself killed by PHILOCTETES.

**The Judgment of Paris** This is how Paris's abduction of Helen, wife of King MENELAUS came about. ERIS (Discord) was present at the wedding of PELEUS and THETIS, the parents of ACHILLES. She made the goddesses quarrel among themselves by throwing a golden apple ("the apple of discord") among the guests. The apple was inscribed, "To the fairest."

HERA, the chief goddess and wife of ZEUS; ARTEMIS, goddess of the hunt; and APHRODITE, goddess of love, each claimed the apple. Asked to make the choice among the three goddesses, Zeus wisely declined and sent his messenger, HERMES, to ask Paris, the most handsome of men, to make the decision. Each of the goddesses offered Paris bribes. Aphrodite offered him love of the most beautiful woman in the world: Helen of SPARTA. Paris awarded the apple to Aphrodite. On that day, Hera and Artemis became enemies of Paris and of Troy.

**PARNASSUS** *Greek* A mountain in south-central GREECE, a few miles north of the Gulf of CORINTH which separates mainland Greece from the PELOPONNESUS. At the foot of the mountain stands DELPHI, the shrine sacred to APOLLO, whose seer, the PYTHON, was renowned throughout the ancient world. Mount Parnassus was sacred to Apollo, DIONYSUS, and the nine MUSES. Bacchanalian rites took place in its caves and gorges, where, it was said, people could hear the pipes of PAN. On the slopes of Mount Parnassus the Ark landed after the flood in the myth of DEUCALION.

**PASIPHAË** *Greek* Daughter of HELIOS (the Sun); wife of MINOS, king of CRETE; mother with Minos of ARIADNE, ANDROGEUS, and PHAEDRA. From her strange union with a BULL, Pasiphaë brought forth the MINOTAUR, a monster that was half human half bull.

**PATROCLUS** *Greek* The close friend of the hero ACHILLES. When Achilles withdrew from the TROJAN WAR, Patroclus assumed command of the MYRMIDONS, the troops of Achilles. HECTOR killed Patroclus in battle. Determined to avenge the death of his friend, Achilles went back into the war, killed Hector, and dragged his body around the tomb of Patroclus.

**PAX** (Peace) *Roman* The divinity who represented peace. Her feast day was January 3. While Pax was often called upon during civil wars, historical evidence suggests that people worshiped her far more after Augustus became the first emperor of ROME in 27 B.C. He built a temple to Pax in 13 B.C. on the Campus Martius, a large, flat open space between the Capitoline and Quirinal hills in the center of Rome. In A.D. 75, Emperor Vespasian dedicated a temple to her in the Roman Forum. Pax was shown carrying a CADUCEUS or wing-topped staff, a horn of plenty, or an olive branch. The Greeks knew her as EIRENE.

**PEGASUS** *Greek* The famous winged horse of Greek mythology. He was born from the blood of the GORGON MEDUSA, when the hero PERSEUS cut off her head. Pegasus carried Perseus to the rescue of ANDROMEDA. He carried BELLEROPHON to the triumphant fight with the monster CHIMERA. When Bellerophon decided to ride his magical steed up to the home of the gods, OLYMPUS, the god ZEUS sent down a gadfly to annoy Pegasus, who threw off his master. Bellerophon fell to Earth. Pegasus went

Mercury rides the great horse Pegasus (left) and the Fame of France's King Louis XIV (right) rides the mythical winged horse in this pair of marble statues carved by sculptor Antoine Coysevox in 1701-02. The pair was designed for the king's stables and then moved to the Tuileries Gardens in Paris. Replicas of the statues replaced them in the Tuileries in 1986 when the originals were moved to the Louvre. *(Photographs by Marie-Lan Nguyen)*

on to Olympus, where he helped Zeus launch his thunderbolts.

Legend said that Pegasus brought forth the fountain of Hippocrene on Mount HELICON with a stroke of his hoof.

Winged animals were common in Near Eastern mythology.

**PELEUS** *Greek* Son of King Aecus; brother of TELAMON; husband of THETIS; father, with Thetis, of the hero ACHILLES.

Peleus and Telamon murdered their younger half-brother, Phocus, the king's favorite. Peleus fled from the kingdom of AEGINA to Phthia. There, he accidentally killed the king's son in the CALYDONIAN BOAR HUNT and had to flee once again. He came to IOLCUS in THESSALY, but bad luck followed him. There, the wife of King Acatus, Astydameia, fell in love with Peleus. When Peleus spurned her love, she accused him before the king of molesting her. King Acatus took Peleus hunting on Mount PELION. He stole Peleus's sword while the young man slept and left him to die on the mountain, which was famous for its savage CENTAURS. However, CHIRON, their wise leader, took pity on Peleus. Chiron found his sword for him and sent Peleus back to Iolcus, where Peleus killed the treacherous Astydameia.

Eventually Peleus married Thetis, a sea NYMPH. All the gods attended their wedding, for Thetis was a favorite of Zeus. However, the couple neglected to invite ERIS, the goddess of strife, and this oversight was one of the causes of the TROJAN WAR, in which Achilles, son of Thetis and Peleus, was a leading figure and hero. (See also *The Judgment of Paris*, under PARIS.)

**PELIAS** *Greek* Son of Tyro, a half brother of AESON, from whom Pelias stole the throne of IOLCUS, in THESSALY. When his nephew, JASON, son of Aeson, reached manhood and demanded his share of the kingdom, Pelias sent him on what was thought to be a hopeless quest—to find and bring back the GOLDEN FLEECE. Jason returned, triumphant, bringing with him MEDEA, the sorceress-queen. Meanwhile, Pelias had put Aeson to death. To avenge his father, Jason urged Medea to use her magic powers. Medea persuaded the daughters of the aging Pelias to slay their father and cook him in a stew, promising that he would arise, rejuvenated. Of course, Pelias did not survive. Acastus succeeded his father as king.

**PELION** *Greek* A mountain in the north of THESSALY, connected with Mount Ossa on the northwest.

In Greek mythology, the giant brothers Ephialtes and Otus, known as the ALOEIDS, "piled Pelion upon Ossa" in an attempt to reach the heavens (OLYMPUS). The phrase has come to mean adding difficulty upon difficulty. Mount Pelion was the home of CHIRON, the gentle CENTAUR.

**PELOPONNESUS** (PELOPONNESE) *Greek* The peninsula that lies south of the Greek mainland, connected to the mainland by the Isthmus of CORINTH. It is named after PELOPS, in Greek mythology the son of TANTALUS and the founder of the Atreid dynasty. In the ancient world, the chief divisions of the Peloponnesus were Elis, Achaea, ARGOS, and Corinth in the north; and LACONIA and Messenia in the south. SPARTA, Corinth, Argos, and Megalopolis were the chief cities.

**PELOPS** *Greek* Son of DIONE and TANTALUS; brother of NIOBE. He married HIPPODAMEIA and became the father of ATREUS AND THYESTES.

Pelops's first appearance in mythology was an unfortunate one. He was served up in a stew made by his wicked father to test the gods. All the gods and goddesses realized what was happening, except for DEMETER, who was distracted with grief from losing her daughter, PERSEPHONE. Demeter ate a shoulder of the infant, but it was later restored when the gods brought the child back to life. The gods had to remake the missing shoulder from ivory.

Though Pelops became the rich and successful king of Pisa in Elis, he and his descendants were forever followed by the dreadful curse of the charioteer MYRTILUS. Pelops's descendants were called the ATREIDS after his son, Atreus.

**Pelops and the Charioteer** When Pelops, son of the wicked Tantalus, grew up, he set off to look for a kingdom of his own. On his way he met the sea god, POSEIDON, who befriended the youth and presented him with a fine chariot and a marvelous team of horses. These gifts led Pelops to challenge OENOMAUS, king of Pisa in Elis, in a chariot race.

King Oenomaus had a passion not only for fine horses, but for his daughter, Hippodameia. Whenever a suitor asked for his daughter's hand in marriage, Oenomaus challenged him to a chariot race, which the suitor invariably lost. The penalty for losing the race was death. By the time Pelops arrived on the scene, 13 suitors of Hippodameia had died. Their heads were hung around the gates of the palace of Oenomaus.

Pelops bribed the king's charioteer, Myrtilus, asking him to loosen the wheels of Oenomaus's chariot. (The king always drove his own chariot in the competitions for his daughter's hand.) This Myrtilus did, on the condition that Pelops would allow him to spend one night with Hippodaemia, whom he loved.

Pelops won the race, Oenomaus was killed, and then Pelops killed Myrtilus. With his dying breath, the charioteer cursed Pelops and all his descendants. The curse took hold, for Myrtilus was the son of the god HERMES, and the gods knew how to make curses work. (See also AGAMEMNON and MENELAUS, the descendants of Atreus and grandchildren of Pelops.)

**PENATES** *Roman* Each household had two Penates, spirits or gods who protected the family storeroom. These were family gods, honored at dinnertime when people gave part of every meal to them, pushing part of the dinner—not merely the leftovers—into the family fire. Guarding the pantry was a critical job in the early Roman agricultural society, and people worshiped their Penates in private, often around the hearth where they cooked their food. While the Penates watched over the food supply, the LARES watched over the general well-being of the house.

**PENELOPE** *Greek* The daughter of ICARIUS and Periboea; the wife of the hero ODYSSEUS; mother of TELEMACHUS. During the long absence of Odysseus during the TROJAN WAR and his long voyage home to Ithaca (see *ODYSSEY*) many men saw Penelope as a wealthy and desirable widow. Suitors overwhelmed the palace and Penelope was obliged to entertain them at great cost. Penelope held them off by claiming that she had to finish weaving a shroud for her father-in-law, LAERTES, before she could choose a husband. She wove all day and secretly undid her work by night. Her secret was disclosed by one of her servants, but Odysseus arrived in time to kill the suitors and reclaim his bride. Penelope's name has come to personify wifely virtues such as patience and faithfulness.

**PENTHESILEA** *Greek* AMAZON queen who led her female warriors to TROY to help the Trojans in the TROJAN WAR. Penthesilea fought bravely against ACHILLES, the Greek hero. It is said that she was so brave and beautiful that Achilles fell in love with her even as he killed her. King PRIAM of Troy gave her a magnificent funeral.

In some accounts Penthesilea inadvertently killed her sister, HIPPOLYTA, and was forever after pursued by the FURIES.

**PERSEPHONE** (KORE) *Greek* Daughter of DEMETER and ZEUS; called PROSERPINA by the Romans.

Persephone was stolen from her mother by HADES, god of the UNDERWORLD (1). Demeter went mad with grief and caused drought and famine on Earth while she searched in vain for her daughter. At last, Zeus sent HERMES to bring Persephone back to her mother, but Persephone was obliged to spend one-third of the year underground. Persephone personified the corn seed that lies underground in winter and springs up in the warm months.

Persephone is considered by many scholars to be the same person as Demeter. Ancient Greek artists pictured them as being identical.

**PERSES** (Destroyer) *Greek* A little-known second-generation TITAN, the son of CRIUS and EURYBIA. He married the Titaness ASTERIA, and together they were the parents of the goddess HECATE.

Perses was considered by some ancient Greek writers to be a god of wisdom and by others a god of war, as was his brother PALLAS. Perses was credited with laying waste to battlefields. A different Perses was the son of PERSEUS.

**PERSEUS** *Greek* Son of the god ZEUS and DANAE; husband of ANDROMEDA; father of PERSES; slayer of the GORGON MEDUSA. After many exploits, Perseus may have become king of ARGOS, but legends differ about what actually happened. Some say that Perseus, Andromeda, and their son, Perses, went to Asia and founded the land of Persia; others say that Perseus accepted the throne of TIRYNS and founded the city of MYCENAE.

**The Childhood of Perseus** Danae, daughter of King Acrisius of Argos was mother of Perseus. An ORACLE had predicted that Acrisius would die at the hands of a son of Danae. Acrisius locked Danae in a bronze tower or chamber. The great god Zeus entered the tower and covered Danae with a shower of gold, after which she bore the son that she named Perseus. Acrisius put mother and son into a wooden chest and cast them upon the sea, hoping thus to avoid the fate the oracle had foreseen.

The fisherman DICTYS spotted the chest and rescued the pair. He took them to the court of King POLYDECTES on the island of SERIPHOS.

Some years later Polydectes fell in love with Danae and wanted to marry her. Perseus, now a robust young warrior, knew that his mother did not want the attentions of the king. To get the young man out of the way, Polydectes contrived to send him on a dangerous and impossible quest. Polydectes asked Perseus to bring back the head of Medusa.

**Perseus and Medusa**   Perseus and his mother had been cast away from Argos by King Acrisius, the father of Danae. They found shelter at the court of King Polydectes on the island of Seriphos. When Perseus became a young man, Polydectes sent him on a quest: to bring back the head of Medusa, the sight of whom turned men to stone.

Fortunately, Perseus had allies among the gods. ATHENE, who had turned Medusa from a beautiful maiden into a hideous monster with snakes for hair, still hated Medusa for defiling one of her temples. Athene warned Perseus never to look directly at Medusa lest he be turned to stone, and gave him a burnished shield to use as a mirror. HERMES gave him a sickle, a leather bag in which to carry the severed head, and a pair of winged sandals so that he could fly. Hermes also told Perseus where to find the GRAEA and how to borrow the helmet of HADES, which would allow him to become invisible.

The Graea (Gray Women) were the sisters of the Gorgons. They had only one eye and one tooth among the three of them, which they used in turn. Perseus snatched away the eye and gave it back only when the Graea told him where to find Medusa.

Now well protected by the weapons of the gods, Perseus slew Medusa and cut off her head, which he carefully stowed in his leather bag. From the blood of Medusa sprang Chrysaor and the winged horse, PEGASUS, children of Medusa and the sea god, POSEIDON.

**Perseus and Andromeda**   With Medusa's head in his leather bag, Perseus set off on his winged sandals to take the head to King Polydectes of Seriphos.

As he flew along the coast, he saw a beautiful woman chained to a rock, weeping. She was Andromeda, daughter of King CEPHEUS of ETHIOPIA, in northeast Africa, and of CASSIOPEIA. Perseus saved Andromeda from being devoured by a sea monster. He uncovered the head of Medusa and turned the monster to stone.

Perseus and Andromeda fell in love and decided to marry. At the wedding feast, Perseus defeated another suitor of Andromeda, PHINEUS, by using the Gorgon's head to turn Phineus and his soldiers into an army of stone.

**Perseus and Polydectes**   When Danae and her infant son Perseus were cast adrift in a wooden box on the Aegean Sea, they were rescued by a fisherman, Dictys, and taken to the court of King Polydectes.

Polydectes and Dictys (who may have been the brother of the king) took good care of the mother and child. As the years went by, Polydectes became enamored of Danae. To get the son out of the way, Polydectes sent Perseus on the quest to bring back the head of Medusa. Danae was protected from the amorous king by Dictys. They took refuge in a temple. Polydectes amassed an army and went after them. Perseus came to the rescue and turned the king and his soldiers into stone, again using the head of Medusa.

Dictys became the new king of Seriphos. Perseus, Danae, and Andromeda returned to Argos, the birthplace of Perseus.

**Perseus and Acrisius**   After Perseus had killed Medusa and turned Polydectes to stone, he and his wife, Andromeda, and his mother, Danae, returned to Argos.

The now aging King Acrisius, who had long ago set his daughter and her infant son adrift, fled the arrival of Perseus, the young hero, remembering an ancient prophecy that said a son of Danae would kill Acrisius. But he could not escape his fate. Acrisius went to Larissa, where games were being held. Perseus also attended the games. Perseus threw a discus that went awry and hit Acrisius, who died from the blow. Thus the prophecy that Acrisius would be killed by a son of Danae was fulfilled.

**PERSONAL GODS** *Roman*   The earliest Romans, those living on the hills that would eventually form the center of the great city and those living in nearby regions in the 700s and 600s B.C., believed in a large number of spiritual forces that guided their individual lives. As ROME grew from a small community to a vast empire, the culture adopted the beliefs of the many people who became part of first the kingdom, then the republic, and finally the empire. This multitude of personal gods influenced family life throughout the empire until the coming of Christianity in the fourth century.

From conception to death, these gods and goddesses influenced almost every detail of life. People called upon these deities to protect them, guide them, and advise them and their loved ones. People prayed to them to help with the happiest, saddest, and, at that time, some of the most dangerous times in life, pregnancy, childhood, and illness.

| God/Goddess | Gender | Area of influence |
| --- | --- | --- |
| Domiducus | M | Bringer of the bride to the husband's household |
| Cinxia | F | Marriage; bride's attire |
| Concordia | F | Marital harmony |
| Viriplaca | F | Restored harmony between married people |
| Mena | F | Menstruation |
| Alemonia | F | Children in the womb |
| Vitumnus | M | Gave life to the child in the womb |
| Pilumnus | M | Proper growth of child in the womb |
| Partula | F | Length of pregnancy |
| Candelifera | F | Childbirth |
| Carmenta | F | Childbirth and midwives |
| Deverra | F | Women in labor and midwives |
| Lucina | F | Childbirth, particularly easing pain |
| Porrima | F | Birth of children who came from the womb head first |
| Postverta | F | Birth of children who came from the womb feet first |
| Orbona | F | Orphans; brought children to childless couples |
| Cuba | F | Infants, particularly in cribs and as they fall asleep |
| Levana | F | Infants, particularly the father's acceptance of the child |
| Cunina | F | Guarded the cradle |
| Nundina | F | Naming of children, which took place on ninth day of life |
| Rumina (Rumilla) | F | Breastfeeding mothers and infants |
| Volumna | F | Nursery |
| Statanus (Statinus) | F | Child's first attempt to stand |
| Fabulinus | M | Taught children to speak |
| Sentia | F | Child's mental development |
| Edusa (Edula) | F | Children learning to eat solids |
| Potina | F | Children's drinks |
| Cardea | F | Protected children from vampires and witches |
| Abeona | F | Children leaving home |
| Domiduca | F | Children on their way to their parents' home |
| Angerona | F | Keeping secrets |
| Angita | F | Healing through magic |
| Febris | F | Protection from fevers and malaria |
| Viduus | M | Separated the soul from the body after death |
| Libitina | F | Corpses and funerals |
| Naenia | F | Songs of lamentation, particularly at funerals |

Many of these personal gods had only one function in protecting the person. Some, such as Concordia, developed broader roles and took on functions across Roman culture. Below is a partial list of some of these gods and goddesses who reigned over the stages of life, including illness.

Another group of divine beings influences the emotions and the thought process, keeping them in balance and helping those whose lives were in turmoil. Among the gods and goddess of the emotions and the abstractions of life were:

| God/Goddess | Gender | Area of influence |
| --- | --- | --- |
| Abundantia | F | Good luck, fortune |
| Clementia | F | Forgiveness, mercy |
| Disciplina | F | Discipline |
| Honos | M | Honor, chivalry |

| God/Goddess | Gender | Area of influence |
|---|---|---|
| Invidia | F | Envy and jealousy |
| Liberalitas | M | Generosity |
| Mens | F | Right or proper thinking |
| Sors | M | Luck |
| Spes | F | Hope |
| Strenua | F | Endurance |
| Suadela | F | Romance, seduction, love |
| Veritas | F | Truth |

The belief in gods and goddesses with distinct functions in life permeated all aspects of the lives of early Roman citizens. In addition to personal gods, there were HOUSEHOLD GODS who cared for the hearth and the threshold, AGRICULTURAL GODS, who watched over the details of the crops, and STATE GODS, who influenced a person's relationship to Rome itself.

See also INDIGETES.

**PHAEDRA** *Greek*  Daughter of MINOS of CRETE and of PASIPHAË; sister of ARIADNE and ANDROGEUS; wife of THESEUS, king of ATHENS. The love goddess APHRODITE caused Phaedra to fall in love with her chaste young stepson, HIPPOLYTUS. The youth fled from her in horror and Phaedra killed herself, leaving a letter to her husband accusing Hippolytus of trying to violate her. Theseus then caused the death of his son. This episode, where Theseus lost both his wife and his son, seemed to mark the end of his heroic life.

**PHAETON** *Greek*  Son of HELIOS, the sun god, and the NYMPH CLYMENE. The companions of Pha-

Phaeton (in blue) asks his father Helios, god of the Sun, if he may drive the Sun's chariot across the sky. Saturn (wings) is in attendance, as are the four seasons. Nicolas Poussin (1594-1665) painted this scene. It is now in the National Museum of Berlin.

eton would not believe that he was the son of Helios. Phaeton went to his father and demanded that he be allowed to drive the Sun's chariot across the skies. With great misgivings, Helios agreed. Young Phaeton could not control the high-spirited horses and plunged the chariot to Earth, causing the devastation of the land now called LIBYA, in North Africa. ZEUS hurled a thunderbolt at Phaeton to stop the destruction. Phaeton instantly turned into a swan and lived out his life on the legendary river Eridanus, surrounded by his sisters, the Heliades, who had been transformed into weeping willow trees forever mourning the death of their brother.

The most complete version of this story is told by the Roman poet OVID in *Metamorphoses*.

**PHILOCTETES** *Greek* The most famous archer in the TROJAN WAR. The hero HERACLES had bequeathed his poisoned arrows to the archer. On the voyage to TROY, Philoctetes was bitten by a venomous snake or, some say, wounded by one of the poisoned arrows and left on the island of Lemnos to die. But it had been prophesied by an ORACLE that Troy could not be taken without Philoctetes. In the 10th year of the siege of Troy, ODYSSEUS sent for Philoctetes. Philoctetes was brought to Troy, where his arrows slew PARIS, and Troy thereafter fell to the Greeks.

**PHINEUS** *Greek* Brother of CEPHEUS, the king of ETHIOPIA; uncle of ANDROMEDA, whom he wished to marry. The hero PERSEUS rescued Andromeda and claimed her as his bride. Phineus and his soldiers appeared at the wedding feast but were transformed into stone by the sight of the head of the GORGON MEDUSA, wielded by Perseus.

**PHOEBE** (Bright) *Greek* A TITAN, one of the daughters of URANUS and GAIA. Phoebe was the wife of COEUS, also a Titan, and the mother of LETO and ASTERIA. Her name, which means "bright" or "shining," was sometimes given to the Moon and was associated with ARTEMIS and DIANA.

**PHOENICIA** (Purple) *Greek* An ancient kingdom on the eastern Mediterranean, in the region of modern Syria, Lebanon, and Israel. Phoenicia was a major trade center of the ancient world. In HOMER and in the Old Testament, its people were known as Canaanites. In the ninth century B.C., the Greeks gave the name *Phoenician* to those Canaanites who lived on the seacoast and traded with the Greeks. It is said that the name came from PHOENIX, brother of CADMUS, CILIX and EUROPA.

The Phoenicians were famous as traders, navigators, and artisans. They obtained a purple dye, "Tyre purple," from shellfish. However, their greatest contribution to Western civilization is thought to be the alphabet, an idea later adopted by the Greeks. The use of symbols for sounds in place of more cumbersome cuneiform and hieroglyphic images was a tremendous advance to learning.

Tyre was the best-known seaport of Phoenicia, lying between Sidon to the north and Acre to the south.

**PHOENIX** *Greek* Son of AGENOR brother of CADMUS, CILIX, and EUROPA. After ZEUS stole Europa, King Agenor sent his three sons to search for her. The brothers could not find her, and not daring to return to the king, they settled down elsewhere. Some accounts say that Phoenix traveled westward, beyond LIBYA, to what is now CARTHAGE, in North Africa. After Agenor's death Phoenix returned to Canaan, since renamed PHOENICIA in his honor.

**PHORCYS** (PHORCUS; Old man of the sea) *Greek* An ancient sea god; son of GAIA and PONTUS; husband to his sister CETO.

Phorcys and Ceto lived together in the sea, most likely the distant western sea at the edge of the world. They were the parents of the following: the GORGONS, three monstrous women; the GRAEA, two or three sisters who were the gray foam of the sea; and, some sources say, the three sisters known as the HESPERIDES and the dragon LADON, all of whom guarded the golden apples of HERA.

Phorcys was also the father of the NYMPH Thoosa, one of the NEREIDS, and of Scylla, a monster with the body of a woman but with six long necks growing from her waist each ending in the head of a dog. (See SCYLLA AND CHARYBDIS.)

Some sources say the Phorcys and NEREUS were brothers, while others say they were different names for the same god.

**PHRIXUS** *Greek* Son of ATHAMAS and NEPHELE; brother of HELLE. His stepmother, INO, demanded that Phrixus be sacrificed to the corn goddess to ensure good crops. Phrixus and his sister, Helle, escaped on the back of the winged ram that had a fleece of gold. When Phrixus reached Colchis, he sacrificed the ram to the god ZEUS and gave the fleece to AEETES, king of Colchis. The flight of Phrixus and Helle on the winged ram was important in the myth of the GOLDEN FLEECE (see *Jason and the Argonauts*, under JASON).

**PHRYGIA** *Greek* An ancient region of central ASIA MINOR (now central Turkey). The goddess CYBELE was worshiped there (as well as, later, in GREECE and ROME). With Gordius, legendary king of Phrygia, Cybele bore a son, MIDAS, who became king of Phrygia after Gordius.

**PICUS** (Woodpecker) *Roman* An ancient Italian god of the wild country, perhaps a SATYR. In this very early mythology, Picus was said to be the son of a laborer whose name meant "dung heap." He had the power to see into the future and to change his shape. He often chose to be a woodpecker, an animal sacred to the god MARS. Picus, the woodpecker, was believed to have helped the she-wolf protect the infants ROMULUS AND REMUS, who would start the city of ROME, after they were abandoned in the wild.

Over time, the myths surrounding Picus changed. Eventually, he evolved into an early legendary king of LATIUM. In this role he was the son of King Saturnus, who would be deified as the god SATURN; father of the FAUNUS, another ancient god whose story evolved in a way to give him human ancestry; and grandfather of LATINUS, king of Latium when AENEAS arrived from TROY.

In this version of his story, Picus was a great warrior with the power to see into the future, a gift that helped him in battle. He used his skills to his advantage. He kept as a pet a green woodpecker, for woodpeckers also had the gift of prophecy. Eventually, the king fell victim to jealousy. Though Picus was married to the NYMPH Canens, he loved the goddess POMONA, but the goddess CIRCE also fell in love with Picus. When he did not return her love, Circe, in a fit of rage, turned Picus into a woodpecker.

**PINDAR** (518–438 B.C.) *Greek* The great lyric poet of ancient GREECE. He was born near THEBES into a distinguished family. When he was 20 years old, another noble family commissioned Pindar to write a poem in honor of one of their sons, who won the footrace at the PYTHIAN GAMES held at DELPHI. Pindar's fame dates from then. He was asked to write more poems to celebrate similar events. In all of them, he alluded to the mythology of Greece and is therefore a most valuable source of knowledge of the ancient religion.

**PIRITHOÜS** *Greek* Son of ZEUS and Dia, the wife of Ixion; king of the LAPITHS, a mythical people inhabiting the mountains of THESSALY; friend of the hero THESEUS. Pirithoüs married HIPPODAMEIA. At the wedding feast, to which the CENTAURS had been invited, a great fight broke out between the Lapiths and the Centaurs, wild creatures that were half man and half horse. The Lapiths and Theseus, who was among the guests, defeated the centaurs and drove them from their home on Mount PELION.

Theseus accompanied Pirithoüs to the UNDERWORLD (1), where the two attempted to steal away PERSEPHONE, the reluctant bride of HADES, god of the underworld. Hades trapped both Theseus and Pirithoüs in deep chairs from which they could not arise. HERACLES rescued Theseus, but Pirithoüs was trapped in his chair for all eternity.

**PLEIADES** (Sailing Ones) *Greek* Seven daughters of ATLAS and PLEIONE, one of the OCEANIDS; sisters of the Hyades. Their names were Alcyone, Asterope, Celaene, ELECTRA, MAIA (1), MEROPE, and TAYGETE. They were placed among the stars to save them from being pursued by ORION. They are sometimes called "the Seven Sisters."

Astronomically, the Pleiades is a cluster of stars easily seen in the Taurus constellation. One of the stars is invisible to the naked eye. Some say that the "Lost Pleiad" is Merope, who married a mortal and hides herself in shame. Others say that the lost star is Electra, who fades away from grief at the fall of TROY.

The ancients believed that when they could see the cluster of stars ("the Sailing Ones") the weather was auspicious for sailing.

**PLEIONE** *Greek* Daughter of the TITANS OCEANUS and TETHYS; a NYMPH, one of the eldest among the thousands of daughters born of this union who were themselves considered by many writers to be Titans. Pleione and her sisters were guardians of bodies of water. She was the consort of ATLAS and with him the mother of the PLEIADES.

Pleione means "to increase in number." Some scholars think she may have been a nymph of flocks and herds. Her grandson, HERMES, one of the OLYMPIAN GODS, was the god of animal husbandry.

**PLUTO** *Greek and Roman* A name used to refer to the god of the UNDERWORLD. *Pluto* was a euphemism, a substitute name, for this much-feared god. In GREECE, *Pluto* referred to HADES. In ROME, after Greek mythology came to strongly influence its religions, people used *Pluto* to refer to Dis or Orcus. People developed this alternative name to protect themselves from this dangerous god who was not easily influenced by the actions or offerings of humans.

In Roman mythology, Pluto was the son of Saturn and brother to Jupiter, Juno, Neptune, and Vesta.

**PLUTUS** *Greek*   Son of Demeter and Iasion, son of Zeus and Electra (2); god of wealth and of the Earth's abundant harvests. (He is not to be confused with Pluto, god of the Underworld.) Plutus was believed to be blind because he distributed wealth to good and bad alike. Plutus appears in Hesiod's *Theogony*, Aristophanes' *Plutus*, and the *Divine Comedy* of Italian poet Dante (1265–1321).

**POLYDECTES** *Greek*   King of the island of Seriphos, protector of Danae and her son, Perseus. Polydectes sent Perseus on a dangerous mission, asking him to bring back the head of the Gorgon Medusa, which turned men to stone. While Perseus was away, Polydectes pursued Danae, trying to win her love. Danae was protected by Dictys, who was possibly the brother of Polydectes. Perseus returned with the head of Medusa and turned Polydectes into stone. Dictys then became king of Seriphos.

**POLYPHEMUS** *Greek*   The savage, one-eyed giant of Homer's *Odyssey*. Polyphemus entraps the hero, Odysseus, and his companions, and devours six of them. Odysseus blinds Polyphemus's one eye and with great cunning escapes. Homer's Polyphemus is identified with the Cyclopes, who were supposed to have one eye in the middle of their foreheads and live on the island of Sicily. Polyphemus appears also in Virgil's *Aeneid* as a threat to the hero Aeneas and his crew.

**POMONA** *Roman*   The young, beautiful Roman goddess of fruit trees and fruit. Her Latin name means "fruit" or "apple." Little is known of Pomona. She is considered one of the lesser goddesses, but she did have her own priests who were responsible only for her care and worship. Romans also dedicated to her a sacred grove that lay 12 miles outside of the city.

In *Metamorphoses*, the Roman poet Ovid told the story of how Vertumnus, the ancient Roman god of fruit and fruit trees, fell in love with Pomona. Though she resisted his courting, Vertumnus disguised himself as a harvester and then as an old woman and finally won this goddess's love.

The Roman goddess Pomona displays her fruits of plenty in the painting by French artist Nicholas Fouche (1653-1733).

Together, Pomona and Vertumnus influenced the growing season of spring and the changing of the trees in autumn.

**PONTUS** (Pontos) *Greek*   An ancient sea god; the first sea god.

Pontus was the son of the great Earth goddess Gaia. Some sources say he had no father, but came forth from his mother through her own will. Others say that Ether, the god of the pure upper air, was his father. Gaia mated with Pontus. Their children were Ceto, Phorcys, Thaumas, Nereus, and Eurybia, though some sources say Nereus was another name for Phorcys. These children are known more for who they married and for their children than for any other role they played in the Greek myths.

With his female counterpart, the female personification of the sea, Thalassa, Pontus was the father of the fish and animals of the sea.

**POSEIDON** *Greek*   Sea god and one of the Olympian gods; son of Cronus and Rhea; brother of Zeus, Hades, Demeter, Hera, and Hestia; husband of AMPHITRITE. The Romans identified Poseidon with NEPTUNE, an Italian water god.

Although Poseidon is best known as a sea god, in ancient times among migrating people he had been a god of fertility and of herdsmen. His emblem, the trident, was a symbol for the thunderbolt, which would make Poseidon a sky god of very ancient times. Some legends say that Poseidon could cause earthquakes.

Like all of his siblings except Zeus, Poseidon was swallowed by his father, Cronus, and then, thanks to Zeus, later disgorged unharmed. In other legends, to save Poseidon, Rhea hid him in a flock of lambs near Mantinea, in ARCADIA, in the care of a nurse named Arne. In yet another story, Rhea put Poseidon in the care of Capheira, a daughter of OCEANUS, who brought up the child in RHODES.

**Poseidon and Amphitrite**   Amphitrite, a NEREID (sea NYMPH), was wooed and won for Poseidon, god of the sea, by Delphinus. In gratitude, Poseidon set the image of Delphinus among the stars as the Dolphin.

Amphitrite bore Poseidon three children: TRI-TON, Rhode, and Benthescyme. They lived in an underwater cave in Eubol, off Aegae. In its spacious stables, Poseidon kept white chariot horses with golden manes. Some people call large, white-capped waves "white horses" in memory of Poseidon's horses.

**Poseidon and Athene**   Poseidon was greedy for earthly kingdoms. He tried to claim the city of ATHENS from the goddess ATHENE, saying that he could do more good for the city than she could. The two appeared before a court of gods and goddesses. Poseidon struck his trident into a rock, and water immediately gushed forth, but it was seawater, salty and therefore not very useful. Athene planted the first olive tree, which gave fruit, oil, and wood. The court decreed that Athene's gift was the more beneficial and that she thus had more right to the land. The olive branch became a symbol of peace.

**Poseidon and Horses**   Poseidon created the horse, according to some ancient writers, with a blow of his trident. He also invented the bridle, which

The ruins of the temple to Poseidon, built around 440 B.C., still stand overlooking the sea on the Cape of Sounion, 67 kilometers (about 42 miles) south-southeast of Athens. *(Photograph by Frank van Mierlo. Used under a Creative Commons License.)*

controls a horse. He probably started horse racing too. The horse was sacred to Poseidon. One myth has it that Poseidon changed himself into a horse to capture the love of the goddess Demeter, who had at one time transformed herself into a mare.

**PRIAM** *Greek* King of TROY during the TROJAN WAR, though too old to take an active part in the war. He was the son of LAOMEDON and, some say, the father of 50 children, some of them with his second wife, HECUBA. Among them were the Trojan heroes HECTOR and PARIS and the prophetess CASSANDRA.

The death of Hector and the lack of respect paid to his body were severe blows to King Priam. Alone, he went to the Achaean (Greek) camp to bargain with the hero ACHILLES for his son's body. There, NEOPTOLEMUS, one of Achilles' sons, killed Priam.

**PRIAPUS** *Greek* An ancient god of fertility, protector of herds, bees, fish, and the vine. Priapus was a latecomer to Greek mythology. In most accounts, Priapus was the son of DIONYSUS and APHRODITE. In others, his mother was CHIONE and his father Dionysus, ADONIS, HERMES, or PAN. Though his parentage may be in doubt, it is certain that Priapus was associated with the ancient Greek worship of Dionysus, the wine god. Many scholars think that Priapus was another name for Pan, an ancient pastoral deity.

**PROMETHEUS** (Forethought) *Greek* One of the TITANS, descended from the EARTH MOTHER (GAIA) and the Sky Father (URANUS); son of IAPETUS and one of the daughters of OCEANUS, possibly CLYMENE; brother of ATLAS and EPIMETHEUS; father of DEUCALION.

Prometheus was a remarkable figure in Greek mythology. Some stories say that he was the creator of man. He was certainly the main champion of humankind, bringing the gift of fire and teaching people how to use it. He also taught humans astronomy, medicine, navigation, metalworking, architecture, and writing.

ZEUS grew angry with Prometheus for stealing fire and giving it to people. He had Prometheus chained to a rock on Mount Caucasus, where an eagle or a vulture plucked at his liver all day. Prometheus healed every night, so that his suffering seemed destined to go on for all eternity. HERACLES eventually rescued Prometheus, and CHIRON, the CENTAUR gave his own immortality to Prometheus.

To revenge himself on humankind, Zeus sent PANDORA into the world and with her all the troubles and sicknesses of humankind.

Some scholars say that in earlier mythologies Prometheus remained chained to his rock through all eternity. But to the fair-minded ancient Greek poets who recorded the myths, it was unthinkable that the champion of humankind should be so punished, hence the story of Heracles, the hero who broke the bonds of Prometheus, and of Chiron, the gentle centaur who conferred his immortality on Prometheus to end his own suffering.

The story of the enmity between Zeus and Prometheus may represent the antagonism between an ancient god, Prometheus, and the more modern OLYMPIAN GODS, personified by Zeus.

References to Prometheus are found in most of the classical poets, such as HESIOD and AESCHYLUS (*Prometheus Bound*). In the 18th century, German poet and scholar Johann Wolfgang von Goethe saw Prometheus as a symbol of humanity's creative striving and rebellion against the restraints of society. The 19th-century English poet Percy Bysshe Shelley, in *Prometheus Unbound*, glorified the Titan who dared to revolt against the gods and triumph over tyranny.

**Prometheus, Fire-bringer and Champion of Humankind** Stories say that on one occasion Prometheus, a Titan, made two bundles out of the remains of an ox that had been sacrificed. One bundle contained the meat, the other, the bones. He wrapped the bones in succulent-looking fat; the meat he placed inside the stomach sac of the ox.

Asked to choose which package he preferred, the god Zeus chose the package that looked succulent but contained nothing but bones. In his anger at being tricked, although some say that the great god surely knew he was being tricked, Zeus decided to keep the knowledge of fire-making from humankind.

Prometheus, undaunted, stole fire from heaven, or from the forge of the smith-god, HEPHAESTUS, and took it to Earth hidden in the hollow stalk of the fennel plant. He then began to teach people all the uses of fire—how to make tools and fashion metal, how to build, and how to cook. He also taught people how to sow and reap, and how to use herbs for healing.

**Prometheus, Bound and Unbound** Prometheus, the champion of humankind, had thwarted the great god Zeus in his attempt to conceal knowledge of fire from humans. To punish the law-breaker, Zeus chained Prometheus to a rock on Mount Caucasus, where an eagle or a vulture plucked at his liver all through the day. Prometheus healed every night, so this torture would go on through all eternity.

Eventually, the hero Heracles slew the bird and unbound Prometheus. The gentle centaur, Chiron,

The god Prometheus, chained to a rock by Zeus for giving fire to humans, suffers each day as an eagle plucks at his liver. Flemish artist Peter Paul Rubens (1577-1640) portrayed the scene in this oil painting which now hangs in the Philadelphia Museum of Art.

then conferred his own immortality upon Prometheus, so that he would die but Prometheus would live.

As well as being punished for bringing fire to men, Zeus held Prometheus captive because he knew a secret to which Zeus wanted an answer: The sea nymph THETIS was soon to bear a child that would be greater than its father. The father could be either Zeus or POSEIDON; the child could cause chaos among the Olympian Gods. Prometheus would not reveal his secret as long as he was held captive.

**Prometheus and Pandora** Prometheus was a cause of great anger to Zeus. Prometheus had tricked Zeus in the matter of sacrifices made by humans and he had eventually escaped from the terrible torture inflicted by Zeus as punishment. Zeus decided that humankind must be punished for having received the forbidden gift of fire.

Zeus ordered Hephaestus, the smith-god, to make a woman out of clay. The gods breathed life into her and made her irresistibly beautiful. She was named Pandora (All-giving) and sent to Earth, bearing a sealed vase, of which she was forbidden to know the contents. In spite of warnings from Prometheus, Epimetheus, his brother, immediately took Pandora to be his wife. Then Pandora opened the vase, sometimes called Pandora's Box, and every disaster that humans were ever to know was released upon the world. Only Hope remained in the vase, giving humankind the will to go on living.

**PROSERPINA** *Roman* Queen of the UNDERWORLD (2) and the consort or wife of DIS, the Roman god of the underworld. The Romans believed Proserpina had power over growing plants and honored her as a springtime goddess. Proserpina was an ancient goddess of Italian origins. The people of ROME honored her and Dis in games held about every 100 years.

Some scholars see Proserpina as the simple translation of the name PERSEPHONE, a Greek goddess, daughter of DEMETER and ZEUS, whom HADES, the Greek god of the underworld, abducted to become his wife. Other scholars identify Proserpina with the ancient Greek goddess HECATE, who, in some stories, becomes Persephone's companion in the underworld.

**PROTESILAUS** *Greek* A hero from Thessaly, son of IPHICLES; husband of Laodamia. Protesilaus was the first of the Greeks to spring ashore at Troy (see TROJAN WAR) and the first to die. Laodamia begged the gods to allow Protesilaus to return to Earth so that they might spend three more hours together. The gods granted her wish and the lovers were reunited. Then Laodamia committed suicide and went to the UNDERWORLD with her husband.

**PROTEUS** *Greek* A minor but ancient sea god who served POSEIDON. Proteus had enormous knowledge and the ability to change his shape at will if he did not want to stay around to answer questions. When finally cornered, he advised MENELAUS, whose ship was becalmed off the coast of Egypt, that to escape he should pay proper honor to the god ZEUS. Menelaus listened to the advice of the sea god and was eventually able to sail home to SPARTA.

In another story, ARISTAEUS, the son of APOLLO, sought the advice of Proteus, who advised him to sacrifice cattle to the gods. Aristaeus did, and was rewarded by seeing swarms of bees emerging from the corpses of the slain cattle. (Aristaeus was an expert in the art of beekeeping.)

**PSYCHE** (Soul) *Greek* A mortal woman so beautiful that the goddess APHRODITE was jealous of her and ordered EROS to punish her.

**PYGMAEI** (PYGMIES) *Greek* A mythological race of very short people, only 13.5 inches tall, found mostly in ancient Greek folklore but also mentioned often in the stories of the great gods. The pygmaei lived by a stream which most sources say was in Egypt, though others say it was in Thrace or India. They wore their hair very long and did not wear clothes. These farmers waged war against the cranes, sometimes called storks, that came each year in the late summer to eat the crops.

A beautiful woman was born among the pygmaei. Her name was Gerana or Oenoe. As she grew, Gerana became very vain and believed she was even more beautiful than HERA, queen of the OLYMPIAN GODS and the wife and sister of ZEUS. Hera finally realized that the only way to correct Gerana's vanity was to punish her, and Hera turned the pygmaei woman into a crane. By that time, Gerana had a son and wanted desperately to be reunited with him. As a crane, she flew back to the pygmaeis but they rejected her and beat her off with sticks. In some versions, Gerana was a human woman who married a pygmaei.

The pygmaei also tried to capture HERACLES after he fell asleep in their lands while on his famous journeys. He awoke and laughed at their efforts, scooped up several pygmaei, and carried them off.

**PYGMALION** *Greek* Son of Belus, a sculptor from Cyprus who despised women but adored the goddess APHRODITE. He made an ivory statue of her of such extraordinary beauty that he fell in love with it. As he embraced the statue, Aphrodite answered his prayers and made the statue come to life, giving it the name GALATEA (3). This story, from OVID's *Metamorphoses*, enhances the legendary power of Aphrodite over all creation. It has been told many times, most famously in the play *Pygmalion* by George Bernard Shaw (1856–1950), the source of the musical *My Fair Lady* by Alan Jay Lerner and Frederick Loewe.

**PYRRHA** *Greek* Daughter of EPIMETHEUS; wife of DEUCALION. Together Pyrrha and Deucalion repeopled the Earth after the great rain sent by ZEUS.

**PYTHIAN GAMES** *Greek* A sacred rite enacted in ancient GREECE to honor the ancient serpent-monster, PYTHON, slain by the god APOLLO. It was one of the great Hellenic festivals celebrated in DELPHI, second only to the OLYMPIC GAMES in importance.

**PYTHON** *Greek* A female serpent born of the Earth. The goddess HERA sent Python to torment her rival LETO, one of the many loves of ZEUS, and the mother of APOLLO. The young Apollo slew the Python and bid the serpent to rot where it had fallen. The spot where this encounter took place was called Pytho, from the Greek word *pytho*, "to rot." The name was later changed to DELPHI. The site became the most venerated shrine in ancient GREECE, sacred to Apollo. The Pythian Games were held every four years in honor of the ancient Python and were next in importance to the famous OLYMPIC GAMES.

**QUIRINUS** (QUIRINIUS) *Roman* An ancient god, perhaps of warfare or of citizenship. The surviving information on Quirinus is confusing and sketchy. Roman historians and poets and modern scholars disagree over just what role he played in Roman society.

Quirinus was the third most important god in the PANTHEON of early ROME, behind JUPITER and MARS. These three were honored together as a trio of the most powerful deities, though JUNO and MINERVA eventually replaced Quirinus and Mars. Much information remains about Jupiter and Mars, including their connection to Greek mythology, but Quirinus was not associated with a Greek counterpart. The details of his origin faded from popularity, and much has been lost.

A cult to Quirinus centered on the Quirinal Hill, one of the seven hills in Rome, named in his honor. A huge temple to Quirinus stood on that hill. The people of Rome celebrated his festival, known as the Quirinalia, on February 17.

Some scholars and stories suggest that Quirinus was the peaceful side of the Roman god of war, Mars: not the soldier, but the citizen. The name *Quirinus* may have come from the Roman word for citizen, *quirite*.

Like Mars, Quirinus may have begun as a god of the Sabine people (see SABINES). Some histories of Rome say that Quirinus was the name given to ROMULUS, the twin brother of REMUS and founder of Rome, when he transformed from a mortal into a god.

# R

**RHADAMANTHUS** (RHADAMANTHYS) *Greek* Son of EUROPA and the god ZEUS; brother of MINOS and SARPEDON. According to HOMER in the *ODYSSEY*, Rhadamanthus was the ruler of the Elysian Fields, where fortunate shades, or spirits, of mortals went after death. Later legends say that he was one of the judges of the UNDERWORLD (1).

**RHEA** (Earth) *Greek* A TITAN, the mother of the great ruling gods of OLYMPUS. She was the daughter of GAIA and URANUS (Heaven); the sister-wife of CRONUS; and the mother of DEMETER, HADES, HERA, HESTIA, POSEIDON, and ZEUS.

The story of Rhea is a near-repetition of that of her mother Gaia. Her father, Uranus, jealous of Gaia's children, had them confined under the Earth, but with Gaia's help the bravest son, Cronus, overcame his father and banished him. When Cronus became the husband of his sister Rhea, they had many children, of whom Cronus was so jealous that he swallowed them. Rhea managed to save Zeus, who rescued his siblings and went to war with Cronus.

Rhea was identified with the EARTH MOTHER and goddess of fertility. Her cult was strongest in CRETE, which some say was the birthplace of Zeus. She was identified with CYBELE and also known as AGDISTIS. In Roman mythology she was identified with OPS, goddess of the harvest. Rhea, though a shadowy figure herself, was widely worshiped under various names as an Earth goddess.

**RHEA SILVIA** (ILIA) *Roman* A VESTAL VIRGIN. Rhea Silvia was raped or loved by the god MARS, which resulted in her becoming the mother of ROMULUS AND REMUS, twin brothers who became the legendary founders of ROME. She was the daughter of King Numitor of ALBA LONGA a city in LATIUM, or according to some legends, the daughter of the hero AENEAS, who was honored by people of Rome as the founder of their race.

Not knowing who had fathered the twins, Rhea Silvia's uncle, King Amulius, who had taken the throne from his brother, Numitor, ordered that the children be taken from their mother at their birth and thrown in the Tiber River and left to die. One legend has it that Amulius imprisoned Rhea Silvia before the birth and kept her there after the birth. Another says that he tried to kill her by throwing her into the Tiber, too, but the god of that body of water rescued her and made her his wife. Meanwhile, a she-wolf found the babies and nursed them until a shepherd, FAUSTULUS, found them and raised them with his wife, ACCA LARENTIA (1).

**RHODES** *Greek* The easternmost island of the Aegean Sea. In Greek mythology, it was the favored abode of the sun god HELIOS, whose wife was the NYMPH Rhodos. Their children were the first inhabitants of Rhodes.

**ROBIGO AND ROBIGUS** *Roman* Two deities, a goddess and god, who watched over growing fields of wheat and grain and who, if not treated well, brought rust or mildew to crops. Robigo, which means blight or mildew in Latin, was female, and Robigus was male.

Each year, on April 25, the time when mildew most commonly attacked young plants, the Romans held the festival of the Robigalia. Worshipers, led by their priest, sacrificed a dog to Robigo and Robigus, preferably a rust red dog to symbolize the color of mildew on plants. Their ceremony was held five miles north of ROME, next to the city's fields. Races and games followed the ceremony.

**ROMA** *Roman* A legendary figure who came to be worshiped as a goddess, Roma was the personification of the city of ROME. According to modern historians and archaeologists, she was first worshiped as a deity in about 195 B.C. when a popular cult to her developed outside of the city and in GREECE, which was, by then, a part of the Roman Republic. Rome had become an important city in the lives of the people in these outlying areas, and they developed a worship of this goddess as an expression of that importance. Augustus, the first emperor of Rome, became associated with Roma. After Augustus died in A.D. 14, people believed he became a god and worshiped him with Roma. In A.D. 118, Emperor Hadrian built a temple to Roma within the city.

The legends of Roma are much older than her worship as a goddess. According to some ancient sources, she was a Trojan prisoner of AENEAS who took her and other captives with him when he left TROY. After years of wandering the seas, Aeneas's ship finally reached the western shores of Italy. The captives were tired of the journey and Roma convinced them to set fire to the ship so Aeneas could not leave. Eventually, the community they created became so prosperous they named the city after her in thanks for her courage.

In other legends, Roma was sometimes named as the granddaughter of Aeneas, as the wife of his son, and even as his wife. She was also said to be the daughter of HERACLES. Some say she was also the sister of LATINUS, legendary king and founder of the Latin people.

Still another tradition says that Roma was the daughter of EVANDER, the legendary king who fled Greece and formed a community on the Palatine Hill before Romulus founded Rome. Evander, stories say, named the city that grew up around that hill and its six neighbors after his daughter.

**ROME** *Roman*  A city on the Tiber River in west central Italy, which by the first millennium B.C., had grown into a major urban center and the seat of an empire that surrounded the Mediterranean Sea and reached as far north as the British Isles. Rome's beginnings are hidden behind many myths and legends. According to the most common myth, Rome was founded by ROMULUS on April 21, an event celebrated in ancient times by the festival of Parilia, the festival of PALES. The year of that event is reported by some ancient sources as between 772 and 754 B.C. Other legends tell of the founding of the city by the descendants of AENEAS, the Greek hero who settled in central Italy after the end of the TROJAN WAR.

Archaeological evidence shows very early settlements built by farming people on or near the seven famous hills that formed the center of the city that became Rome. The first hill people settled appears to have been the Capitoline Hill. Archaeologists have discovered some of the oldest temples to the supreme Roman god, JUPITER, on this hill. According to legend, it was on this hill that Romulus founded his city.

The next hill that settlers developed was the nearby Palatine, 1,250 yards to the southeast of the Capitoline Hill. Legend says that EVANDER, a leader from the ARCADIA region of ancient GREECE, settled this hill even before Romulus was born.

Rulers, citizens, and cult followers also built sites of worship on the Quirinal Hill, 2,100 yards to the north-northwest of the Capitoline Hill, and the Aventine Hill, 2,500 yards to the south of Capitoline Hill. Rome's other three hills are the Viminal, Esquiline, and Caelian.

The community of Rome grew surrounded by the lands of many different cultures which, over time, interacted with and then became part of the Roman culture. No more than 20 miles to the northwest was ETRURIA, a region more than a kingdom, whose religions strongly influenced the people of Rome. The SABINES lived about 25 miles to the northeast. Twenty-five miles to the southeast lived the Latini people who gave their name to the language that came to dominate central Italy, Latin. RUTULI lay 20 miles to the south.

According to legend, Rome's earliest rulers were kings, some of them rulers of nearby regions, who were honored over time as great heroes. One such was LATINUS, king of the Latini people. The last king, Tarquinius Superbus, who ruled from 534 to 510 B.C., at first refused the books of prophecy offered him for sale by the SIBYL OF CUMAE. After she had destroyed the first six books, he realized the worth of the last three and bought them at the price of the original nine. During this time, also, Greek mythology began influencing the religions of the people of Rome and the surrounding areas, primarily through contact with Greek colonies in southern Italy and on the island of Sicily. This process of influence by the cultures of Greece is known as HELLENIZATION.

After this era, the people of Rome rejected kingship as a form of government and turned to a representative republic, whereby each year the people chose two chief executives to govern the city. At this time, too, Rome's history becomes a matter of authentic records available for modern study. During the Republic era (510 to 264 B.C.), Rome extended its rule to most of central Italy through military force. Romans also conquered many of the Greek colonies and brought those lands into their nation.

Ruins of an ancient temple to Saturn (foreground) remain today in the Roman Forum, which stood between the Capitoline and Palatine hills. *(Photograph by Marcok. Used under a Creative Commons License.)*

Rome became a world power in the third and second centuries B.C., expanding its rule to North Africa, Spain, and the eastern Mediterranean. Rome's conquests included Greece. In the Macedonian Wars of the third century B.C., Roman armies defeated the ruler of the northern portion of the Greek peninsula and then took over rule of the southern portion, home to the great Greek myths and the philosophical and cultural center of that part of the world.

Rome became an empire after the reign of Julius Caesar in the first century B.C. As the Romans spread their influence, they colonized many lands and built temples to their gods, as well as civic and cultural buildings, across the region. Temples to Jupiter, Minerva, Juno, and Mars stood on hills across the lands of the Mediterranean and western Europe. The ruins of many still stand today and provide evidence of the widespread influence of the Roman empire.

Today, Rome is the economic, cultural, and political center of Italy. Monuments to the ancient societies stand amid modern buildings. Archaeologists continue to discover the past of this city and its influences, including evidence of its religions and myths. New discoveries continue to contribute to the understanding of the nature of Rome's great beliefs.

**ROMULUS AND REMUS** *Roman*   The twin sons of the god Mars and Rhea Silvia. They were the legendary founders of Rome, the greatest city of the ancient world. Their mother, Rhea Silvia, was a Vestal Virgin. In the most common story, she was condemned to death for losing her virginity. Her uncle, King Amulius, commanded that the two infants be thrown into the Tiber River. A she-wolf who had just given birth found the boys and fed them with her own milk. Some sources say that Mars, the divine father of Romulus and Remus, sent the wolf, his sacred animal, to watch over his sons. A shepherd of the king, Faustulus, found the boys and took them home where his wife, Acca Laurentia (1), raised them. After they grew up, they founded the city of Rome on the Palatine Hill. They quarreled over the plans for the city, and Romulus slew Remus. Romulus became king of Rome and ruled for 40 years. He provided wives for the new settlers of Rome by capturing Sabine women. Romulus was at last taken up to the heavens in a mysterious whirlwind, said to be sent by Mars.

The best-known artistic representation of Romulus and Remus is the bronze sculpture of a she-wolf nursing the two infants, now in the Capitoline Museum Rome.

**Rutuli** (Rutulians) A people of ancient Italy inhabiting Ardea and the land surrounding Latium. Their king was Turnus, who was killed in battle with the Aeneas, a hero of the Trojan War, who settled in Italy.

# S

**SABINES** (SABINI) *Roman* One of the oldest peoples of central Italy. In a famous Roman legend, the new Roman settlers, subjects of ROMULUS, needed wives, so they abducted the Sabine women. War immediately broke out between the Sabine men and the Romans. The Sabine women helped to make peace by placing themselves and their infants between the warring tribes. The Sabines and the Romans became united as one people.

The seizure, or rape, of the Sabine women is frequently portrayed in art. One of the most famous is the painting by the Flemish artist Peter Paul Rubens (1577–1640) in the National Gallery, London.

**SAGITTARIUS** (The Archer) *Greek* A constellation in the night sky of the Northern Hemisphere between Scorpio and CAPRICORN; the ninth sign in the Zodiac. Star charts show Sagittarius wielding a bow and arrow, pointing as if to shoot at Scorpio.

Experts debate the mythological identity of Sagittarius. Some scholars believe that Sagittarius, who is often shown as human from the waist up and horse from the waist down, represents a CENTAUR, and conclude that he was a symbol of CHIRON, the wise centaur of Greek mythology. Because Chiron was skilled at archery and hunting, they believe ZEUS placed him in the night sky in this position to make him immortal.

However, other scholars and the Latin poet Hyginus, who lived in the first century B.C., argue that Sagittarius is not half horse but half goat, which would make him a SATYR and a servant of the god DIONYSUS (known as BACCHUS to the Romans). These experts suggest that Chiron's constellation is CENTAURUS, which shines in the night sky of the Southern Hemisphere.

Italian Renaissance sculptor Giambologna (1529-1608) portrayed Roman men carrying off a Sabine woman in this statue, which now stands in Florence, Italy. *(Photo by Yair-haklai. Used under a Creative Commons License.)*

**SALACIA** (The salty one) *Roman* A goddess of the sea, usually associated with the sea god NEPTUNE, likely his wife. Salacia personified salt water and was said to have fled from Neptune to the Atlantic Ocean, which became her domain. Eventually, she married the great sea god. Salacia took on many of the stories of the Greek goddess AMPHITRITE.

**SALUS** *Roman* The goddess of health and preservation, also of success and good fortune. Salus was more of an abstraction than a character in myths and became closely associated with the Greek goddess of health, HYGEIA. In 302 B.C., the Romans dedicated a new temple on the Quirinal Hill to Salus. People celebrated her feast on April 30. Salus was often shown standing on a globe and pouring liquid from a cup onto an altar around which curled a snake. Her name was part of the popular phrase "Salus Publica," referring to the public health, or well-being of the state and society of ROME.

**SARPEDON** *Greek* A son of ZEUS and Laodemia or EUROPA. In the TROJAN WAR, Sarpedon was a hero, the ally of King PRIAM. His particular friend was GLAUCUS (1), who mourned his death (in HOMER's *ILIAD*) at the hands of PATROCLUS. Zeus had APOLLO carry the body of Sarpedon from the battlefield to be buried in LYDIA, his homeland.

In an earlier legend, Sarpedon was the son of Zeus and Europa, and the brother of MINOS and RHADAMANTHUS. He became king of Lydia. Zeus granted him the privilege of living for three generations.

**SATURN** (SATURNUS) *Roman* Originally a god of agriculture, of the sowing of seeds and corn; also the god of the passage of time. Saturn may have been an early Etruscan family god who grew in importance in the culture of ETRURIA before developing a larger following.

To the Romans, Saturn represented a primitive golden age, a time of great happiness that myths say existed before people needed to farm to survive. Saturn was king of that longed-for mythical time. LUA was his wife in that wonderful land.

Eventually, the characteristics of Saturn merged with those of the Greek god CRONUS, and Saturn was honored as the father of JUPITER, NEPTUNE, JUNO, and PLUTO. The role of Saturn's wife shifted to RHEA. Saturn, whose symbol was the scythe, also served as the keeper or guardian of the treasury in ROME, and because of that responsibility people saw him as the god of money.

The Saturnalia, the week-long feast in honor of Saturn, began on December 17, the time of winter sowing. People celebrated with riotous feasting and exchange of gifts. This festival eventually influenced the Christian celebration of Christmas.

In astronomy, Saturn is the sixth planet from the Sun and the second-largest planet, after Jupiter, in this SOLAR SYSTEM. This gas giant is surrounded by as many as 21 moons. The largest, TITAN, is named

for the first race of Greek gods. Other Saturn moons named after Greek and Roman gods include TETHYS, DIONE, Rhea, HYPERION, and PHOEBE.

**SATYRS** *Greek* One of a class of woodland and mountain spirits attendant on DIONYSUS. They are usually shown as part human and part goat or monkey. The satyrs were noted for riotousness and mischief, terrifying herdsmen and shepherds, and chasing after NYMPHS. One legend relates that the satyrs were originally men, sons of HERMES and Iphthima. The goddess HERA turned them into half human beasts to punish them for neglecting to keep watch over Dionysus. They were ever after faithful to the god and accompanied him to all his festivals. Medieval Christian art used the satyrs as images of the devil.

**SCYLLA** *Greek* Daughter of Nisus. She was cruelly treated by MINOS. This Scylla has no connection with the monster named Scylla (see SCYLLA AND CHARYBDIS).

**SCYLLA AND CHARYBDIS** *Greek* Two mythical characters who inhabited the Straits of Messina, between mainland Italy and the island of Sicily. On the Italian side lived the monster Scylla. She had the body of a woman, but around her waist grew six long necks with the heads of dogs armed with three rows of teeth, who emitted ferocious and terrifying barks. On the Sicilian side lived Charybdis, who dwelled under a great fig tree. Three times each day, Charybdis swallowed up the sea and then spat it out again in a boiling whirlpool.

Although the witch CIRCE had warned the hero ODYSSEUS of the dangers of Scylla and Charybdis, Scylla managed to devour six of Odysseus's crewmen. The legend represents the dangers of navigation faced by early mariners in those waters, where there are treacherous currents akin to whirlpools.

The expression "to fall between Scylla and Charybdis," similar to the more modern "to jump from the frying pan into the fire," means to be caught in a dilemma—that is, to have to choose between two unsatisfactory alternatives.

**SELENE** (Moon) *Greek* An ancient moon goddess. Daughter of the TITANS THEIA and HYPERION; sister of HELIOS (the Sun) and EOS (the Dawn). Selene is also called PHOEBE. She is LUNA in Roman mythology, and sometimes identified with ARTEMIS.

Selene was a beautiful woman, usually depicted with long wings and a golden crown that shed a

Selene, the Greek goddess of the moon, watches over the sleeping Endymion, a shepherd boy whom she loves. Sabastiano Ricci (1659-1734) captured the scene in this painting, which now hangs in Chiswick House in London.

gentle light in the darkness of night. White horses pulled her chariot across the skies. She was the mother of three daughters by ZEUS: Pandia, Erse (the Dew), and Nemea. It is said that the Nemean Lion was born to Selene and Zeus, and that it fell from the Moon to the Earth (see under HERACLES). Selene was also loved by PAN. The best-known legend of Selene was that of her love for the youth ENDYMION.

**SEMELE** (Moon) *Greek* Daughter of CADMUS and HARMONIA, lover of ZEUS, mother of DIONYSUS. After her death in the flames created by Zeus, Semele was conducted from the UNDERWORLD to OLYMPUS, home of the gods, where she became immortal under the

name Thyone. Semele was worshiped in ATHENS during the Leneitai (Festival of Wild Women), when every year a BULL representing Dionysus was sacrificed to her.

Some say that Semele is a form of SELENE, an ancient moon goddess.

**SERIPHOS** (SERIFOS) *Greek* An island in the Western Cyclades group in the Aegean Sea. This was the island where the infant PERSEUS and his mother, DANAE, came to rest after escaping from Acrisius.

**SEVEN AGAINST THEBES** *Greek* The name given to the conflict between the rulers of the kingdom of THEBES and the rebels who challenged the king for the throne. It was the subject of a tragedy by AESCHYLUS.

At the death of their father, OEDIPUS, Eteocles and Polynices (who were probably twins), had made a pact to rule the kingdom of Thebes jointly, each one taking over the kingdom for a year at a time. However, Eteocles refused to give up his kingship at the end of his year. Polynices appealed to King ADRASTUS of ARGOS for military help and the war began. The seven were the champions Adrastus brought together to help Polynices gain the throne.

The city of Thebes had seven gates. Eteocles set a champion to guard each one. Adrastus delegated a champion to capture each gate. It was fated that, at the end of the battle, the two brothers, Eteocles and Polynices, should meet in one-to-one combat and kill each other.

Creon, the new king of Thebes, ordered that Eteocles be left to lie on the battlefield rather than be buried. He was opposed by ANTIGONE, the sister of Eteocles and Polynices, who herself performed the forbidden burial service.

The EPIGONI, sons of the Seven, continued the war years later.

**SIBYL** (SIBYLLA) *Greek* Originally, a young girl, the daughter of a Trojan, who had the gift of prophecy. Her name was Sibylla, and she dedicated her gift to APOLLO, who inspired her to make predictions. Over time, people shortened her name to Sibyl. Eventually, her legend came to identify Sibyl as the daughter of ZEUS and Lamia, a daughter of the sea god POSEIDON.

People then began using the name *Sibyl* for any woman who had the same gift of foretelling the future. The most famous Greek woman given this name was the Sibyl of Erythia in LYDIA, a region of GREECE. The most famous Roman prophetess was the SIBYL OF CUMAE, who lived in a cave on the Bay of Naples.

**SIBYL OF CUMAE** *Roman*   A prophetess who lived in a cave below a temple to APOLLO in Cumae, a port in the Bay of Naples on Italy's western coast on the shores of Lake Averna.

Some historians believe the Sibyl of Cumae was first known as the Sibyl of Erythrae, a city in GREECE. This SIBYL, which was the woman's name and came to identify a female prophet, is said to have left Greece and settled in Italy after the god Apollo promised her as many years of life as the grains of sand she could hold in her hand if she left her homeland and never returned.

In Italy, the Sibyl of Cumae is said to have offered to sell nine prophetic books to one of the last kings of ROME, Tarquinius Superbus, but, not recognizing her or her power, he refused to pay the price. The Sibyl left, burned three of the books and returned to offer Tarquinius six for the same price as nine. He refused. She burned three more and returned again to offer him three books for the price of nine. Having learned who she was, Tarquinius bought the three, and then and there the sibyl vanished.

Her written words of prophecy, which came to be known as the SYBILLINE BOOKS, gained a powerful influence over the development of Roman religion, particularly as it was influenced by Greek religion.

**SIBYLLINE BOOKS** *Roman*   A collection of prophecies written by the SIBYL OF CUMAE, perhaps brought with her from GREECE, which contained advice for fortune-telling, predictions of the future of ROME, and a set of instructions that influenced Roman religion for centuries.

In the mid-500s B.C., this sibyl offered the original nine volumes of her predictions to the last Roman king, Tarquinius Superbus, but he refused twice to buy them, not knowing their worth. With each refusal, the sibyl burned three books. Then the king, having learned of her reputation as a prophetess, bought the three remaining books at the same price as the original nine. The sibyl vanished and Tarquinius had the manuscripts preserved in a lower chamber of a temple of JUPITER. Special priests guarded the books. In times of strife and conflict, Roman leaders consulted these prophecies. Often they instructed the people of Rome to bring a new cult or worship of a specific Greek god to Rome.

In 83 B.C., the temple in which the books were kept burned and they were destroyed. The Roman leaders sent for copies of the verses from across the empire, which included all of Italy and Greece, stretched from Spain to Turkey, and included portions of northern Africa. The last known time Rome consulted the Sibylline Books was in A.D. 363.

**SILENUS** (SELINI) *Greek*   Son of HERMES or of PAN; tutor of DIONYSUS. An immensely wise old man, Silenus knew both past and future. He is often shown as a hairy, plump old man with the ears and legs of a horse, seated astride a wine cask or a donkey.

In its plural form, the Sileni denoted a category of rural divinities, personifying the genii of springs and rivers. As such they were associated with the SATYRS who followed Dionysus in his revels.

**SILVANUS** *Roman*   An ancient god of northern Italy and then of the Romans. Silvanus was, in his earliest form, a god of uncultivated lands, of forests and woods, fields and flocks. People believed that he either lived among the mysterious forces of these places or was himself one of those mysterious forces. Later, people came to worship Silvanus as a god of agriculture, a rural god. Artists portrayed him as a peasant or a man of the country.

Silvanus was often worshiped with FAUNUS, another Roman god of rural life, who was seen as a protector of farmers and shepherds. As the Romans adopted many of the stories of the gods of classical GREECE (see HELLENIZATION), the characteristics of Silvanaus and Faunus merged with those of PAN, the god of fields and forests whom artists portrayed as half man, half goat.

**SIRENS** *Greek*   The NYMPHS whose sweet song lured sailors to destruction by making them go mad and therefore become shipwrecked on the coast where the Sirens lived. In HOMER'S *ODYSSEY*, CIRCE warned the hero, ODYSSEUS, about the Sirens. He plugged the ears of his crewmen with wax, then had himself tied to the mast of the ship, while the crew rowed out of danger. In the myth of the ARGONAUTS, the sailors were able to sail safely by the nymphs because the poet ORPHEUS was on board and sang more sweetly than the Sirens.

**SISYPHUS** *Greek*   Son of AEOLUS; brother of ATHAMAS; husband of MEROPE. Although Sisyphus is described as a cunning rogue in HOMER'S *ODYSSEY*, he is most famous for a terrible punishment visited on him by ZEUS. He was condemned to push an enormous boulder to the top of a hill. Once at the top, the boulder would come crashing down, and Sisyphus had to begin his task all over again. Thus,

Sisyphus has become the symbol for a fruitless task. It is not known for what crime Sisyphus was being punished in this manner.

Another story about Sisyphus tells how he outwitted THANATOS (Death). Zeus had sent Thanatos to seize Sisyphus. Sisyphus asked Thanatos to demonstrate how the manacles that he carried worked. During the demonstration, Sisyphus managed to lock up Thanatos. Zeus had to send ARES from OLYMPUS to release Death upon the Earth again, for no one was dying.

Meanwhile Sisyphus asked his wife, Merope, to leave his body unburied when he died—for he knew that Thanatos would come for him a second time. When Sisyphus died, he went straight to HADES, god of the UNDERWORLD (1), and complained that his corpse had not received a proper burial. Hades, a just god, sent Sisyphus back to Earth to arrange a decent burial. Sisyphus had a joyous reunion with his wife, broke his word to Hades to return, and lived to an old age.

**SOL** *Roman*  In the earliest Roman religion, a sun god worshiped by the SABINES, who introduced the cult of Sol to the Roman people when a Sabine king ruled over that city. As Greek religions gained influence over the religions of ROME, people identified Sol with HELIOS, the Greek sun god, and with APOLLO, who also had attributes of the Sun in his myths.

Later, the Roman emperor Aurelian (A.D. 270–275) introduced the worship of Sol Invictus (Invincible Sun) to Rome, but this Sol is known to have been of Syrian origins and is not the Sol of the older religions of Rome. The worship of Sol Invictus was one of the last cults introduced into Roman culture before the emperor Constantine converted to Christianity in the A.D. 300s.

Sol is the name given to the Sun at the center of our SOLAR SYSTEM that is 98 million miles from Earth. It is 109 times the diameter of Earth and has been shining for more than 4 billion years, according to scientific estimates.

**SOLAR SYSTEM**  The Sun, known also as SOL, named after a Roman god, and the astronomical bodies that orbit it. In modern times, the English names for six of the planets are Roman gods and the names for two of the planets are Greek gods. (Earth is an Old English word that refers to the planet we live on.) These gods are

> MERCURY—The Roman god of trade and
> merchants
> VENUS—The Roman goddess of the productive
> power of nature

> MARS—A Roman god of fertility and war
> JUPITER—The supreme Roman god
> SATURN—A very old Roman god of agriculture,
> father of Jupiter
> URANUS—A very ancient Greek deity, husband
> of GAIA
> NEPTUNE—An ancient Roman sea god
> PLUTO (no longer considered a planet)—A ritual
> title for HADES, Greek god of the UNDER-
> WORLD and Roman god DIS

Many of the moons of these planets were discovered since about A.D. 1500. They, too, were given mythological names, most of them from the Greek stories. Some of Jupiter's 16 moons are GANYMEDE, EUROPA, IO, and CALLISTO. Some of Saturn's 20 moons are TETHYS, PROMETHEUS, PANDORA, and ATLAS. Neptune's moons, too, have been named after beings from Greek mythology. TRITON is the largest, discovered soon after the planet in 1846. Most of the moons were discovered in 1989, but also received Greek names, including PROTEUS, GALATEA and THALASSA.

The first known asteroid, CERES, named after a Roman goddess, was discovered in 1801. Since then, many asteroids have received mythological names. JUNO, VESTA, and ICARUS, as well as EROS, the first asteroid to be orbited by a humanmade probe, are also named after Greek and Roman gods and goddesses.

**SOPHOCLES** (496–406 B.C.)  Along with AESCHYLUS and EURIPIDES, one of the great tragic poets of ancient GREECE. Not much is known about his life. Sophocles was born at Colonus, near ATHENS. He died at the age of 90, having written more than 100 plays, only seven of which survive. These include *Ajax*, *Antigone*, *Oedipus*, and *Electra*, all of which are concerned with Greek mythology and are important sources of our knowledge of that subject. Surviving scraps of evidence from the fifth century B.C. show that Sophocles was an actor and a dancer. Drama took a great stride forward when he increased the number of actors from two to three, and made the chorus a more integral part of the play. Sophocles was active as an Athenian citizen, serving in the army, in the treasury, and as a priest. He seems to have possessed serenity and he lived a long life.

**SPARTA** (LACEDAEMON) *Greek*  City and capital of LACONIA in the southern PELOPONNESUS. The ancient Spartans were famous for their cruelty to slaves and for their rigorous military training.

**SPHINX** *Greek*   A monster, half woman, half beast, the offspring of ECHIDNA and Orthos. She lived near THEBES and was supposed to set impossible riddles, one of which went something like this:

What goes on four feet, on two feet, and three,
But the more feet it goes on, the weaker it be?

The answer is a human being, who as an infant crawls on all fours, as an adult walks on two feet, and in old age supports both legs with a walking stick. It is said that OEDIPUS solved this riddle and thus delivered the Thebans from the curse of the Sphinx.

The Greek Sphinx has nothing to do with the Egyptian Sphinx, except that both creatures were half beast, half human.

The marble statue known as the Sphinx of Naxos, which dates back to 560 B.C., was a gift from the island nation to the temple at Delphi in Greece. The half woman/half lion stands on the top of a column and now fills a room in the Delphi Museum in Greece. *(Photo by Fingalo. Used under a Creative Commons License.)*

**STATA MATER** (STATUA MATER; STATIS MATER) *Roman*   A goddess called upon to help protect against fire. Specifically, people placed a statue to this lesser goddess in the Roman Forum, located between the Palatine and Capitoline hills, and a central area in the ancient city. Here the goddess could protect the city from the threat of fire and other damage at night. Stata Mater also guarded a city fire that burned there on the community hearth.

Stata Mater was closely associated with VULCAN, Roman god of fire and blacksmiths, and VESTA, goddess of the home and the household hearth.

**STATE GODS** *Roman*   As the city of ROME grew into a regional power and then into the center of a vast empire, rulers and members of the Senate brought into the culture gods and goddesses to protect society. Often these deities had been honored and worshipped first in the home, but rulers saw for them roles they could play in society. Many of these deities were originally influential in the cultures of Central Italy, such as LATIUM and ETRURIA. By broadening the scope of the deities's influence from the family to society, the rulers, and eventually the citizens, believed they would be protected in all walks of life.

These state gods included the major PANTHEON of Roman gods. They also included lesser known gods and goddesses who influenced a citizen's responsibility to the state or government, to Rome's ability in warfare and success at conquering enemies, and to the physical city itself.

First among the gods and goddess who protected all of Rome and its power was QUIRINUS, who represented the good citizen and a person's responsibility to society. The goddess Pietas, whose name means devotion, represented duty to the family and to the state of Rome. FIDES was the goddess who helped citizens remain trustworthy and faithful to Rome. Securitas was the goddess who, as her name suggests, protected the state. Eventually, the people of Rome adopted a goddess named ROMA who represented the very essence of Rome itself.

Some divine beings watched over the physical aspects of life in Rome. CLOACINA, for example, protected the great sewers of Rome, and STATA MATER protected the city from fire. The goddess VESTA watched over communal hearths in cities across the Roman Empire and kept their fires burning, and JANUS protected the gates of cities across the empire.

MARS was the greatest of the war gods by the time of the Roman Empire, which began in the first century B.C. He was supported in his work by a retinue of goddesses, who were themselves called upon by Roman soldiers of all ranks for protection and success. BELLONA, a frequent companion of Mars, brought a warlike spirit and enthusiasm to hearts of soldiers. VIRTUS gave soldiers courage and skill. To Lua and NERIO soldiers dedicated the weapons captured from their enemy, often burning those weapons as a sign to the goddesses that the soldiers appreciated their help and desired more help as they continued their conquests. The goddess VICTORIA, who may also have been called by the name Vica Pota, represented victory over the enemy.

In commerce as well as in patriotism and warfare, Romans had special gods that they called upon for help. This aspect of their public lives was influenced by their principle gods and gods of specific tasks. MERCURY oversaw merchants, and MINERVA was the patroness of craftsmen and manufacturers. The goddess Felicitas brought success to all in business, and the Dei Lucrii, a group of early gods, ensured profit and good trade. Aequitas helped merchants to be honest and fair in their dealings with customers.

See also AGRICULTURAL GODS; HOUSEHOLD GODS; INDIGETES; PERSONAL GODS.

**STHENO** (Strong) *Greek* One of the three GORGONS, female monsters; daughter of CETO, an ancient sea goddess, and PHORCYS; her sisters were EURYALE and MEDUSA. Stheno and Euryale were immortal, while their sister, Medusa, was mortal.

The hero PERSEUS was sent by POLYDECTES to retrieve the head of a Gorgon. Of course, he chose Medusa because she was mortal. Her sisters shared with Medusa the power to turn people to stone when the mortals looked into the Gorgon's eyes. The sisters chased Perseus after his theft of Medusa's head, raking the air with their great claws.

**STYX** *Greek* One of the eldest OCEANIDS, or water NYMPHS, of which there were thousands, all daughters of the TITANS OCEANUS and TETHYS. Styx, like many of the oldest Oceanids, was often counted among the Titans. She guarded the river in the UNDERWORLD (1) that carried her name, Styx.

The god PALLAS fell in love with Styx and together they had four children: ZELUS (Zeal), NIKE (Victory), CRATUS (Strength), and BIA (Violence). An ardent follower of ZEUS, the great OLYMPIAN GOD, in his battle with the Titans, Styx persuaded her children to fight with the Olympians in the battle against their father and the rest of the Titans. Zeus rewarded her by granting all of the oaths made in her name.

**STYX, RIVER** *Greek* The principle river, or system of rivers, in HADES, the Greek UNDERWORLD (1); named for the goddess who carried the same name, STYX. The river formed the boundary between Earth and the land of the dead.

The OLYMPIAN GODS made oaths to the waters of the Styx River. Whenever the gods wanted to make a strenuous, binding oath, they sent the goddess IRIS to the Styx and Iris brought back a sacred cup of the river's water. The god would make the oath then drink the water. If the god or goddess broke that oath, he or she would fall into a deep sleep or lose his or her voice, for nine years. Sources very on the details of the penalty for breaking the oath.

The River Styx contained magical powers, good and bad. It was the river in which the goddess THETIS dipped her infant son ACHILLES in an effort to make him invulnerable to all weapons, though she missed his heel and it was there that an arrow later struck and killed the great Trojan hero. The waters of the Styx corroded gold and, when sprinkled on the island of RHODES, turned Rhodes barren.

**SUMMANUS** *Roman* God of the night; specifically, the god who sent thunder and lightning during the night, as opposed to JUPITER, who sent these forces of nature during the day. Perhaps one of the many gods of the dead. Summanus was most likely a god of the SABINES who was later brought into the religions of the people of ROME.

A temple on the Aventine Hill, or perhaps in the Circus Maximus, was dedicated to him and his feast day was June 20. Little is known of Summanus, and some modern scholars believe he was merely a representation of Jupiter.

**SYRINX** *Greek* A NYMPH, daughter of LADON. When she was being pursued by PAN, Syrinx called upon her father for help. He turned her into a reed. Pan consoled himself by fashioning the syrinx reeds into a seven-reed pipe. The syrinx, or panpipes, is an instrument still played by shepherds in GREECE.

**TALUS** (TALOS) *Greek*   The nephew and apprentice of the great inventor DAEDALUS. Talus, who is said to have invented the saw and also the compass, incurred the jealousy of Daedalus, who murdered him. Some stories say that Daedalus threw the boy from the top of the Acropolis and that the gods changed Talus into a partridge ("perdix"). Perdix was a nickname for Talus or his mother, Polycaste, or for both.

**TANTALUS** *Greek*   A king of LYDIA in ASIA MINOR; father of PELOPS and NIOBE. Tantalus stole food from the gods and served it to mortals. He even attempted to serve up his son, Pelops, in a stew at a banquet for the gods but the gods rescued Pelops. Tantalus was punished for his misdeeds by the downfall of his kingdom and eternal hunger and thirst. It is said that he stands in a pool of water, but whenever he bends down to drink, the water recedes, and that over his head hang branches laden with fruit, but they are just out of reach.

**TARTARUS** *Greek*   A realm of eternal darkness, the deepest, most terrible part of the UNDERWORLD, the opposite of the dome of the sky. Tartarus was even deeper below the Earth than HADES, farther below Hades than the Earth was below the sky, a realm of darkness and death. The OLYMPIAN GODS exiled the TITANS to Tartarus after the great war between the two generations of gods.

The Olympians sent other supernatural beings there as well, such as the CYCLOPES. Humans were also sent there for punishment, including TANTALUS, SISYPHUS, and the 50 daughters of DANAUS, known as the Danaides. Some poets said that evil men who had nothing to do with the gods and their stories were also punished in Tartarus. In later stories, the realm was more closely associated with Hades.

**TAYGETE** *Greek*   A NYMPH, born on Mount Cyllene, one of the PLEIADES, who served the goddess ARTEMIS; daughter of ATLAS and PLEIONE, who was a nymph and one of the OCEANIDS.

Taygete was, like other nymphs, coveted by the great god ZEUS. She refused his advances and, afraid of the god, begged Artemis to help, and the goddess changed her into a doe. In that form, Zeus made love to Taygete. Back in human form, Taygete gave birth to Lacedaemon, who became the founder of SPARTA, a prominent city in ancient GREECE.

**TELAMON** (TELEMON) *Greek*   Son of King Aecus of AEGINA; brother of PELEUS; father, with HESIONE, of TEUCER, the great archer.

Telamon and Peleus killed their half-brother, Phocus. After the murder, Telamon fled the country. He lived a heroic life, taking part in the CALYDONIAN BOAR HUNT, sailing with the ARGONAUTS, and accompanying HERACLES on his expedition against LAOMEDON of TROY.

**TELEGONUS** *Greek*   In some accounts, the son of hero ODYSSEUS and the witch CIRCE. Circe sent her son to find Odysseus in his kingdom of Ithaca. Telegonus killed his father (the two were unknown to each other) with a poisoned spear given to him by Circe. Later Telegonus married PENELOPE, the widow of Odysseus.

**TELEMACHUS** *Greek*   Son of ODYSSEUS and PENELOPE. As an infant, Telemachus was placed in the path of his father's plow as a test of the father's pretended madness. When the TROJAN WAR ended, Telemachus searched unsuccessfully for his father, returned to Ithaca, and recognized Odysseus; together he and Odysseus slew all the would-be usurpers to the throne who had been imposing upon Penelope to choose a husband from among them. (See *Odysseus Returns to Ithaca*, under *ODYSSEY*.)

**TELEPHUS** *Greek*   The son of HERACLES and Auge, a Tegean princess. Telephus became the king of Mysia, in ASIA MINOR, where the Greeks landed on their way to TROY. The Greek hero ACHILLES wounded Telephus in an ensuing scuffle. He was told by an ORACLE that his wound could be cured only by the one who had inflicted it. Telephus went to the Greek camp and sought out Achilles. Since another oracle had told Achilles that only Telephus could show him the way to Troy, Achilles obligingly scraped some rust from his spear into the wound of Telephus, curing him. Telephus showed the Greeks the way to Troy, where they were victorious.

**TELLUS** (TERRA MATER) *Roman* A goddess of fecundity, or the ability to produce young. People sought her protection and help even before they developed formalized religion in Italy. Many scholars see Tellus as an equivalent of the Greek GAIA, the EARTH MOTHER. Tellus means "Earth," as the name of the third planet from the Sun, though the word "Terra" in her alternative name refers to soil or land. Tellus was also the divinity who watched over wedding ceremonies and whose goodwill couples sought before their marriages.

On April 15, people gathered to sacrifice a pregnant cow to Tellus. They cut the unborn calf from its mother and burned it, too. In this ceremony, people sought protection of their own fertility.

Romans seem to have worshiped Tellus in conjunction with the goddesses CERES and FLORA, both Roman goddesses of fertility, though Tellus is more ancient. All three were feared as goddesses of the dead, Tellus as their queen. This image seems to have evolved from people's understanding that death was the opposite of birth and the belief the goddess of one function must have an influence over the other. On December 13, people honored Tellus, Ceres, and Flora together.

**TEMPE** *Greek* A valley in THESSALY, famous for its beautiful scenery. There are many references to the Vale of Tempe in Greek mythology. It was the scene of APOLLO's purification after the slaying of PYTHON. It was the scene of the metamorphosis of DAPHNE (from NYMPH pursued by APOLLO into laurel tree). It was also where CYCNUS, son of ARES, killed unwary travelers and used their bones to build a temple to his father.

**TERMINUS** *Roman* God of boundaries and frontiers. Specifically, Terminus was the god of the sacred boundaries of pieces of land that were dedicated to JUPITER, the supreme god in Roman mythology. In Latin, "terminus" means boundary.

In daily life, Terminus protected the good relationship between owners of neighboring properties. He supported and encouraged harmony among neighbors, a task that was very important in an agrarian or farming culture such as ancient ROME.

New neighbors would dig a hole at the boundary of their properties and consecrate that hole with wine, offerings, and the blood of a sacrificial animal. They then took a large stone, coated it in oil, added garlands of plants to it, and buried it in the hole. Each year after that first ceremony, the neighbors met at the stone and offered a sacrifice to Terminus to seek his help in protecting their land.

Terminus also guarded boundaries in time and marked the end of events as well as pieces of property. His festival in the Roman calendar of festivals, Terminalia, on February 23, marked the end of the year.

**TETHYS** *Greek* The daughter of two TITANS, URANUS and GAIA; sister-wife of OCEANUS. With him she bore the OCEANIDS (sea NYMPHS). She was also the mother of STYX, and, some say, the mentor of the goddess HERA.

**TEUCER** *Greek* The son of TELAMON and HESIONE; half-brother of the great AJAX (1). He was the best archer among the Greeks and played an important part in the TROJAN WAR, fighting alongside Ajax. Teucer founded the town of Salamis in Cyprus.

**THALASSA** *Greek* An ancient sea goddess; daughter of ETHER, the upper air, and HEMERA, day. With PONTUS, an ancient god of the sea, Thalassa was the mother of the fish and animals of the sea.

Thalassa is featured in the stories of classical Greek writers as the form of a woman, made of water. She rises out of the sea and talks with humans who become stranded on her shores. Some say Thalassa was the mother of APHRODITE, for, as the sea, Thalassa carried the goddess out of the ocean after she had formed from the dismembered parts of URANUS.

**THANATOS** (Death) *Greek* The personification of death (Mors in Latin). The son of NYX (Night), with no father (according to HESIOD); twin brother of HYPNOS (Sleep). The only mortal who managed to outwit Thanatos (at least for a while) was SISYPHUS.

**THAUMUS** (Wonder) *Greek* An ancient sea god, ranked among the second-generation of TITANS; son of Gaia and Pontus; brother of Ceto, Phorcys, Nereus, and Eurybia.

Few stories are told of this god. He is known most for being the father, with the Oceanid Electra (3), of Iris, the goddess of rainbows, and of the strong storm winds known as the Harpies.

**THEBES** *Greek* A city of ancient Greece, in Boeotia, reputedly founded by Cadmus. Thebes was also associated with other Greek myths, such as those of Oedipus, the Seven Against Thebes, and the Epigoni.

**THEIA** (Radiant) *Greek* A first-generation Titan goddess of sight and the shining light of the blue sky; daughter of Gaia and Uranus; mother, with Hyperion, of the gods who brought light to humans: Helios (Sun), Selene (Moon), and Eos (Dawn). She was known also as the female counterpart of Ether, the upper air.

Theia's association with the concept of brilliant light made her also the goddess of gems and gold, because she gave to them their great value. She had the ability to see into the future. The people of Thessaly built a temple in her name.

**THEMIS** *Greek* A Titan, daughter of Gaia and Uranus; one of the many loves of Zeus. Mother of the Horae (Seasons) the Moirae (Fates), Astraea, and, some say, of Prometheus. Themis presided over law and order, justice, hospitality, and prophecy. One legend has it that Themis communicated with the Oracle at Delphi before Delphi became the favored shrine of the god Apollo. Another says that she appeared before Deucalion and told him to repeople the Earth after the deluge.

**THESEUS** *Greek* Chief hero of Athens, the major city of Attica. Son of Aegeus, king of Athens, and Aethra, daughter of King Pittheus of Troezen. Theseus was brought up under the protection of Pittheus and Aethra until he was 16. Then he set off to Athens to claim his birthright. On his way and afterward, he had countless adventures, of which the most famous was the slaying of the Minotaur. Upon the death of Aegeus, Theseus became king of Athens and was the hero of many battles. At the end, he retired to Skyros, an island in the Aegean, where he was murdered by Lycomedes.

Scholars believe that the character of Theseus may have been based on a real person, a hero of ancient times, similar in many ways to the demigod Heracles. Mythologists may have adapted the character of Theseus to make him a suitable hero for their city of Athens.

**Some Adventures of Theseus** Theseus, the great hero of ancient Athens, had countless adventures. Among them were some showing that he let the punishment fit the crime.

Periphetes was crippled and used a huge bronze club to kill wayfarers. Theseus, on his way to Athens, killed Periphetes with the club, which he carried ever afterward as one of his weapons.

Sinis, "The Pinebender," was so strong and monstrously cruel that he bent young pine trees down to the ground, then lashed his victim, a hapless traveler, to the trees so that the victim would be killed by having his limbs torn apart after Sinis let the trees loose. Theseus inflicted the same punishment on Sinis.

Procrustes, also called Polypemon, was the father of Sinis. He was another scourge of travelers. He would invite them into his house, where he had an iron bed. If the victim did not fit the bed, Procrustes would either chop off the victim's overhanging parts or stretch his limbs to fit the bed. Theseus forced Procrustes to lie in his own bed, where Theseus slew the villain. The word *procrustean* has come to denote any cruel attempt to reduce people or ideas to fit one arbitrary standard.

In Eleusis, a city northwest of Athens, Theseus defeated the king in a wrestling match. Theseus is said to have perfected the art of wrestling. Eleusis had no king from that day on and came under the leadership of Athens.

**Theseus and Aegeus** Theseus, the great hero of Athens, was the son of King Aegeus, king of Athens. His mother was Princess Aethra, the daughter of King Pittheus of Troezen. Before he left Troezen, Aegeus lifted a heavy rock and hid his sword and sandals beneath it. He instructed Aethra to bring his son to this rock when he became a young man and to remove the sword and sandals. If Theseus succeeded in doing this, he was to bring the items to Athens to claim his birthright from his father, the king.

Aethra took Theseus, when he was 16, to the rock, which the lad lifted easily, and sent him on his way to Athens.

Theseus had many adventures on his journey and entered Athens as a hero. Warmly welcomed by his father, Theseus then went on to his greatest adventure, the slaying of the Minotaur, the dreaded bull-monster of King Minos of Crete. Every year, Minos demanded seven men and seven maids from Athens to be sacrificed to the Minotaur, thus bringing great sorrow to the people of that city. Theseus determined to put an end to this tragedy. In spite of his father's protests, he went aboard the fateful ship that took the victims to Crete. Theseus promised Aegeus that if he succeeded in killing the monster, he would bring the ship back flying white sails in place of the black sails it left with. Theseus did indeed defeat the beast, but he forgot to hoist the white sails. Aegeus, watching anxiously from the top of a cliff, saw the black sails and cast himself into the sea in despair. That sea—the Aegean—today bears his name.

**Theseus, Ariadne, and the Minotaur**  The slaying of the Minotaur was Theseus's greatest and most famous deed, in which he was helped by ARIADNE, daughter of King Minos of Crete. Minos demanded a yearly tribute from Athens because of the murder of his son, ANDROGEUS, by the Athenians. Each year, seven Athenian men and seven maidens were sent to Crete to feed the Minotaur.

Theseus determined to end the yearly tragedy suffered by the Athenians. He boarded the ship that bore the victims to Crete. When she saw him, Ariadne fell in love with the hero. She gave him a ball of string that would help him find his way out of the LABYRINTH where the bull lived. Theseus unwound the string as he followed the tortuous mazes that led him to the Minotaur. He slew the bull after a ferocious battle and then made his way triumphantly back to the entrance of the labyrinthine palace. When he went back to Athens, Theseus took the lovely Ariadne with him, but he abandoned her on the island of NAXOS and went on his way.

**Theseus and Medea**  When Theseus was a young man, he set forth to claim his birthright from Aegeus. Aegeus had married the sorceress MEDEA, who knew at once that Theseus was the king's son. She tried to poison the lad; just in time, Theseus revealed the sacred sword that his father had left behind in Troezen. Aegeus dashed the poisoned cup from the boy's hand and embraced his son. Medea fled from Athens with her son, Medus.

**Theseus and Pirithous**  Theseus was also famous for having a deep and enduring friendship with PIRITHOÜS, king of the LAPITHS, a mythical people of THESSALY. The friendship originated when Pirithoüs mischievously stole some of Theseus's cattle. Theseus went in pursuit, but the two young men were so filled with admiration for each other that they forgot their quarrel and swore eternal brotherhood. The young heroes had many adventures together.

In a fight that started at the wedding feast of Pirithoüs and HIPPODAMEIA, Theseus helped his friend to drive the CENTAURS, wild creatures that were half human, half horse, out of Thessaly.

Pirithoüs later helped Theseus carry off HELEN. In return, Theseus descended to the UNDERWORLD (1) to help his friend in his attempt to abduct PERSEPHONE, reluctant bride of HADES. Hades caught the two friends and they had to remain in the underworld until the hero Heracles came to attempt their rescue. Theseus was freed, but Pirithoüs had to remain a captive for eternity.

**Theseus and the Amazons**  Theseus, great hero of Athens, accompanied the demigod Heracles on his ninth labor, which was to capture the girdle of HIPPOLYTA, queen of the AMAZONS. Heracles captured the girdle, whereupon Hippolyta made war on Athens. Theseus vanquished Hippolyta and made her his wife. She bore him a son, HIPPOLYTUS.

After the death of Hippolyta, Theseus married PHAEDRA, with disastrous consequences. Phaedra fell in love with her young stepson, Hippolytus, and killed herself in despair, whereupon Theseus invoked the help of the sea god, POSEIDON, in causing his son's death.

**The Death of Theseus**  Theseus led a life full of triumphant adventures. His most famous exploit was the killing of the dreaded Minotaur. But his end was a sad one. He lost both his wife, Phaedra, and his son, Hippolytus, and finally was driven out of Athens by Menesthius, of the ancient line of ERECHTHEUS.

Theseus set sail for Crete, now ruled by Phaedra's brother, DEUCALION, who had promised him refuge. Theseus's ship was blown off course and he took shelter on the island of Skyros, where he had a small estate. King Lycomedes of Skyros seemed to welcome the sad and aging king, but he treacherously pushed Theseus off a cliff. Thus the great Theseus died. Later his bones were taken to Athens and enshrined there.

**THESSALY** *Greek*  The largest division of GREECE, located in the eastern mainland, encircled by mountains except for the valley of TEMPE in the northeast corner. Thessaly's mythical inhabitants were the LAPITHS, whose king, IXION, had fathered the CENTAURS, creatures that were half human and half horse. It was also the home of the mythical MYRMIDONS, created by ZEUS to increase Thessaly's population.

**THETIS** *Greek*  One of the NEREIDS, sea NYMPH daughters of NEREUS; wife of PELEUS; mother of ACHILLES. Both ZEUS and POSEIDON had pursued Thetis, but on being told by the seeress THEMIS that a son borne by Thetis would overthrow the OLYMPIAN GODS, Zeus persuaded Thetis to marry Peleus. When her son, Achilles, was born, Thetis wanted to make him invulnerable. She dipped the baby into the river STYX, holding him by one heel. Since that heel did not touch the magical water, it remained vulnerable. It was this heel that later caused Achilles' death in the TROJAN WAR.

**THYESTES** *Greek* Son of PELOPS and HIPPODAMEIA; brother of ATREUS; father of AEGISTHUS by his own daughter, Pelopia.

Thyestes and Atreus, rivals since childhood, were the victims of the curse made upon their house by the actions of their father, PELOPS. (See also under ATREUS and THYESTES.)

Thyestes ruled for a short time as king of MYCENAE, one of the most important cities of ancient GREECE, with Aegisthus as his heir, but he was eventually driven out by AGAMEMNON and Aegisthus was deposed.

**TIBERINUS** *Roman* The god of the river Tiber, upon which the city of ROME was founded. The river was vital to the fortunes of Rome. Numerous festivals were held in honor of its god. Some say that RHEA SILVIA, the mother of the twins ROMULUS AND REMUS, was thrown into the river and became its spouse. In VIRGIL's *AENEID*, Tiberinus visits AENEAS, who is asleep on the banks of the river, and tells him in a dream that his destiny is to found a city on the banks of the river.

**TIRESIAS** *Greek* The blind seer of THEBES, a figure who appears several times in Greek mythology.

According to some legends, ATHENE struck Tiresias blind because he saw her bathing. Another legend says that it was HERA who struck Tiresias blind.

Some scholars think that the figure of Tiresias as a wise man is a mythological embodiment of the person who is out of the ordinary (blind, lame, or otherwise afflicted), endowed with special gifts such as those of Tiresias and HEPHAESTUS, the lame smith-god.

**TIRYNS** *Greek* A town in the ARGOS region of the northern PELOPONNESUS. PROETUS, brother of Acrisius, founded the city and built massive walls with the help of the CYCLOPES.

**TITAN** *Greek* The race of Greek gods that preceded and gave birth to the OLYMPIAN GODS; the children of GAIA (Earth) and URANUS (Heaven), who were the first gods of Greek mythology. According to most Greek writers, there were 12 Titans, six male and six female. The sons were OCEANUS, HYPERION, COEUS, CRONUS, IAPETUS, and CRIUS. The daughters were MNEMOSYNE, PHOEBE, RHEA, TETHYS, THEIA, and THEMIS.

Some scholars, however, rank Gaia's children by the ancient sea god PONTUS among the Titans. They were CETO, PHORCYS, THAUMAS, EURYBIA, and NEREUS.

The children of Gaia's children were also known as Titans, or second-generation Titans. Hyperion had three children, EOS, HELIOS and SELENE. Coeus had two daughters, LETO and ASTERIA. Iapetus had four sons, ATLAS, PROMETHEUS, EPIMETHEUS, and MENOETIUS. Crius three children, ASTRAEUS, PALLAS, and PERSES.

Also commonly counted among the Titans were the eldest of the OCEANIDS, a group of water NYMPHS, daughters of OCEANUS and TETHYS. They were STYX, DIONE, NEDA, METIS, CLYMENE, EURYNOME, DORIS, ELECTRA (3), and PLEIONE.

The children of Cronus and Rhea became the first and perhaps most prominent Olympian Gods. They were ZEUS, POSEIDON, HADES, HERA, DEMETER, and HESTIA.

The Titans were the primary gods of GREECE during the Golden Age, before the rise of the HELLENES as the dominant culture. The Hellenes brought their Olympian gods to the peninsula and supplanted the gods of earlier peoples. In the mythology, of the Hellenes, Zeus led the battle of the generations and defeated the Titans, sending most of them to TARTARUS, the deepest pit of the UNDERWORLD.

**TITHONUS** *Greek* The son of LAOMEDON, king of TROY, and brother of PRIAM. Eos, goddess of the dawn, loved him. She bore him a son, Memnon, one of the heroes of the TROJAN WAR. Eos begged ZEUS to make her husband immortal. Zeus granted her wish and Tithonus lived for a very long time. However, eternal youth was not given to him, and the young man became a shriveled old thing with little more than a strident voice. At last the gods took pity on him and turned him into a cicada.

**TRIPTOLEMUS** *Greek* Son of CELEUS and Metaneira, brother of DEMOPHON. A favorite of the goddess DEMETER, Triptolemus received from her the secrets of corn and of agriculture. It is said that he invented the plow and the science of agriculture and was thus a pioneer of civilization. He was a central figure in the Eleusinian Mysteries.

**TRITON** *Greek* A water god; the son of POSEIDON and AMPHITRITE. He was often represented as a merman, with the head and body of a man and a fishtail instead of legs.

It is said that he blew on a conch shell trumpet to calm the waves for Poseidon. Sometimes Poseidon is depicted as being escorted by many Tritons.

Triton was a benevolent, helpful deity. During the Olympian war with the TITANS, Triton used his conch shell to terrify the giants. In HOMER's *ODYSSEY*, Triton saved the ARGONAUTS from a storm and helped them find the Mediterranean Sea.

In astronomy, Triton is one of the moons of the planet NEPTUNE.

**TROJAN WAR** *Greek* A legendary war fought between Achaean (Greek) invaders and the defenders of TROY, a seaport at the northwestern tip of ASIA MINOR, around 1200–1300 B.C. (See below for an account of recent archaeological discoveries that make it certain that such a war, or series of wars, took place.) The events of this war and the return to their homes of some of the Greek generals make up a body of myth that was recounted over the centuries and eventually reshaped and written down by the great poet HOMER in two epics: the *ILIAD*, which describes the end of the Trojan War, and the *ODYSSEY*, the journeys of one of the Greek heroes, ODYSSEUS.

The story of the 10-year struggle between the Greeks and Trojans is complex. The cause of the war, according to Greek mythology, was said to be a beauty contest between three goddesses. The silver-footed sea NYMPH, THETIS, and the king of AEGINA, PELEUS, neglected to invite ERIS, goddess of strife, to their wedding. In her anger, Eris threw "the apple of discord" into the midst of the wedding throng. The apple was inscribed "To the Fairest."

Three goddesses immediately claimed the apple: HERA, the chief goddess and wife of ZEUS; ATHENE, goddess of war; and APHRODITE, goddess of love and beauty. When asked to make a choice among the three goddesses, Zeus wisely declined and gave the task to a young Trojan prince, PARIS, who was said to be exceedingly handsome.

The three goddesses wooed young Paris, tempting him with bribes. Paris succumbed to the offer of Aphrodite, who promised him the love of the most beautiful woman in the world in return for the apple.

At that time, the most beautiful woman in the world was HELEN, the young queen of King MENELAUS of SPARTA. Paris went to the court of Menelaus, won Helen, and carried her away to Troy.

King Menelaus immediately rallied around him all the former lovelorn suitors of Helen, who had promised to fight anyone who might try to steal Helen away from GREECE. Menelaus chose his

brother, AGAMEMNON, king of MYCENAE, as leader of the army. Agamemnon soon had a fleet of 1,000 ships ready to sail for Troy. (In later literature, Helen's face was described as "the face that launched a thousand ships.") Among the first victims of the war was one of Agamemnon's daughters, IPHIGENIA, sacrificed in order to gain fair winds to Troy.

ACHILLES was the principal hero of the Greeks who took part in the Trojan War. His contingent numbered about 50 ships and he led his own army, unlike the other Greeks who acknowledged the leadership of Agamemnon and his huge fleet. Achilles captured a number of towns on the coast near Troy. Among his prizes was the beautiful slave girl BRISEIS. Agamemnon stole Briseis away from Achilles. Furious, Achilles withdrew from the war, causing a serious setback to the Greeks. The quarrel between Achilles and Agamemnon was one of the starting points of the events of the latter part of the Trojan War described by Homer in the *Iliad*. Later, Achilles would rejoin the war and help bring the Greeks to victory, this time under the leadership of his dear friend PATROCLUS. HECTOR killed Patroclus. Achilles then slew Hector and dragged his dead body around the ruins of Troy.

Led by the hero Hector, the Trojans were successful in many major engagements, especially when Achilles temporarily left the conflict after the quarrel with Agamemnon. Eventually, the Trojans lost the war when the Greek hero Odysseus had the cunning idea of hiding troops within a huge wooden horse delivered as a gift within the walls of Troy. The selected troops broke out of their hiding place in the dead of night, slew the Trojans, and looted and set fire to their city.

The gods themselves took sides in the Trojan War and played an active part in the hostilities. APOLLO and the war god ARES supported the Trojans, as did Aphrodite, the champion of Paris. Athene, Hera, and POSEIDON backed the Greeks, and HEPHAESTUS, the smith-god, made armor for Achilles.

The Trojan War was the last great communal enterprise of the Greek heroes. Although it succeeded in its aim to rescue Helen, the difficulties were great and long, and an air of failure and defeat seemed to hang over the enterprise. Few of the heroes returned to find their homes secure.

**The Trojan War: Fact or Fiction?**  The Trojan War of Greek mythology lasted for 10 years, ending in the sack of Troy and a victory for the Greeks.

Scholars now think that such a war did indeed take place, around 1200–1300 B.C. Recent archaeological finds confirm that there was a city of Troy. Extensive

Bronze Age burial grounds and many crematory urns, perhaps some of slain heroes, have been excavated. In addition, caches of food have been found buried beneath the walls of the city, very likely by people from the countryside who were taking refuge within the city walls during a lengthy siege by marauding tribes.

It seems certain that there were numerous trade routes common to the Greeks and the Trojans. Troy, at the northwestern tip of Asia Minor, controlled the seaway between the Aegean and the Black seas, through the narrow inlet called, in ancient times, the HELLES-PONT, now known as the DARDANELLES. This strait led to the Sea of Marmara, which in turn led to the Black Sea via the passageway known as the Bosporus.

Once Troy had fallen, the Greeks were able to establish colonies along the coast of Asia Minor. They dealt in gold, silver, iron, cinnabar, timber, linen, hemp, dried fish, oil, and Chinese jade. In fact, the return of Helen to the Greeks may have symbolized the restoration of Greek rights to enter the Hellespont. The *Iliad* may be an assemblage of folk memories of a series of raids by the Greeks against the shores of Anatolia (Asia Minor)—and, in particular, Troy, the guardian of the Dardanelles—to ensure vital passage to the Black Sea and its valuable trade.

**The Wooden Horse of Troy**  The Trojan War came to an end when the Greek hero Odysseus had the idea of building a huge wooden horse, inside which would be hidden hundreds of Greek soldiers. The horse was given as a gift to the Trojans and dragged within their walls. In the dark of night, the Greek soldiers burst forth from their clever hiding place, fought the unprepared soldiers and citizens of Troy, and destroyed the city, thus winning the war.

Many explanations for the Trojan horse have been put forth. The most likely is that it was a battering ram, a device used to knock down walls since ancient times. The massive walls of Troy, with their sloping bases, presented an almost unsolvable problem to enemy forces. It seems likely that the Greeks constructed a towering "ram" that would be capable of attacking the more vulnerable upper structure of the walls. The "legs" raised the battering ram up to the level of the superstructure. The tool would be moved up to the wall on rollers. To the soldiers, the battering ram may have looked somewhat like a gigantic horse. In the ancient world, it was common for soldiers to give animal nicknames to pieces of equipment. For example, the Romans called their catapults *scorpions*. The word *ram* comes from the name for a male sheep or goat, which has a solid, sturdy shape.

**TROY** *Greek*  One of the most famous cities in Western literature and the site of the 10-year-long siege and battle of Troy (see TROJAN WAR). Excavations during the 19th and 20th centuries prove that there were no fewer than nine cities built—one after and on top of the other—on the mound of Hissarlik, a strategic position overlooking the DARDANELLES, the strait that leads to the Black Sea. The founder of Troy was DARDANUS, a son of ZEUS. PRIAM, king of Troy, was a descendant of Dardanus. Troy commanded the trade routes between the Mediterranean and the Black Sea. It was, in fact, at the crossroads between east and west. In mythology, the Trojan War was caused by the abduction of HELEN, wife of the king of SPARTA, by the Trojan prince PARIS. Many scholars think the abduction was a metaphor for the rivalry between the Greeks and Trojans over the lucrative trade route to the Black Sea.

The city discovered by the archaeologists was in fact only about 200 yards across, more of a citadel than a city. Excavations in 1984 and 1985 revealed many burial urns. They have also revealed caches of food buried beneath the walls of the citadel, perhaps the supplies of the people from the neighboring countryside who came inside the walls of the citadel for refuge from the marauding tribes.

**TURNUS** *Roman*  King of the RUTULI people, who lived in a region 20 miles southeast of the hills of ROME, at the time that AENEAS arrived in Italy after the TROJAN WAR; son of Daunus and his wife, the NYMPH VENILIA, and sister of JUTURNA.

Turnus was betrothed to LAVINIA, daughter of LATINUS, king of neighboring LATIUM, but when Aeneas arrived on the shores of Italy, he fell in love with Lavinia. Facing pressure from Aeneas and his army, Latinus and his wife Amata broke their promise to Turnus and betrothed their daughter to the Trojan hero. This led to a war between the Rutuli king and the Trojan hero that involved the great gods who watched over Aeneas.

Near the end of the war, which caused many deaths on both sides, Aeneas fought Turnus in one-to-one combat. The Trojan finally defeated Turnus, and was about to spare his life, when Aeneas noticed that Turnus was wearing the belt of PALLAS, a fallen Trojan. In vengeance, Aeneas killed Turnus.

**TYCHE** *Greek*  A goddess, the personification of plenty, also of chance and fate, both good and bad. Very few stories surround Tyche, but she was an important concept and figure in the lives of Greek citizens and, later, in the lives of Romans as the goddess FORTUNA. People recognized the power of good and bad luck in their lives and considered Tyche the provider of that luck. Her influence was so great that each individual had his or her own Tyche. Over time, people believed she had power over the fates of entire cities and each city had its own Tyche. A wheel symbolized her ever-changing nature and a balance showed her power to weigh the good and bad events in a person's life.

The Greek poet HESIOD, who wrote in the 800s B.C., named her as one of the OCEANIDS, daughters of the sea TITANS OCEANUS and TETHYS.

**TYPHON** (TYPHOEUS) *Greek* A hundred-headed monster whose parents were GAIA (Earth) and TARTARUS. Although it was the largest monster ever born, according to Greek mythology, with coiled serpents for legs, ZEUS defeated the monster and threw it into HADES.

Another version of the Typhon myth was that Typhon did mighty battle with Zeus, hurling rocks and mountains against the thunderbolts of the god and eventually capturing Zeus. Typhon cut the sinews from the hands and feet of Zeus, thus rendering him powerless. He thrust Zeus into a mountain cave, and stuffed the precious sinews into a bearskin sack or leather bag. HERMES and PAN found Zeus and managed to steal back the sinews and restore them to Zeus's appendages.

The struggle between Typhon and Zeus continued. Delicious food given to Typhon by the Fates weakened him. He made a final stand on Mount Haemus (Blood Mountain) in Thrace, where Zeus injured him so severely that his blood made the streams run red, giving the mountain its name. Typhon was able to flee to Sicily, but Zeus caught up with him and finally crushed him into the Earth under a volcano, Mount Etna, which is one of the most active volcanoes in the world.

Before he was imprisoned Typhon fathered with ECHIDNA a host of monsters, among them CERBERUS, the CHIMERA, the Lernaean HYDRA, the Nemean Lion, Orthos, and the SPHINX.

# U

**ULYSSES** *Roman* The Latin spelling of ODYSSEUS, the Greek hero whose stories are told by HOMER in the *ODYSSEY*. The Roman spelling was Ulixes.

The Romans and other peoples of central Italy apparently had no unique stories to add to the legends of this hero. They learned of him from the Greek colonists who settled on the southeastern shores of the Italian peninsula.

**UNDERWORLD (1)** *Greek* The black abyss known as HADES and the dwelling place of the dead. The lord of the Greek underworld was Hades or, sometimes, PLUTO. The consort of Hades was PERSEPHONE, who lived in the underworld for four months of the year. (See *Demeter and Persephone*, under DEMETER.)

In Greek mythology, the location of the underworld changed over time. In ancient times, it was supposed to be in "the Far West," the place that lay beyond the sea that encircled the Earth, which then was thought to be flat. The Far West was thought to be barren and uninhabited. However, as geographic knowledge progressed, it became evident that other lands lay beyond the ocean and were fruitful and peopled. Consequently, the underworld was placed under the Earth, a region of dark shadows and mystery, where the dead were buried.

Travelers seeking access to the underworld had first to cross the Grove of Persephone. At the gate to Hades waited the dog CERBERUS, who had at least three heads, in some accounts as many as 50. A monstrous watchdog, Cerberus had a roaring bark to terrify all, but he could be appeased by a "sop," a piece of honeyed bread.

Surrounding Hades and leading to its subterranean depths were many rivers: ACHERON (River of Sadness), Cocytus (River of Lamentation), LETHE (River of Oblivion), and STYX (River of Hate).

To cross the Styx, a soul needed to pay old CHARON, the miserly ferryman. Once in Hades the

souls of the dead drank from the Lethe to obtain forgetfulness of their former lives and thoughts.

The fortunate few who had won the favor of the gods went to ELYSIUM, a special section of the underworld, or perhaps that magical place called "the Far West." Here the shades, or spirits, of the dead lived in great happiness until eternity.

Those who were truly evil were sent to TARTARUS, the deepest, darkest, vilest section of the underworld.

**UNDERWORLD (2)** *Roman* While most strongly influenced by Greek mythology, the Roman view of an underworld, was, in the earliest ages, simply a realm below the Earth, a realm of riches, a place where gods and goddesses awaited the spring.

DIS PATER, originally an Etruscan god of riches, became the early Roman god who ruled over the underworld. He was the god of the precious gems and metals found deep below the surface of the Earth. PROSERPINA, an ancient goddess of fertility and of the germination of seeds, was originally associated with Dis. Over time, however, the underworld became connected with death, not only of people but of nature, as winter settled in and people awaited spring. Dis Pater and Proserpina emerged from the underworld to plant seeds and return life to the Earth.

By the middle of the third century B.C., Dis Pater and Proserpina had also become the rulers of the realm of dead spirits. Together they became an official part of the Roman religious ceremonies. Beginning in 249 B.C., Romans held games known as the Ludi Tarentini or Tarentine Games, to recognize, honor, and appease these two gods. Much of the mythology of Dis Pater and Proserpina had by this time taken on the stories of the Greek gods HADES (or PLUTO) and PERSEPHONE, who ruled over a realm also known as HADES.

However, Roman mythology also included spirits of the dead who did not appear to inhabit this underworld. The MANES, beneficial spirits of the dead, were called upon in ceremonies held over graves in February to watch over and protect the living. They were in turn ruled over by the goddess Mania, an ancient goddess of crossroads. The LARES, HOUSEHOLD GODS, were believed to be the spirits of a family's ancestors who watched over the home.

Romans also deified their founders, AENEAS and ROMULUS AND REMUS, and their emperors, without associating them with this underworld.

By the first century B.C., Roman historians and poets were describing the underworld as a rugged, craggy, gloomy place inhabited by the spirits of the night and the souls of the dead. According to VIRGIL, in his masterpiece the *AENEID*, the entrance to hell was located on the edge of Lake Averna, a lake in the center of a dormant volcanic crater near Naples, and also near the cave of the SIBYL OF CUMAE.

**URANUS** (OURANOS; Heaven) *Greek* The personification of heaven and the starlit sky. Uranus was the son of GAIA (Earth) and with her the father of the TITANS, the CYCLOPES, and the HECATONCHEIRES. Uranus did not care for his offspring and banished them to the UNDERWORLD. Gaia, mourning for her children, bade her son CRONUS to wound and mutilate Uranus. This Cronus did, with a flint sickle made by Gaia. From the spilled blood of Uranus sprang the FURIES, the GIGANTES (Giants), and the goddess APHRODITE. Uranus, defeated and wounded, left the Earth to the Titans. Before he died, he prophesied that Cronus, in his turn, would be overthrown by one of his sons. His prophecy came true when ZEUS deposed Cronus.

The Greek poet HESIOD tells the story of Uranus.

Uranus is the seventh planet from the Sun in the SOLAR SYSTEM. The English astronomer Sir William Herschel discovered the gas giant in 1781. Uranus was the first planet to receive the name of a Greek god. Uranus has five moons, none of which is named after a Greek or Roman deity or hero, unlike the moons of other planets.

# V

**VENILIA** *Roman* A spirit of the sea and wind, most likely a NYMPH, known for her kindness. Some ancient sources identify her as the wife of the god JANUS. Others say she was the wife of Daunus, an early king of the RUTULI, and with him the mother of TURNUS and JUTURNA. Venilia's sister, Amata, was the wife of LATINUS, an early king of LATIUM, a kingdom in Central Italy near ROME.

**VENUS** *Roman* An ancient goddess originally of springtime, crop cultivation, and gardens. By the end of the third century B.C., the Romans had given Venus the characteristics of the Greek goddess APHRODITE, and Venus became the goddess of love and beauty.

The name *Venus* means desire, charm, and grace in Latin, though the name is much older than the Roman civilization.

In some accounts, Venus was the daughter of JUPITER and DIONE, who was a NYMPH. Venus became the wife of VULCAN and the mother of CUPID. According to the Roman poet VIRGIL, Venus was also the mother of the hero AENEAS. Though scholars believe that people in Italy worshiped Venus long before the Greek influence arrived, one story says that Aeneas

Venus rises from the sea on a shell, the zephyrs blowing her to shore, in the masterpiece of Italian art by Sandro Botticelli (1445-1510). The painting now hangs in the Uffizi Gallery in Florence, Italy.

brought her cult with him when he arrived there after fleeing TROY.

The Romans regarded Venus as one of the founders of their people. Julius Caesar, who ruled ROME from 49 to 44 B.C., and Augustus, who became emperor in 27 B.C., both considered her their patroness and guardian.

Many artists chose this goddess of beauty as their subject. The *Venus de Milo*, now in the Louvre museum in Paris, is one of the most famous statues in the world. It was sculpted in the second or first century B.C. and was found on the island of Melos in A.D. 1820. The 15th-century Italian painter known as Botticelli (Alessandro di Mariano Filipepi) portrayed her as rising from the sea and standing on a half scallop shell in *Birth of Venus*, which hangs in the Uffizi Gallery in Florence, Italy.

Venus is the name of the second planet from the Sun in the SOLAR SYSTEM. It is the brightest object to appear in the night sky, shining as either the morning star or the evening star, depending on the season and the planet's position relative to Earth. Early Greeks and Romans believed they saw two different planets until Pythagoras (c. 500 B.C.), a Greek philosopher and mathematician who settled in Italy, demonstrated that they were the same object.

**VERTUMNUS** *Roman*  An ancient god of fertility and harvest to the people of ETRURIA, but a lesser god among the Romans; the protector of harvests and vegetation. Vertumnus is best known for his ability to change shape and for using that ability to woo and win the love of POMONA, a goddess of fruit trees and harvest.

He was portrayed as both handsome and youthful and old and gray-bearded, symbols of the changing seasons which he also represented. A statue of Vertumnus stood at the entrance to the Etruscan district of ROME during the days of the republic and the empire.

**VESTA** *Roman*  Goddess of the hearth, worshiped in every household of ancient ROME. She was identified with the Greek goddess HESTIA, one of the OLYMPIAN GODS.

Primitive Roman religion was a domestic affair, concerned with the welfare of the family, house, and farm. The focus of the home was the hearth. (The Latin word *focus* means "hearth.") The caretakers of the hearth were the young females of the family (the males of the family being out in the fields, the mother and older females working at the loom or in the kitchen). As families became more extended,

richer, and more sophisticated, the caretakers of the hearth became young women (see VESTAL VIRGINS) who were designated to guard the fires of the goddess Vesta rather than their own family hearths.

**VESTAL VIRGINS** *Roman*  Priestesses who guarded the temple of the goddess VESTA. They were guardians of the hearth who kept the sacred fires of Vesta burning. Vestal Virgins served for 30 years. If one was found to be unchaste, she was buried alive or otherwise punished.

**VICTORIA** (Victory) *Roman*  An ancient goddess of agriculture.

Victoria had the power to bring military success to ROME and was a favorite of soldiers. She was the humanlike representation of the concept of victory. Victoria was also a favorite of many of the ruling families in Roman history and was often pictured as a winged figure holding a wreath with which to crown the conqueror. She became a prominent symbol of the growing Roman Empire. Victoria was worshiped at a temple on the Aventine Hill.

Very late in Roman history, Victoria became associated with the Greek goddess NIKE and was made a member of the Roman PANTHEON.

**VIRGIL** (VERGIL) (70–19 B.C.)  A great Roman poet, born Publius Vergilius Maro near present-day Mantua (now Italy, then Cisalpine Gaul). Virgil's education took him to Cremona, Milan, and ROME.

Virgil's first works were the *Eclogues*, short pastoral poems. Later he wrote the *Georgics*, more poems about country life. His final work was the *AENEID*, an epic poem that took him the last 11 years of his life to write and remained unfinished, as far as he was concerned. People consider it one of the great literary works of the world.

Virgil enjoyed admiration and a great reputation during his lifetime. The *Aeneid* became a school textbook almost as soon as it appeared. It was known and quoted by people of all classes. The *Aeneid* had great influence on worldwide thought but particularly on Roman thought, since it was a uniquely Roman myth that glorified the city and inspired all with pride and patriotic fervor. Furthermore, Virgil's fame and popularity continued into the Christian era, for the Christians saw his poetic epic as having foretold the birth of Christ and the advent of Christianity, which occurred only 40 years after Virgil wrote the fourth *Eclogue*.

Virgil's influence on Roman thought derives more from the *Aeneid* than the *Eclogues* or the *Georgics*, for it foretells the glory of Rome, expressing the feelings of the time and the country of Virgil.

**VIRGO** (Virgin) *Greek*  One of the constellations; sixth sign of the Zodiac, named for the maiden ERIGONE, who hanged herself from a tree after finding the grave of her murdered father, ICARIUS of ATTICA. The gods took Erigone up to the heavens and transformed her into the constellation Virgo.

**VIRTUS** *Roman*  Goddess of courage and bravery, called upon by soldiers in battle. While her origins appear to be very old, Virtus was often worshiped in more recent Roman times with HONOS, the god of honor. Military leaders also built temples to Virtus near the sites of successful battles and conquests.

Virtus appears frequently on Roman coins, wearing a helmet and carrying a sword.

She eventually took on the characteristics of ARETE, a minor Greek goddess of virtue.

**VULCAN** *Roman*  Ancient god of fire, worshiped by the Romans throughout their early history. Vulcan was associated with volcanoes and volcanic fire. Later, he was identified with the Greek god HEPHAESTUS and therefore supposed to have workshops under Mount Etna and other volcanoes, where he was assisted by the CYCLOPES in forging thunderbolts for JUPITER. However, while the Greek Hephaestus was "the divine artificer," a great craftsman, Vulcan was only a fire god. He was also called Mulciber (Softener or Smelter).

Vulcan's parents were JUPITER and JUNO. His wife was VENUS, with whom he fathered CUPID.

**WINDS** *Greek and Roman* Both Greek and Roman cultures in classical times personified the winds, recognizing the power of these forces.

In Greek mythology, the four principle winds were known as the Anemoi, and were the children of the Titans Astreus and Eos, goddess of the dawn. However, the god Aeolus was known as the father of the winds and was said to have kept them in a bag to protect people from their power.

In Rome, the winds were called the Venti, and their characteristics often varied depending on the storyteller.

Winds were described by their moods—anger for a cold north wind, pleasant for a warm west wind. Some Greek winds, such as Boreas and Zephyrus, had important roles to play in stories. Boreas, for example, was the father of two of the fastest Argonauts, Calais and Zetes, and of the marvelous horses that belonged to King Erichthonius, which could gallop across water without causing a ripple. Zephyrus carried Psyche to Cupid and pushed Apollo's discus off course, causing it to kill Hyancinthus. People invoked the names of the other winds when they needed favors related to those winds or their fates.

The wind gods were among the oldest invoked by the Romans and the people of Central Italy who preceded them. The oldest was, according to some writers, the god of the northwest wind Corus (Caurus) or perhaps Africus, a warm wind from across the Mediterranean Sea.

Surviving documents, from poets, historians, and scientists, provide a jumbled picture of the importance of the winds in mythology and in explaining the world around them. However, the frequency with which the eight winds are named shows scholars that the people of classical Rome and Greece had significant respect for the power of these natural forces.

| Direction | Greek name | Roman name | Attributes |
| --- | --- | --- | --- |
| North | Boreas | Aquilo | Winter, cold |
| South | Notus | Auster | Summer, stormy, wet |
| East | Argestes/Eurus | Vulturnus | Autumn |
| West | Zephyrus | Favonius | Spring, warmth |
| Northeast | Kaikias | Caecius/Caicias | Bad, evil, harsh |
| Southeast | Eurus/Euros | Apeliotes/Subsolanus | Refreshing rain, help to farmers |
| Northwest | Skiron | Corus | Signaled the coming of winter |
| Southwest | Lips/Livus | Africus/Afer ventus | Quickly brings clouds and clears skies |

# Z

**ZAGREUS** *Greek*  The son of Zeus and his own daughter, Persephone. In order to save his child from the Titans, Zeus repeats his own history by hiding Zagreus on Mount Ida (2) and setting the Curetes to clashing their armor and shouting, just as they did for the infant Zeus. However, Zagreus slips away as the Curetes sleep and in spite of brave efforts to save himself by magical transformations into various animals, the Titans seize Zagreus and eat him. This myth represents the annual sacrifice of a boy, which took place in ancient Crete in honor of Minos, the Bull king.

**ZELUS** (Zelos; Zeal, Strife) *Greek*  The personification of rivalry, envy, jealousy, and eagerness; a demigod or lesser god; son of the Titan Pallas and the water Nymph Styx; brother of Nike (Victory), Bia (Force), and Cratus (Strength).

With his sisters and brother, Zelus stood beside the throne of Zeus, carrying out the great god's commands and guarding his home against intruders. When their mother, Styx, sided with Zeus in his battle with his father, Cronus, and the Titans, she brought Zelus, Nike, Cratus, and Bia into service with her, though their father was a Titan.

Zelus was seen as a force, often a negative influence, that encouraged rivalry, that separated families due to envy and that caused an almost blind drive by some people to surpass the abilities and successes of others. People used his name as an oath, sometimes almost a curse. He was seen as a companion to the spirits of competition, jealousy, and strife.

Zelus' Roman counterpart was Invidia, the goddess of envy.

**ZEPHYRUS** (West Wind) *Greek*  The personification of the West Wind. Zephyrus was the son of Eos, goddess of the dawn, and of Astraeus, a Titan, or Aeolus, the king of the winds.

Zephyrus was a balmy, gentle wind. Among his many adventures, he blew Aphrodite to the shores of Cyprus after she was born full grown in the foam of the sea. He helped Cupid protect Psyche from the anger of Aphrodite. With the one of the Harpies, Zephyrus fathered the divine horses of Achilles and the white horses of the dioscuri.

**ZETHUS** *Greek*  Son of Zeus and Antiope, who was the daughter of a prince of Thebes; twin brother of Amphion; husband of Thebe. Zethus was an important character, with his brother, in the story of the founding of the Greek city of Thebes.

After growing up in a shepherd village, unaware that their grandfather had been king of Thebes, the brothers gathered an army to claim Thebes as their birthright. They captured the city and decided to build a wall around it. While Zethus, a strong warrior, struggled to move the great stones, his brother, a gifted musician, played beautiful music on the lyre given to him by Hermes and moved the stones easily.

Zethus was a great hunter and herdsman, well practiced in the art of war. According to the *ODYSSEY*, Zethus's wife killed their only son in a fit of madness and Zethus died of heartbreak.

**ZEUS** (Day, Bright Sky) *Greek*  The chief god of Greek mythology. He was the son of Cronus and Rhea, both Titans; brother of Hades, Hestia, Demeter, Poseidon, and Hera, who was also his wife. Over time the Romans attributed many of the legends of Zeus to their own supreme god, Jupiter.

Zeus was a sky and weather god, having authority over the sky, the winds, the clouds, rain, thunder, and lightning. His name has a close connection with the Latin word for day, *dies*. Zeus was also the god of battle, the patron of games and agriculture and protector of the state. He was called the father of both

This ancient Roman copy of a Greek bust of Zeus was made in the third century and found in 1775 in excavations of the ancient site at Otricoli, north of Rome. It is now in the Vatican Museums in Vatican City. *(Photograph by Marie-Lan Nguyen.)*

gods and humans. After defeating his father, Cronus, Zeus reigned supreme over the gods of OLYMPUS, the home of the gods. He was the father of many children by Titanesses, goddesses, NYMPHS, and mortal women. Among his offspring were APOLLO, ARES, ARTEMIS, ATHENE, and DIONYSUS. (See *The Loves of Zeus*, below.) His most famous sanctuary was at DODONA.

Zeus is often depicted as wearing a crown of oak leaves (the oak tree was sacred to him), and bearing a scepter in one hand and a thunderbolt in the other. Often he wore his shield, called an AEGIS, and had an eagle at his feet.

**The Childhood of Zeus**  Cronus the Titan, father of Zeus, learned that one of his children would kill him, so he swallowed his children as soon as they were born. Thus Hades, Hestia, Demeter, Hera, and Poseidon disappeared into his mouth. But Rhea, wife of Cronus and mother of Zeus, saved her last child by wrapping a stone in swaddling clothes and presenting it to Cronus, who promptly swallowed it. The stone was called the OMPHALOS, later set up at DELPHI as the "navel of the Earth." Rhea hid Zeus in a cave on Mount IDA (2), in CRETE. There he was nursed by the she-goat AMALTHEA and the NYMPHS ADRASTIA and IDA (1). Young warriors known as the CURETES clashed their weapons together to disguise the infant's cries.

**Zeus Rescues His Siblings**  After young Zeus grew to manhood, he left Mount Ida, where he had been sheltered by Nymphs, and went to visit the Titaness METIS. Metis was very wise. She advised Zeus how to get Cronus, the Titan father of Zeus, to disgorge his brothers and sisters, whom Cronus had swallowed. Zeus was to disguise himself as a cupbearer and offer Cronus a drink so vile that the Titan would immediately vomit and his offspring would reappear. This Zeus did and all went according to plan. His brothers and sisters, Hestia, Demeter, Hera, Hades, and Poseidon were expelled alive and well from the body of their father. The stone, which Cronus had been made to believe was Zeus wrapped in baby clothes, was also expelled and later set up at Delphi as the Omphalos, or navel, of the Earth.

**The War with the Titans**  Once Zeus had induced Cronus into releasing his brothers and sisters, the siblings decided to go to war against Cronus and the Titans. For 10 long years, Zeus fought against the Titans, who were led by the mighty ATLAS, for Cronus was now old. Finally Zeus enlisted the help of GAIA (Earth), who advised him to release the CYCLOPES and the Hundred-Handed Ones (the HECATONCHEIRES), who had been imprisoned in the UNDERWORLD. Zeus did this, and in gratitude the Cyclopes gave Zeus the thunderbolt as a weapon. They gave a helmet of invisibility to Hades, and to Poseidon, a trident. With these weapons and the help of the Hundred-Handed Ones, Cronus and all the Titans were overthrown, and never troubled GREECE again. Atlas was ordered, as punishment, to carry the sky on his shoulders forevermore.

When the war was over, the three brothers, Zeus, Poseidon, and Hades, drew lots to see who should rule the universe. To Poseidon fell the rule of the seas and rivers; to Hades, the Underworld; and to Zeus all the rest of the universe, except for Olympus, which was to be the realm of all the gods and goddesses.

The war between the Titans and the OLYMPIAN GODS may have been a symbolic description of the invasion of the land now called Greece, by the migrating tribes who became the first Greeks. They brought their gods with them, including Zeus. The ancient gods were displaced or absorbed by those of the conquerors.

**Zeus and Hera** The wife of Zeus was his sister, Hera. One of the most famous myths about their coming together was that Zeus took the form of a cuckoo, who appeared before her wet and shivering. Touched by pity, Hera wrapped the bird in her arms to warm it. Then Zeus resumed his usual form and persuaded Hera to become his wife. They were solemnly married on Mount Olympus. Although Hera remained the official consort of Zeus, the god continued to court goddesses, nymphs, and mortal women, so that Hera lived in constant anger and jealousy.

By Hera, Zeus had two sons, Ares and HEPHAESTUS, and one daughter, HEBE. Some versions of the myth say that Hera gave birth to Hephaestus, the smith god, without any help from Zeus. Hera and Zeus were also the parents of EILEITHYA, according to some sources.

**Zeus and Metis** According to the Greek poet HESIOD, Zeus's first wife was not Hera, but METIS, the wise one. She conceived a child by Zeus. Warned by URANUS and GAIA that the child would pose a threat to him, Zeus swallowed Metis, thus absorbing wisdom into himself. The child was born, nevertheless. It was the great goddess Athene, who sprang fully grown and clad in armor from the forehead of Zeus.

**The Loves of Zeus** Zeus was a wise and just ruler but, in spite of the anger and jealousy of his wife, Hera, he was inclined to have numerous love affairs. Scholars explain the amorous exploits of Zeus as symbols of the new and powerful religion taking over lesser religious traditions and merging with them, which is what happened in ancient Greece as various migrating tribes overcame and sometimes absorbed the ancient inhabitants and their cults. Perhaps, more simply, the ancient Greeks were trying to create for themselves the noble ancestry that would have come from the union of the great god Zeus with their ancestors.

To make a conquest, Zeus sometimes assumed a different shape. He became a cuckoo for Hera, a swan for LEDA, a BULL for EUROPA, and a quail for LETO.

The few remains of the great temple known as the Olympian Temple of Zeus stand on a huge block of land in Athens, Greece. Begun in the seventh century, B.C. the temple was completed in the second century A.D. It was the largest temple in Athens, but only a small portion of its pillars still stand. One pillar, which fell in 1852, lies in pieces in the foreground. *(Photograph by Chris Fleming. Used under a Creative Commons License.)*

Among the supernatural females Zeus dallied with were

ELECTRA (2), daughter of Atlas, mother of HARMONIA (though some say that Harmonia was the daughter of Ares and APHRODITE)

EURYNOME, daughter of OCEANUS and TETHYS, who bore THE THREE GRACES

Leto, who became the mother of Apollo and Artemis

MAIA (1), daughter of Atlas and Pleione, mother of HERMES

MNEMOSYNE (Memory), who gave birth to nine daughters who were the MUSES

TAYGETE, daughter of Atlas, mother of Lacedaemon

THEMIS (Law), who bore the HORAE (Seasons); EUNOMIA (Wise Legislation); DIKE (Justice); EIRENE (Peace); and the Fates, who are the daughters of NYX (Night)

Among the mortal women Zeus mated with were

ANTIOPE, daughter of King Nycteus of THEBES, who bore twin sons AMPHION and ZETHUS.

DANAE, daughter of Acrisius, who bore PERSEUS

EUROPA, daughter of AGENOR and Telephassa

Io, sister of Phoroneus, who bore EPAPHUS

Leda, wife of Tyndareus, who bore Pollux and HELEN by Zeus and Castor and CLYTEMNESTRA by Tyndareus

NIOBE, daughter of Tantalus and the nymph Laodice, who bore Argos, founder of the city of ARGOS.

SEMELE, daughter of CADMUS, who bore DIONYSUS

Among the Olympian goddesses was Demeter, who bore PERSEPHONE. He also had an affair with Lamia, a queen of LIBYA, whose children Hera killed as they were born. Lamia became a demon who devoured children.

# SELECTED BIBLIOGRAPHY

Aken, Andreas R. A. van. *The Encyclopedia of Classical Mythology*. Trans. R. Welsh. Englewood Cliffs, N.J.: Prentice-Hall, 1965.

Barber, Richard A. *A Companion to World Mythology*. New York: Delacorte Press, 1979.

Bell, Robert E. *Dictionary of Classical Mythology: Symbols, Attributes & Associations*. Santa Barbara, Calif.: ABC-CLIO, 1982.

Burn, Lucilla. *The Legendary Past: Greek Myths*. Austin: University of Texas Press, 1990.

Bulfinch, Thomas. *Bulfinch's Mythology*. New York: Crowell, 1970.

Campbell, Joseph. *The Hero with a Thousand Faces*. New York: Pantheon Books, 1949; paperback, Bollingen Series, Princeton, N.J.: Princeton Press, 1968.

———. *The Power of Myth*, with Bill Moyers. New York: Doubleday, 1988.

Cotterell, Arthur. *A Dictionary of World Mythology*. Oxford: Oxford University Press, 1979, 1986.

Dixon-Kennedy, Mike. *Encyclopedia of Greco-Roman Mythology*. Santa Barbara, Calif.: ABC-CLIO, 1998.

Dowden, Ken. *The Uses of Greek Mythology*. London: Routledge, 1992.

Eliot, Alexander, ed. *Myths*. New York: McGraw-Hill, 1976.

Flaum, Eric. *The Encyclopedia of Mythology: Gods, Heroes, and Legends of the Greeks and Romans*. Philadelphia: Courage Books—Running Press, 1993.

Frazer, James G. *The Golden Bough*. London: Macmillan, 1912; abridged edition, 1922; paperback, 1957.

Gardner, Jane F. *The Legendary Past: Roman Myths*. Austin: University of Texas Press, 1993.

Gaster, Theodore H., ed. *The New Golden Bough: A New Abridgement of the Classic Work by Sir James Frazer*. New York: Criterion Books, 1959.

Gayley, L. M. *The Classic Myths in English Literature and Art*. Boston: Ginn & Co., 1983.

Grant, M. *Myths of the Greeks and Romans*. Cleveland: World Publishing, 1962.

———. *Roman Myths*. New York: Scribner, 1972.

Graves, Robert. *The Greek Myths*. Mt. Kisco, N.Y.: Moyer Bell, Ltd., 1988.

———. *Greek Gods and Heroes*. New York: Dell (Laurel Leaf Library), 1965.

Grimal, Pierre. *The Dictionary of Classical Mythology*. Trans. A. R. Maxwell-Hyslop. Oxford: Basil Blackwell, 1986.

Guthrie, W. K. C. *The Greeks and Their Gods*. Boston: Beacon Press, 1954.

Hamilton, Edith. *Mythology*. Boston: Little, Brown, 1942.

Hawkes, Jacquetta. *The Dawn of the Gods*. London: Chatto & Windus, 1968.

Heyden, A. Van Der, ed. *Atlas of the Classical World*. London: Nelson, 1963.

Howe, George, and G. A. Harrer. *A Handbook of Classical Mythology*. New York: F. S. Crofts & Company, 1947. Reprint, Detroit: Gale Research Company, 1970.

Jobes, Gertrude. *Dictionary of Mythology, Folklore and Symbols*. 2 vols. New York: Scarecrow Press, 1961.

Leach, Marjorie. *Guide to the Gods*. Santa Barbara, Calif.: ABC-CLIO, 1992.

Mercatante, Anthony S., *Facts On File Encyclopedia of World Mythology and Legend*. New York: Facts On File, 1988.

Otto, Walter. *The Homeric Gods*. New York: Pantheon Books, 1954.

Oswalt, Sabine G. *Concise Encyclopedia of Greek and Roman Mythology*. Glasgow: Collins, 1969.

Perowne, Stewart. *The Archaeology of Greece and the Aegean*. London: Hamlyn Publishing Group, 1974.

———. *Roman Mythology*. New York: Peter Bedrick Books, 1974.

Pinsent, John. *Greek Mythology*. New York: Peter Bedrick Books, 1983.

Pomeroy, Sarah B., Walter Donlan, Stanley M. Burstein, and Jennifer Tolbert Roberts. *Ancient Greece: A Political, Social, and Cultural History*. New York: Oxford University Press, 1999.

Powell, Anton. *Ancient Greece, Cultural Atlas for Young People*. New York: Facts On File, 1989.

Room, Adrian. *Room's Classical Dictionary: The Origins of the Names of Characters in Classical Mythology*. London: Routledge and Kegan Paul, 1983.

Stapleton, Michael. *The Illustrated Dictionary of Greek and Roman Mythology*. Introduction by Stewart Perowne. New York: Peter Bedrick Books, 1986.

Wiseman, T.P. *The Myths of Rome*. Exeter, UK: University of Exeter Press, 2004.

Woodward, Roger. *The Cambridge Companion to Greek Mythology*. Cambridge: Cambridge University Press, 2007.

# INDEX

**Boldface** page numbers indicate main entries. Page numbers followed by *f* indicate figures.